ELDERS in the LIFE
of the CHURCH

IX 9Marks

Building Healthy Churches

Other books in the 9Marks Life in the Church series:

Biblical Theology in the Life of the Church by Michael Lawrence (Crossway)

Is your church healthy? 9Marks wants to help churches grow in these nine marks of health:

    (1) Expositional Preaching

    (2) Biblical Theology

    (3) A Biblical Understanding of the Good News

    (4) A Biblical Understanding of Conversion

    (5) A Biblical Understanding of Evangelism

    (6) Biblical Church Membership

    (7) Biblical Church Discipline

    (8) Biblical Discipleship and Growth.

    (9) Biblical Church Leadership

9Marks exists to equip church leaders with a biblical vision and practical resources for displaying God's glory to the nations through healthy churches.

For a list of all 9Marks books, see www.9Marks.org/books/book-store.

ELDERS in the LIFE of the CHURCH

Rediscovering the Biblical Model for Church Leadership

PHIL A. NEWTON
MATT SCHMUCKER

Elders in the Life of the Church: Rediscovering the Biblical Model for Church Leadership

© 2014 by Phil A. Newton and Matt Schmucker

This is a comprehensive update of the previous edition, *Elders in Congregational Life*, © 2005 by Phil A. Newton.

Published by Kregel Publications, a division of Kregel, Inc., P.O. Box 2607, Grand Rapids, MI 49501.

The Library of Congress cataloged the first edition as follows:
Newton, Phil A.
    Elders in congregational life: rediscovering the biblical model for church leadership / by Phil A. Newton.
        p. cm.
    Included bibliographical references and indexes.
    ISBN 0-8254-3331-2 (first edition)
    1. Elders (Church officers)—Baptists. 2. Baptists—Government. 3. Baptists—History. 4. Elders (Church officers)—Biblical teaching. I. Title.
    BX6346.N48   2005
    262'.146—dc22   2005006561

ISBN 978-0-8254-4272-8

Printed in the United States of America

14 15 16 17 18 / 5 4 3 2 1

For Karen,
in honor and celebration
of our life together!

For Eli,
whom I love
¨Absolutely!¨

CONTENTS

FOREWORD

The church is a reflection of God's Son. That's why leadership of the church is of utmost importance. The church is how the great hope—eternity with God in Christ—is to be seen. In the time between Christ's ascension and His return, Christians in covenant with one another—loving and caring, encouraging and sharing, correcting and bearing over the years—present the clearest picture of God's love that this world can see.

The Lord's church, His bride, is comprised of not merely a list of individuals who are redeemed and being sanctified. Rather, in the society of the saints is something that seems more human than in the life outside of it. Furthermore, its radiance should shine out of our life together.

That was the plan from the beginning. From eternity past, God enjoyed full fellowship with Himself—Father, Son, and Holy Spirit. In the fullness of His love, He made this world, and then came Himself to redeem it. Those redeemed from the mass of this fallen world are ultimately to be with God forever.[1] In that great assembly, our union with Christ will know new depth, richness, and permanence. It will sparkle and shine, it will irradiate and warm, it will add passion and understanding that we can scarcely dream of now.

When speaking of leadership of the church—that is, the local church—is it any wonder, then, that *who should lead the church and how* is so critical? Phil Newton is the right man to write on this subject. He is a humble and joyful Christian who knows what it means to be united with Christ. More than that, he has decades of practice in leadership as a husband and father, and as a pastor of his own local church in Memphis. His understanding of God's Word is even deeper than his voice—a considerable statement, if you've ever talked with Phil or heard him preach! He's lived out the experience of leading a church as a single elder-pastor,

---

1 See 1 Thessalonians 5 and 2 Thessalonians 2 for some early words of Paul on this great reality.

9

and leading it through the transition to elder plurality. I, too, am a pastor who has led a church and lived through such a transition. For that reason, I salute Phil and commend his work to you.

Perhaps you have questions about leadership. Perhaps you're a deacon and you're worried about the ideas your pastor has been sharing. Maybe you're a member of many years, and you wonder how you should think about your church's structure. Perhaps you're a pastor, and through study of Scripture, your own experience, or from watching other churches, you question the way your church is being led. You'll find help in this book, where biblical wisdom and pastoral warmth meet and give you the help you need. The answers and suggestions offered come with plenty of biblical and personal examples.

While many objections to having elders in a church can be imagined, this book addresses three superbly.

Is it Baptist? You might be thinking that this whole idea of having elders just "isn't Baptist!" When our church was considering the change, an older member said that very thing to me in front of a large Sunday school class.[2] If you share that concern, Phil's first chapter should be of interest to you. It looks at Baptists in history—in both England and America—and in particular at the question of having multiple elders in one local church. Phil cites primary sources to show that Baptists from their earliest times have acknowledged that pastors are elders (in that sense, Baptists have always had elders) and that Baptists have frequently preached, taught, and written in favor of having multiple elders in one local congregation. So, while it's true that other groups— Presbyterians, Dutch Reformed, Bible churches, Churches of Christ, and so on—have advocated having elders, Baptists too have so believed and taught. While it has certainly become a minority position among Baptists—and Phil even investigates this interesting fact—it has always been present, and today seems to be undergoing a renaissance. After reading this book, you'll see that having elders, indeed, "is Baptist."

Is it biblical? Others reading this book couldn't care less about whether eldership is Baptist. Perhaps you're in an Evangelical Free church, an independent church, or some other church, and you're in the process of reconsidering your structure. For you, the abiding concern is not one of denominational identity,

2 I've written a short booklet that addresses this concern head on: Mark Dever, *By Whose Authority?* (Washington DC: 9Marks, 2005). For a short summary of the Bible's teaching on elders, see Mark Dever, *Nine Marks of a Healthy Church*, 3rd edition (Wheaton, IL: Crossway, 2013). For a look at how elders work in conjunction with Baptist polity more broadly, see Mark Dever, *A Display of God's Glory* (Washington DC: 9Marks, 2001).

but of biblical faithfulness. That's really the concern of the best Baptists—and the best Presbyterians, Methodists, Congregationalists, Episcopalians, and Lutherans as well! Christians understand the Bible to be God's revelation of Himself and His will for us, and as such, the Bible is the touchstone for our faith and practice. The Bible is how we learn to approach God both individually and in our churches. The Bible tells us how to run our lives, and the Bible tells us how God's church is to be ordered. So if you're concerned if eldership is biblical, you'll find this book a great help.

Elders in the Life of the Church is full of careful, balanced, informed consideration of Scripture. Chapter 3 surveys the evidence in the New Testament, looking at the various titles that are used for church leaders and addressing the question of multiple elders in a single congregation. Chapter 5 considers the examples in the book of Acts. The whole of part 2 focuses on four central texts—Acts 20, the record of Paul's meeting with the Ephesian elders; 1 Timothy 3, Paul's list of qualifications for holding the office of elder; Hebrews 13, the words to the leaders of congregations; and 1 Peter 5, Peter's words about being an undershepherd of God's flock. In all three parts, Scripture is regularly both referred and deferred to. Phil not only knows the Bible but he intends to obey it. As a pastor himself, he has gone through the difficulties of leading a congregation to change. Why would he do that? He did it because of his belief in the sufficiency of Scripture, and his commitment to be ruled by it, both in how he approaches God and in how he leads his church to do the same. After reading this book, you'll come to agree with Phil, and you'll see that having elders is, in fact, biblical.

Is it best? Finally, your concern may be a more practical one. You may be concerned not so much about your denominational identity, or the deep debates on specific texts of the Bible. Perhaps you think that having a plurality of elders does seem the most biblical way to lead a church, but you wonder, *Is it really best?* Is it the best thing for your church at this time? How would you go about it? Perhaps your pastor is promoting the idea right now. Maybe he gave you this book to read. (Don't you love the way pastors give you books to read, like you don't have anything else to do?) Maybe you're part of a church leadership team studying together on this subject. Maybe you're a pastor who's convinced of having elders in your church, but have no idea of how you would actually do it. Take heart, my friends, you've found the right book!

I know of no other book that gives such particular and practical consideration for transitioning to plural elders. The whole of part 3, "From Theory to Practice," is a wonderfully practical guide for evaluating elders, presenting them, and beginning to have them function in your church. By the wealth of information in these chapters, it's obvious that Phil has lived through the process, and he's willing to share his own experiences—good and bad—in order to help us have even better experiences in our churches. If you read this book, you'll see that having elders is, without doubt, the best way to lead your church.

One more word of testimony: I'm enthusiastic about this book because I'm excited about what having elders has meant to me as a senior pastor. Since 1994 I've had the privilege of serving Capitol Hill Baptist Church in Washington, DC. This church, founded in 1878, had grown large in the early part of the twentieth century, but declined in number during the last half of the century. In the early months and years of my stewardship of this very traditional (and senior) Baptist congregation, I openly taught on having elders—and I didn't mean just more staff members. I meant understanding that Christ gives His church teachers, some of whom may be financially supported by the church, others who are not. I was convinced that it was consistent with Baptist history, that it was biblical, and that it was simply best that we move to having a plurality of elders.

These elders, I taught, would help me guide the flock. I taught from 1 Timothy and Titus, from 1 Peter and from Acts 20, from Hebrews 13 and Ephesians 4. When I had opportunity, I instructed the congregation. I used John MacArthur's booklet on elders,[3] circulating multiple copies of it in the congregation. We had the privilege of D. A. Carson coming to our church, and teaching on this very topic. I cited the example of other well-known Baptist pastors—from C. H. Spurgeon to John Piper—who had elders.

Finally, after two years of careful, committee-filled consideration, the congregation voted to adopt a new constitution with the plurality of elders. Only one member voted against it; at this writing six years later, he's still a happy member of the church in regular attendance. What has been the result? Six years of improved pastoral care, wisdom in decision-making, help in difficulties, and joy for me as I've seen mature, godly men give sacrificially of their time and lives to lead the congregation that God has given them. It's been a wonderful time.

As you read this book, I pray that God will make it useful to you, and that you will experience as did I the goodness and care of God through the order that He has established for His church. If God has deliberately instructed us, let us give ourselves to hear and heed His word on every point—even down to having elders recognized in the church.

---

3 John MacArthur, Jr., *Answering the Key Questions about Elders* (Panorama City, CA: Grace to You, 1984).

Authority is a good gift of God to us. In both exercising and submitting to authority, we come to know God better. And especially because this gift of authority is so little understood and so often misused in our churches, I pray that through this book God will help you and your church.

MARK DEVER
Capitol Hill Baptist Church
Washington, DC

ACKNOWLEDGMENTS

The first edition of this book, *Elders in Congregational Life*, came together through the support and help of numerous colleagues and friends: The members of South Woods Baptist Church in Memphis where I've served since 1987; my fellow elders—Jim Carnes, Tommy Campbell, and Tom Tollett; friends who loaned me a quiet place to write—Richard and Ginger Hamlet; friends that read the manuscript and offered invaluable suggestions to improve it—Suzanne Buchanan, Mark Dever, Ray Pritchard, Danny Akin, Tom Ascol, Matt McCullough, Randy McLendon, and Todd Wilson; and friends who gave me the opportunity to teach on elders—the late Stephen Olford and David Olford. My debt to all of these dear friends can never be repaid!

The present volume builds on the significant influence of those just noted with the addition of several more. Teaming with my long-time friend Matt Schmucker as he contributes insights from many years of experience as an elder, gives the book a new level of application *and* color! Thanks Matt! Jonathan Leeman and Bobby Jamieson of 9Marks have added editorial skills and ecclesiological insight to sharpen the book's usefulness. Thanks brothers!

In addition to the three elders serving with me when the original volume came to print, Dan Meadows and Chris Wilbanks have joined the fellowship of elders, who along with the others already mentioned add many layers to my understanding of the ministry of elders. One of my greatest joys in ministry is serving with these men who pray for me, encourage me, and spur me toward more love for Christ. They help to shoulder the load of shepherding the flock. I love you brothers dearly!

Over the past few years, the Lord has given our church a wonderful group of present and former pastoral interns. They've asked so many important questions that have woven their way into this book. Thanks Drew Harris, Rich Shadden, Mike Beaulieu, Chris Spano, Mike Collins, Steven Hockman, Matt Gentry, and

James Tarrance! Matt Sliger, formerly an intern and now one of our pastors, has helped me in countless ways, as has our administrative assistant, Debbie Jones. I love serving with all of you!

Several of my professors at Southeastern Baptist Theological Seminary have honed my understanding of the subject in this book, especially John Hammett, Andreas Köstenberger, Bruce Ashford, and Alvin Reid. I'm thankful for their investment in me. My PhD cohort members Cris Alley, Dale South, Josh Laxton, Louis Beckwith, and Jason Mitchell have joined together in many long hours of talks about ecclesiology, polity, and leadership—all sharpening my grasp of these important subjects. Thanks for being iron sharpening iron!

My family has been encouraging throughout the writing and editing process. My wife Karen is an incomparable helper and joy to me! She has listened to so much of my rambling about my research and writing, and has done so with patience and encouragement. Karen, you are my love! My children and their spouses have gladly listened to my chatting about this book and never acted exasperated! Thanks Kelly and Adam, Andrew and Jessica, John, Lizzy, and Stephen. And thanks to my mother, Jane Newton, who never tires of asking me about how the writing is coming along. I've also written this book so that my grandchildren's generation might have a stronger leadership foundation as they mature in their grasp of the gospel and Christ's church. Addie, Olivia, Spence, Clara, Stratton, Lyla (d. 2011), and Tripp remind me that the heritage that follows me needs good roots in biblical polity.

Thank you for taking the time to read and think on the subject of elder plurality and church polity. May the Lord give each of us more passion to follow His design for the church!

Phil A. Newton
November 28, 2012

In the fall of 1984 the Lord graciously intervened and rescued me from a sure damnation, breathing life into me through the new birth found only in Jesus Christ. His love is evidenced by his provision and is inextricably tied to one church and a few people without whom I would have lacked the knowledge and heart to write the words found in this book. My story is their story.

Capitol Hill Baptist Church has been my spiritual home since 1991. They welcomed a green, energetic young man (not an elder!) and patiently prodded and pulled me to new levels of dedication and love for Christ's church.

The elders of Capitol Hill Baptist Church have been a source of wisdom and encouragement since we first gathered in the winter of 1998/99. I have loved serving with you guys and apologize for all the times my confusion or stubbornness extended our already late meetings.

Jonathan Leeman who is, no doubt, editing even this paragraph, has been the best of friends and a constant reminder of godliness in word and conduct. Karen Race, Josh Coover, Kevin Hsu, Andrew Sherwood, Marcus Glover, Tim Gosselin, Katy Winsted, Bobby Jamieson, Justin Leighty, John Pastor, Paul Alexander, Paul Curtis, Scott Gurley, Susan Gwilliam, Brooke Santamaria, Zach Moore, Tosan Ogharaerumi, and Samuel Jindoyan have in one way or the other lent their hearts and minds to the cause of building healthy churches through 9Marks. Special thanks to Ryan Townsend, the new executive director of 9Marks, for supporting this project. I pray the Lord blesses all your plans.

Since 1994 Mark Dever has been my friend, pastor, next-door neighbor and fellow elder. Together we have buried dear friends, seen other friends walk away from the faith, labored to protect sheep under attack, seen many baptized and attended what seems like a thousand weddings. Mark has believed the best about me when the evidence was lacking, modeled generosity with his words and gifts, and by his example helped me to believe heaven and the One who sits enthroned will be worth the wait. By nature I'm a pessimist. By experience I've become a bit of an optimist largely because of my friendship with Mark.

I asked a fruitful, loyal, faithful, pretty blonde girl with a nickname of "Eli" to marry me in August of 1987 and she said, "Absolutely!" Her resolve, dedication and love have not wavered in 25 years of marriage, despite my wave-making. I'm not surprised to see those same qualities reproduced in my favorite people on the planet, my children: Chelsea, Jason, Lauren, Katie, and Joanna. I'd rather be with you all at our kitchen table than anywhere else in the world! If I'm qualified to write about being an elder, it is because the six of you have supported me in "managing my household" and filled our home with the aroma and love of Christ.

Matt Schmucker
September 19, 2012

INTRODUCTION

"**W**hy elders?" The question was posed to me as our congregation journeyed through the transition to elder leadership. Elders seemed odd to my denomination's thinking at the time. A good look at Scripture, church history, and practical implications changed the way that we thought. But that was over 20 years ago.

Since first publishing *Elders in Congregational Life* (2005), the discussions on the subject have grown. Matt Schmucker and I have fielded countless phone calls, emails, and visits where new and seasoned pastors and church leaders quizzed us about introducing the subject of elders to their churches. Some asked for biblical reasons for changing their polity. Others asked how to reconcile their way of governing with church history. Most seemed concerned to know how a church functioned with a group of elders leading the congregation. How could they transition their churches to healthy elder plurality? Could they do it without splitting their churches? How would they recognize the men qualified to serve as elders? Many still ask the same questions. That's why we wrote this book.

But before we get into the nuts and bolts of elder plurality, let me tell you a little about my own story of transitioning to elder leadership.

Three primary elements moved me into the direction of a plurality of elders: Scripture, Baptist history, and practical issues of church life. While delivering sermons that dealt with biblical texts teaching elder plurality, I experienced numerous uncomfortable moments—uncomfortable because I softened or ignored the teaching due to my own pastoral context. References to elders abound throughout the New Testament, so it is impossible to not encounter these texts while preaching consecutively through books of the Bible. I adopted the superficial explanation that equated the early church elders with today's pastoral staffs. This satisfied my audience but it was clear to me that I imposed a modern perspective on the ancient text. Before continuing to offer this explanation to my congregation, I had to be sure that this common interpretation was true to the biblical text. If, through studying the Scripture myself, I was not convinced that this interpretation was biblical, how could I convince my congregation? The more I studied the biblical texts, the less support I found for simply equating elders with the modern church staff. Biblical integrity called for a change in the way that I addressed these texts.

History played a vital role in affecting my thought as well. When I was a teenager, I discovered that my home church recognized elders in its early history. The first few pastors were identified as Elder Gibson, Elder Hudson, and Elder Jennings. Why were they called *elder* in the nineteenth century if, indeed, they were pastors? The answer to that question came many years later when a friend sent me a copy of W. B. Johnson's address, "The Rulers of a Church of Christ" from his *The Gospel Developed through the Government and Order of the Churches of Jesus Christ* (1846). Johnson, the first president of the Southern Baptist Convention, clearly set forth the biblical and practical necessity for a plurality of elders in Baptist life. Johnson's notoriety as a leader among early Southern Baptists made his address no small historical marker for elders in congregational life. If the congregational life of some, or perhaps even many, eighteenth- and nineteenth-century Baptists included the practice of elder leadership, then why did Baptists in the nineteenth and twentieth centuries transition to a leadership structure of a single pastor, staff, and deacons?

Lastly, practical concerns gave much reason for questioning the common authority structure in Baptist churches. I had experienced my share of church conflicts, disheartening business meetings, poorly qualified deacons, and power struggles in congregational life. I witnessed firsthand the discontinuity between pastor and deacons that affected the unity and viability of a church. Was this just the way things had to be if you were a Baptist? Many thought so. Yet how would I answer the Lord of the church if I acquiesced to conflict and confusion in church leadership?

Knowing my accountability to the Lord for the way that I led the church I served, I also knew that I had to take a higher road—even if the price were also high. Is there a better way—a more biblical way—to conduct church life? That's the question that I faced in the late 1980s, and one that many are currently facing. The necessity for change must not be ignored, but the methodology need not cause knee-jerk reactions that upset the equilibrium of congregations. Church leaders and congregations must labor, however, to discover God's revealed will in the Scriptures and, then, faithfully obey it.

Elders in the Life of the Church takes a look at elder plurality from the same three angles: historically, biblically, and practically. While Matt and I have written out of our experiences as Baptists transitioning to elders, both of us have talked with plenty of non-Baptists about the same need for establishing healthy church polity.

While most of our examples come out of our Baptist backgrounds, we believe that churches from other traditions will find the historical, biblical, and practical recommendations to be equally useful in aiming toward a healthy church polity.

The historical section, part 1, is the briefest of the three but particularly helps those from Baptist backgrounds—my own denominational heritage—to see how Baptist churches with plural elder leadership are not really so odd after all. The biggest question that I've received regarding the history of elders in Baptist life focuses on what happened to shift Baptist thinking away from elder plurality. Why did Baptists commonly practice elder plurality in the seventeenth, eighteenth, and well into the nineteenth centuries, but moved away from it—at least in the United States—in the 20th century? I think the historical section will help to answer that important question—and others—and demonstrate that elders fit quite well with being Baptist.

Part 2 turns to Scripture. I take a look at four key biblical texts, working through them expositionally to show the biblical teaching on elder leadership. These same texts made me squirm early in ministry because I feared that the churches that I served had no intention of embracing them, yet I had the responsibility to expound upon them. If it's not biblical then we certainly do not need to go through the potential trouble to transition to elder polity! But if it is biblical, then we are compelled to reconsider the way that we govern and lead our churches in light of God's Word. This reconsideration ultimately leads to change.

Part 3 takes us from the theoretical to the practical: How do we move from the biblical text to actual practice of plural elder leadership? How does this reshape the way that we conduct church life? Here's where I caution church leaders to move slowly, deliberately, and gently. No leader should read a book on elder plurality and suddenly announce the change to his congregation! That could be disastrous! Yet he should begin the careful process of teaching, training, and directing his congregation toward a healthier way of church leadership. The questions that I've received from pastors, leaders, and seminary students over the years weave their way into the chapters in this section—at least my attempt to answer them. I've tried to consider many of the pitfalls and objections along the way to transitioning the church's polity. I encourage you to read these chapters carefully before launching into massive change in your church.

Church leadership remains important regardless of the size or location of the church. That's why I added chapter 21, "Leadership Development in Hard Places: Missionaries, New Churches, and Elders." My discussions with mission leaders and nationals led to some serious reflection on how to establish elder leadership when the missionary has only a brief chance to do it, especially where persecution seems the norm. For those engaged in cross-cultural work, you may find this chapter particularly helpful. It may also help congregations involved in mission work to be more sensitive to the challenges that our missionaries face.

The best change to this book came with the addition of Matt Schmucker's candid chapters! Matt has been a friend since the mid-'90s when we met at a conference. We've talked a lot of family, sports, gospel, church polity, and life since that time. We've prayed together and shed tears together. I love his forthrightness and passion for Christ's church! You will find plenty of examples of this in his chapters. His narrative of the Capitol Hill Baptist Church's restoration to vibrant health will give you hope and encouragement, as well as insight into your own setting.

We both pray that this book will serve Christ's church and the faithful leaders who seek to shepherd the flock purchased by His blood (Acts 20:28).

ABBREVIATIONS

ANF   Alexander Roberts and James Donaldson, eds. *Ante-Nicene Fathers*. Repr. 1885. 10 vols. Peabody, MA: Hendrickson, 2004.

BDAG   Frederick W. Danker. *A Greek-English Lexicon of the New Testament and Other Early Christian Literature*. 3rd ed. Chicago, IL: University of Chicago Press, 2000.

CrChr   Philip Schaff, ed. David S. Schaff, rev. ed. *The Creeds of Christendom with a History and Critical Notes*. 3 vols. 6th ed. Grand Rapids, MI: Baker, 1993.

EMQ   *Evangelical Missions Quarterly*

ESV   *English Standard Version*

LKGNT   Fritz Rienecker. *A Linguistic Key to the Greek New Testament*. Cleon L. Rogers Jr., ed. Grand Rapids, MI: Zondervan, 1980.

NAC   *New American Commentary*. Nashville, TN: B&H.

NASB   *New American Standard Bible*

NICNT   *New International Commentary on the New Testament*. Grand Rapids, MI: Eerdmans.

NIGTC   *New International Greek Testament Commentary*. Grand Rapids, MI: Eerdmans.

NTC   *New Testament Commentary*. Grand Rapids, MI: Baker.

TDNT   Geherd Kittel, ed. *Theological Dictionary of the New Testament*. Trans. Geofrey W. Bromiley. 10 vols. Grand Rapids, MI: Eerdmans, 1964.

WBC   *Word Biblical Commentary*. Waco, TX: Word. Nashville, TN: Thomas Nelson.

PART ONE

WHY ELDERS?

CHAPTER ONE

WHY *BAPTIST ELDERS* IS NOT AN OXYMORON

O ld photos of old men raised questions in my young mind. They were the por- traits of the pastors who had served my home church during the nineteenth century, and they piqued my teenage curiosity whenever I walked by them in the hallway. Each one had the caption "Elder" under the man's name.

I knew that Presbyterian and Church of Christ congregations had an office called "elders," but I had never heard of an elder in a Baptist church.

Yet the pictures were not lying. My church, the First Baptist Church of Rus- sellville, Alabama, had once recognized elders. The church had been founded by congregations from neighboring towns in 1867 "with Elders R. J. Jennings and Mike Finney constituting the presbytery."[1]

My church was not unique. In previous centuries, Baptist churches often re- ferred to their pastors as elders. Not only that, they often possessed a plurality of elders, including men who were not paid by the church. Some even called these non-ordained elders "ruling elders."[2] For instance, J. H. Grimes, writing around the turn of the twentieth century, frequently refers to pastors as *elders*. He iden- tifies Elder John Bond in Statesville as "only a licensed minister at this time, but

---

1   Boyce Broadus, *Baptists of Russellville, Alabama, 1867–1967* (Birmingham, AL.: Banner Press, 1967), 3. Miss Broadus was the granddaughter of noted Southern Baptist theologian John Broadus.

2   Gregory A. Wills, *Democratic Religion: Freedom, Authority, and Church Discipline in the Bap- tist South, 1785–1900* (New York: Oxford University Press, 1997), 51, 155 n. 4. Wills derives this conclusion from several eighteenth- and nineteenth-century historical records of Baptists in Georgia.

was regularly ordained by Union Church AD 1820, by a presbytery consisting of Elders Joshua Lester and David Gordon."[3] Bond subsequently served as a pastor, but he was called "elder" before entering the pastorate. Within Tennessee Baptist churches, Grimes identified the men involved in pastoral leadership who did not draw a salary as "lay elders."[4]

ELDER PLURALITY AMONG AMERICAN BAPTISTS

Many Baptist churches in America were led by a plurality of elders, both paid and unpaid.

For instance, David Tinsley, a prominent Baptist serving in Georgia in the late eighteenth century alongside Jesse Mercer's father,[5] Silas Mercer, was ordained four times: first to the office of deacon, then to the office of ruling elder, then to the office of gospel preacher, and finally to the office of evangelist.[6] As an unpaid non-staff elder, he was part of the plural eldership in his church. His service with the noted leader Silas Mercer demonstrates the prominence given to plural eldership among Baptists.[7]

Ample evidence for plural elder leadership can be found in the minutes of the leading association of Baptists in the colonial period, the Philadelphia Baptist Association. In 1738, for instance, the association considered whether if a ruling elder who had already been set apart by the laying on of hands "should afterward be called by the church, by reason of his gifts, to the word and doctrine [i.e., as pastor], must be again ordained by imposition of hands." The answer was simple: "Resolved in the affirmative."[8] Indeed, it appears to have been the norm in the Philadelphia Association to distinguish between ruling elders and those who regularly ministered the word.[9] Plurality was their practice.

---

3 J. H. Grimes, *History of Middle Tennessee Baptists* (Nashville: Baptist and Reflector, 1902), 158.
4 Ibid. Admittedly, the terms *ruling elders* and *lay elders* are not New Testament titles. The distinction in these titles resembles, however, some of the common titles used in modern churches, e.g., *senior* pastor, *associate* pastor, pastor of *education*, and *executive* pastor. All are considered to be serving in pastoral roles but not all have the same function within the local church setting. The adjective qualifies the role just as it has done with the *ruling* elder and *lay* elder titles. I'm indebted to Dr. Daniel Akin for raising questions about this important historical distinction (personal correspondence, July 24, 2003).
5 Jesse Mercer, also a prominent Baptist minister, was the founder of Mercer University.
6 David Benedict, *General History of the Baptist Denomination in America and Other Parts of the World* (Boston: Manning and Loring, 1813), 176.
7 Wills, *Democratic Religion*, 31, identifies Silas Mercer in Georgia and Isaac Backus of Massachusetts as "Revolutionary War-era leaders" among Baptists. So Tinsley's service in plural eldership took place within a prominent church.
8 A. D. Gillette, ed., *Minutes of the Philadelphia Baptist Association 1707–1807: Being the First One Hundred Years of Its Existence* (1851; repr.; Springfield, MO: Particular Baptist Press, 2002), 39.
9 Ibid., 102.

So, too, in Kentucky's Elkhorn Baptist Association. In the minutes from the 1790 meeting, Cooper's Run Church asked, "Whether the office of elder, distinct from that of minister, is a gospel institution or not?" The Association responded, "It is the opinion of the Association it is a gospel institution." These eighteenth-century Baptists recognized non-staff elders as part of the elder plurality in their local churches.[10]

The Charleston Association also recognized that ministers are called "elders" and suggested that churches were led by "presbyteries" which contained a plurality of "ministers" or "elders."[11]

In short, the practice was not universal, but many Baptist churches of the eighteenth and nineteenth centuries practiced plural leadership. Baptist historian Greg Wills observes, "These elders assisted the pastor as necessary in preaching and administering baptism and the Lord's Supper. They were leaders of the congregation by their wisdom, piety, knowledge, and experience. Such churches recognized the gifts and calling of all elders among them."[12] For a while, many Baptists distinguished between "ruling elders" and "teaching elders." Ruling elders focused on the administrative and governing issues of church life, while the teaching elders exercised pastoral responsibilities, including administering the ordinances. By 1820 the title of "ruling elder" had faded, and some contended that the pastor and deacons constituted the eldership. Not all agreed, including the first president of the Southern Baptist Convention, W. B. Johnson, who "taught that Christ strictly required each church to have plural eldership."[13]

AMERICAN BAPTIST DECLINE IN ELDER PLURALITY

It is often asked why Baptists gave up the practice of elder plurality. The late theologian Stanley Grenz identifies Isaac Backus (1724–1806) as one major reason for the decline. Backus, one of the most significant Baptist leaders in the eighteenth century, is best known in our day for his politically oriented work, even meeting with members of the Continental Congress. Yet Backus also widely promoted evangelism and church planting through extended evangelistic preaching

---

10 Basil Manly Jr., "History of the Elkhorn Association," accessed February 9, 2011; http://baptisthistory.page.comelkhorn.assoc.his1.manly.htm1.

11 In "A Summary of Church Discipline," in Mark Dever, ed, *Polity*, 120, and plural reference to ministers on 125.

12 Greg Wills, "The Church: Baptists and Their Churches in the Eighteenth and Nineteenth Centuries," in *Polity: Biblical Arguments on How to Conduct Church Life*, ed. Mark Dever (Washington, DC: Center for Church Reform, 2001), 33–35.

13 Ibid., 34. Wills summarizes Johnson's view.

tours and assisting with establishing new churches. As a prolific writer and gifted orator, he influenced his generation and beyond. He grew up as a Congregation-alist and pastored a New Light church in Titicut, Massachusetts starting in 1748, before adopting Baptist views in 1756. He then served as pastor of the First Bap-tist Church of Middleborough, Massachusetts for fifty-two years until his death.

Backus' family suffered at the hands of the religious hierarchy in the colonies, so he rightly reacted against any kind of religious tyranny or hierarchical heavy-hand-edness. He deplored any polity that depreciated the common individual in the church. Many Baptist churches practiced elder plurality at that time, probably due to the influence of the Philadelphia Association. But Backus' emphasis on individualism, coupled with his hyper-congregationalism, led to a denigration of elder plurality in churches under his influence. Grenz explains, "Backus favored a very 'weak' clergy, with the real power lying in the church members themselves."[14] Consequently, Backus limited the churches that he helped start to only one elder.[15]

Baptist minister John Leland (1754–1841) then picked up Backus' mantle on both religious liberty and polity through his own writing and oratory. Both men had been shaped by the developing colonial culture's emphasis on the individual and had relegated the church to a secondary position relative to the individual.[16] As one historian notes, Backus called for an "unmitigated congregational polity" that best suited individualism, while Leland "equated congregationalism, polity, and Christianity," probably leaning more on Thomas Jefferson than Scripture to solidify his views.[17] Both Baptist leaders feared any ecclesiastical structure that might remove power from the congregation. This led them to denigrate the idea of plural elder leadership, even if those elders led under the congregation's final authority (as with churches in the Philadelphia Baptist Association).

The emphasis on individualism and the decline of elder plurality continued into the mid-nineteenth century with the prolific writing of Francis Wayland. Way-land, along with Edward Hiscox and John Newton Brown, shaped what would be regarded as Baptist orthodoxy for generations.[18] Wayland treated different church polities as historical accidents. He did not believe the New Testament presented

---

14 Stanley Grenz, *Isaac Backus—Puritan and Baptist: His Place in History, His Thought, and Their Implications for Modern Baptist Theology* (NABPR Dissertation Series, 4; Macon, GA: Mercer University Press, 1983), 278–279.
15 Ibid., 279.
16 Edwin S. Gaustad, "The Backus-Leland Tradition," in *Baptist Concepts of the Church: A Survey of the Historical and Theological Issues Which Have Produced Changes in Church Order*, Winthrop S. Hudson, ed. (Chicago: Judson Press, 1959), 106.
17 Ibid., 122–123.
18 Norman H. Maring, "The Individualism of Francis Wayland," in *Baptist Concepts*, Hudson, 135.

a normative organizational structure, so he argued that decisions on church government could vary from church to church, each adopting what it deemed most helpful. Although favoring congregational polity, he carried no torch for it. He instead emphasized individual liberty. This continued emphasis on individualism chipped away at both the corporate nature of the local church and the leadership structure of elder plurality.[19]

In the same era, the emergence of Landmarkism catered to the same growing individualism. Its emphasis on a strict democracy in churches further eroded the leadership pattern established in the New Testament.[20] So the Landmarkist J. M. Pendleton, in his 1893 *Baptist Church Manual,* argued that "pastors and deacons are the only permanent Scriptural church officers."[21]

Despite this diversity, modern Baptists seeking to embrace plural eldership have a viable heritage as a foundation.[22] This heritage radiates clearly through some of the polity documents of earlier Baptists. Two final examples: First, Benjamin Griffith, in "A Short Treatise Concerning a True and Orderly Gospel Church" (1743), clearly taught elder plurality, pointing to ruling elders as those gifted "to assist the pastor or teacher in the government of the church."[23] He further explained, "The works of teaching and ruling belong both to the pastor; but in case he be unable; or the work of ruling too great for him, God hath provided such for his assistance, and they are called ruling elders."[24] Griffith saw the elders coming alongside the pastor who labored at the ministry of the Word, strengthening his hands for the demands of Christian ministry. They were to be helpful "in easing the pastor or teacher, and keeping up the honor of the ministry."[25]

In 1798, the Philadelphia Baptist Association charged Samuel Jones (1735–1814), the influential pastor and scholar in the middle colonies, to revise the disciplines of the Philadelphia Confession of Faith. He did this later in 1805. In his work, Jones admitted that much disputation took place among Baptists on

---

19 Ibid., 152–158, 165–166.
20 See Robert G. Torbet, "Landmarkism," in *Baptist Concepts*, Hudson, 170–195 for a helpful survey of early Landmarkism influence.
21 J. M. Pendleton, *Baptist Church Manual* (Nashville: Broadman Press, 1966), 24, 32.
22 I'm indebted to Shawn Wright, at the Southern Baptist Theological Seminary in Louisville, Kentucky, for research and comments that helped to clarify this point (personal correspondence, January 24, 2003).
23 Benjamin Griffith, "A Short Treatise Concerning a True and Orderly Gospel Church" (Philadelphia: Philadelphia Baptist Association, 1743), in Mark Dever, ed., *Polity: Biblical Arguments on How to Conduct Church Life* (Washington, DC: Center for Church Reform, 2001), 98.
24 Ibid.
25 Ibid.

the legitimacy of "ruling elders." He thought it best that local churches decide for themselves whether to include this particular office in their respective congregations, so he offered arguments in favor of and against the practice. Positively, he asserted that the ruling elder might help "ease the minister of part of his burden," as also deacons do. He said it might deflect "some hard thoughts and ill-will" among members of the congregation that can arise in leadership decisions. He further explained that not all ministers have gifts for leading the business of the congregation, and that others might better handle those responsibilities. Therefore, the congregation needs to allot such men the authority to serve in such capacities.[26] Although I prefer not to make the distinction of "ruling elder," as is common in Presbyterian circles, Jones' argument surely indicates that early Baptists recognized elder plurality as a necessary part of the church's polity.

ENGLISH BAPTISTS

The practice of including elders in Baptist life did not begin in America. Plural eldership was common in England during the seventeenth and eighteenth centuries. Pointing to several examples of lay elders in Baptist churches,[27] historian A. C. Underwood notes that early Baptists not only recognized elder plurality, but also distinguished the functions of elders within local churches. He mentions the seventeenth-century Broadmead Church in Bristol, which had a pastor, ruling elders, deacons, and deaconesses.[28]

Yet Baptist elders differed from Presbyterian elders. The former "recoiled at the prospect" of the elders in one church functioning as elders in another. Hence, they never would have considered the idea of a synod or presbytery outside of the local church. Authority belonged in the local church. The only exception appears to have occurred when the elders of one church would, for necessity's sake, help to ordain officers or administer the ordinances in another church. In such cases, the elders functioned as ministers of the gospel, but without pastoral authority in the other church.[29]

---

26 Samuel Jones, "A Treatise of Church Discipline and a Directory (1798)," in Dever, *Polity*, 145–146.

27 My use of *lay elders* by way of explaining the historical practice of plural eldership is not an endorsement of the term for modern usage. A better distinction might be *non-staff elders* serving with the elders that constitute the church staff. This assumes that, unlike staff elders, the non-staff elders receive no compensation from the church for their service.

28 A. C. Underwood, *A History of the English Baptists* (London: Carey Kingsgate Press, 1947), 130–31.

29 In James M. Renihan, "The Practical Ecclesiology of the English Particular Baptists, 1675–

Most of the English Baptists of this era, unlike Presbyterians, rejected the idea of "ruling elders" as a distinct from "teaching elders." The Devonshire Square Church in London, where William Kiffin pastored, recognized "a parity within the eldership"; each elder shared responsibility and authority within the church. Likewise at a church in Kensworth, Bedfordshire in 1688, "three men were chosen jointly and equally to offitiate [sic]…in breaking bread, and other administration of ordinances, and the church did at the same time agree to provide and mainetane [sic] all at there [sic] one charge."[30] The renowned Benjamin Keach also rejected the idea of ruling elders as a distinct position, but allowed that the church might "choose some able and discreet Brethren to be *Helps* in *Government*," presumably either as a separate alliance or more likely as members of plural eldership.[31] However, a few Baptist churches did make a distinction between teaching and ruling elders. In such cases, "The pastor was the chiefe [sic] of ye Elders of ye Church," while the ruling elders shared oversight with him.[32]

Certainly not all of the English Baptist churches of this era followed elder plurality but "the majority of the Particular Baptists were committed to a plurality and parity of elders in their churches," believing that a plurality of elders were "necessary for a completed church."[33]

Elders were never to lord their position over their churches. They were "stewards responsible to their Master, and servants to their people." Their duties, according to Nehemiah Coxe in a 1681 ordination sermon, were "prayer (leading worship), preaching and the exercise of discipline; and the private duties as visiting the flock, encouraging, exhorting and rebuking them."[34] Hanserd Knollys, another remarkable leader among seventeenth-century English Baptists, described the duties of plural eldership:

> The Office of a *Pastor, Bishop,* and *Presbyter,* or *Elder* in the Church of God, is to take the Charge, Oversight, and Care of those Souls which the Lord Jesus Christ hath committed to them, to feed the Flock of God; to watch for their Souls, to Rule, Guide and Govern them . . . according to the laws, Constitutions and ordinances of the Gospel.[35]

1705: The Doctrine of the Church in the Second London Baptist Confession as Implemented in the Subscribing Churches" (Ph.D. diss., Trinity Evangelical Divinity School, 1997), 196.

30 Ibid., 201.

31 Benjamin Keach, *The Glory of a True Church and Its Discipline Display'd* (London: n.p., 1697), 15–16 (emphasis Keach), quoted in Renihan, "Practical Ecclesiology," 202.

32 Ibid.

33 Ibid., 205.

34 Ibid., 210, summarizing Coxe's comments.

35 Ibid., 210; quoting Hanserd Knollys, *The Word That Now Is* (London: Tho. Snowden, 1681), 52.

BAPTIST CONFESSIONS

Confessional documents and statements on church polity among early Baptists in England and the United States substantiate the practice of plural eldership. The London Confession of 1644 affirmed,

> That being thus joyned [sic], every Church has power given them from Christ for their better well-being, to choose to themselves meet persons into the office of Pastors, Teachers, Elders, Deacons, being qualified according to the Word, as those which Christ has appointed in his Testament, for the feeding, governing, serving, and building up of his Church, and that none other have power to impose them, either these or any other.[36]

Similar to the London Confession of Baptists, the 1658 Savoy Declaration—the Congregationalist confession that contained much of the substance of later Baptist confessions—identified "Pastors, Teachers, Elders, and Deacons" as "the officers appointed by Christ to be chosen and set apart by the church."[37]

The Baptist Confession of 1688 (the Philadelphia Confession) followed the language of the Savoy Declaration with a change only in the offices identified as "bishops or elders and deacons."[38]

The New Hampshire Confession of 1833—the foundational document for the Southern Baptist Convention's 1925 *Baptist Faith and Message*—identifies the local church's only scriptural officers as "Bishops, or Pastors, and Deacons, whose qualifications, claims, and duties are defined in the epistles to Timothy and Titus."[39]

The Abstract of Principles (1858)—the confession still used at the Southern and Southeastern Baptist Theological Seminaries—stated, "The regular officers of a Church are Bishops or Elders, and Deacons."

Although the 1925 *Baptist Faith and Message* of Southern Baptists identifies the office of elders, both the 1963 and 2000 *Baptist Faith and Message* revisions eliminate the titles *bishop* and *elder*: "its Scriptural officers are pastors and deacons." The change demonstrates how plural eldership fell out of use in Baptist practice.[40]

---

36 John Piper, "Biblical Eldership: Shepherd the Flock of God Among You", app.1; accessed March 29, 2003; www.desiringgod.org/resource-library/seminars/biblical-eldership-part-1a. See also John Piper, *Biblical Eldership* (Minneapolis: Desiring God Ministries, 1999).
37 *CrChr*, 3:725.
38 Ibid., 3:739.
39 Ibid., 3:747.
40 Paul Burleson in a sermon, "An Historical Study of Baptist Elders—1 Peter 5:1–4," at Trinity

Admittedly, these confessional statements are somewhat vague, making room for both those who affirm elder plurality and those who object to it. Not all of the English and colonial Baptist churches practiced plural eldership. By some accounts, only a minority did so. Yet the presence of plural eldership among notable leaders and in strong churches contradicts the notion that eldership is an anomaly among Baptists.

W. B. JOHNSON AND SOUTHERN BAPTISTS

As a founder of the Southern Baptist Convention and its first denominational president, W. B. Johnson left a legacy of biblical fidelity and passion for the gospel. His work on church polity, "The Gospel Developed through the Government and Order of the Churches of Jesus Christ" (1846), remains a generally trustworthy guide for encouraging Baptist churches to be faithful to the Word of God. After outlining the biblical evidence of plural eldership in the first century churches, Johnson explained that each elder (or "bishop" or "overseer," as he called them) brought "a particular talent" to the needs of the church. He added, "The importance and necessity of a bishopric for each church, embodying gifts for various services, is thus most obvious for the accomplishment of one of the great ends for which Christ came into the world, and for which, when he ascended up on high, he received gifts for men" (see Eph. 4:7–16).[41] In a plurality, each elder brings a different set of gifts and abilities so that the whole body profits from their shared ministry. Johnson states, "A plurality in the bishopric is of great importance for mutual counsel and aid, that the government and edification of the flock may be promoted in the best manner."[42] In reviewing the scriptural teaching on elders, Johnson explains, "These rulers were all equal in rank and authority, no one having a preeminence over the rest. This satisfactorily appears from the fact, that the

---

Baptist Church in Norman, Oklahoma; accessed November 21, 2002; http://www.hhbc.com/webpages/baptist1.htm, offers three reasons for the decline of elders in Baptist life in the late 1800s to 1900s. First, in the expansion of Baptist churches into the west, the single pastor/church planter often served as a circuit-riding minister, handling the bulk of church duties with plural eldership fading in the process. Presumably, qualified male leadership was scarce in the early days. Second, the rise of Landmarkism, with its emphasis on "democratic rule with no elder rule" had profound influence on Southern Baptist life and practice. Third, "the rise of the Campbelites" [sic]—now called the Church of Christ, who "used the word elder exclusively"—caused Baptists to react and reject the name *elder*, using only the word *pastor* for those involved in church ministry and leadership.

41 W. B. Johnson, "The Gospel Developed through the Government and Order of the Churches of Jesus Christ" (Richmond: H. K. Ellyson, 1846); in Dever, *Polity*, 193.

42 Ibid., 192–193.

same qualifications were required in all, so that though some labored in word and doctrine, and others did not, the distinction between them was not in rank, but in the character of their service."[43] He identified equality among elders regardless of their particular function or role in the church.

Johnson was also realistic. While acknowledging that the Scriptures require elder plurality, he noted that some churches might not be able to establish a plurality immediately: "In a church where more than one [elder] cannot be obtained, that one may be appointed upon the principle, that as soon as another can be procured there shall be a plurality."[44] Further, Johnson distinguished between elders and deacons. The elders' office is spiritual, while the deacons' is temporal. "Whatever of temporal care the interests of the church require, *that* care falls upon the *deacons*, as the *servants* of the church."[45] Of course, deacons function in plurality as well.

Did all Baptist churches of the past have a plurality of elders? Obviously not. But many believed it was the New Testament model. Pastor John Piper, after surveying historical Baptist confessions, drew the same conclusion: "The least we can say from this historical survey of Baptist Confessions is that *it is false to say that the eldership is unbaptistic.* On the contrary, the eldership is more baptistic than its absence, and its disappearance is a modern phenomenon that parallels other developments in doctrine that make its disappearance questionable at best."[46]

RECENT DEMISE IN ELDER PLURALITY

The past two hundred years have witnessed the demise in elder plurality among Baptists. Pastors have begun to resemble CEOs rather than humble New Testament shepherds. Their staffs are hired for their business skills. And their churches are run like big businesses, requiring the corporate structures of a successful company.

A candid look at polity in churches at large today raises questions regarding our diligence to conform to Scripture. Specifically, how well are Christians in the West doing in being different than the world around them? Are we acting as salt and light in our communities? Are our "family values" appreciably different from our neighbors? Connected to theses questions regarding the holiness of the church are the polity questions: Are our congregations nurtured and disciplined like their New Testament counterparts? Are our membership rolls inflated, and

---

43   Ibid., 191.
44   Ibid., 194.
45   Ibid., 196–197.
46   Piper, "Biblical Eldership," app.1.

could this be contributing to our worldliness? Are pastors and staff members held accountable to anyone besides themselves? Might the alarming rate of immoral behavior among ministers be connected to the disconnect between church staff and a plurality of godly elders, both lay and staff? To put it plainly, I believe recent experience teaches what Scripture at least implies—that the holiness of a church is tied to its polity, just as faith is tied to order.

Our Baptist forebears sought to anchor their church structures and practices in the teaching of Holy Scripture. These stalwarts did not conform their churches to the popular designs of the day, but applied the truths of Scripture to forge a path for their heirs. In the end, whether or not Baptists historically practiced plural eldership is secondary. The primary focus for church leaders today must be to understand what God's Word teaches, and then to order their churches accordingly. History merely serves to affirm the veracity of Scripture.

REFLECTIONS

- What part does history play in one's understanding of modern church life?
- Did all of the early Baptist churches practice elder plurality?
- What were the positions of Benjamin Griffith, Samuel Jones, and W. B. Johnson's on plural eldership?
- What influence did Isaac Backus, John Leland, and Francis Wayland have on Baptist church polity?
- Why was there a movement away from elder plurality among nineteenth- and twentieth-century Baptists?

CHAPTER TWO

SHEEP WITHOUT A SHEPHERD

Abandoned. I was sure of it. It was November of 1990. My wife, two young children, and I were trying to find the funeral for my wife's grandmother, Madeline Dunmire. We were standing in front of the Capitol Hill Metropolitan Baptist Church, where Grandma Dunmire had been a member from 1924 until her death. Yet the building looked abandoned.

There were no exterior signs identifying the building; they had fallen off years earlier. Half of the trim on the stained glass windows had been painted probably ten years earlier; the other half was peeling, neglected since who knows when. The church grounds were surrounded with chain-link fence, some of which had collapsed. Planted in front of the fence were pricker bushes for "keeping the homeless out." In fact the bushes may have scared off a number of would-be visitors as well, presenting a nice collection of beer cans and other trash.

We pulled our minivan into an adjacent lot and parked next to half a sedan, the product of a rear-end impact. The four church doors visible to the street were all locked. Nobody could be seen moving inside the darkened building. Standing outside in the freezing cold, the conversation with my wife went something like this:

"There's no one here."

"There must be."

"This place is abandoned."

"It can't be."

"Are you sure this is the right place?"

"I remember coming here as a little girl for mother-daughter banquets."

"This place doesn't look open for business, sweetheart."

Finally, a middle-aged woman with a Southern accent came to the last door we tried. "Can I help you?" she said.

As it turns out, this was Grandma's church, and a funeral was taking place. Nancy, the friendly door-opener from Georgia, led us to the nursery. It looked like an eastern European hospital from an early twentieth-century war, only dirtier. The room was ringed with poorly painted white metal cribs that stood high above a dirty linoleum tile floor. It was lit by three uncovered light bulbs that hung out of the ceiling by wiring. The hired nursery workers didn't speak English.

We decided to keep our kids with us and then wound our way through a series of hallways and into the "sanctuary." The various shades of gray and blue hair on the old women seated in the back rows were as striking as the smell of mothballs emanating from their wool and fur coats.

The service began and, somewhat surprisingly, went off without a hitch. The robed choir sang from the Baptist Hymnal and the gospel was preached to an older audience of a couple hundred people in a dimly lit room that seats a thousand.

In conversations afterward, it became clear that my family was looking at a remnant, a remnant of what were known as the "glory days." In the 1930s through the 1950s, the building was full of young war veterans and their parents. Now they were simply old and dying. One faction of the senior group was known as the "Triple L Club," which stood for Live Long and Like It. They had their own room in the basement across from the Fellowship Hall, formerly known as the Lower Tabernacle. Another faction was known as the "Gray Panthers," a name they adopted when they fought off a young pastor in the 1980s. He had wanted to adopt a contemporary, seeker-sensitive model for church growth, but the Panthers had won and the young pastor left to start a counseling ministry.

This first visit to the Capitol Hill Metropolitan Baptist Church, which a few years later would drop the "Metropolitan," did not exactly entice us to come back. (Since the church is now called Capitol Hill Baptist Church, that is what I will call it moving forward, or CHBC.) Yet my wife and I had recently moved our family to DC, and so decided to join the church. Perhaps we could do a little good, and more importantly the gospel had been clearly preached.

Who knew what God had in store.

Through a series of providential, unplanned appointments I was hired by the church in the summer of 1991 to clean up the business side of the operation. My plan was to help for ninety days and then begin graduate school. And what I had seen of the church from the outside only became more curious on the inside.

I met the church secretary, who was so intimidated by her IBM 286 computer that she kept an extinguisher at her back in case of fire. She also kept five pairs of

shoes underneath her desk, each pair slightly larger than the last for accommodating swelling feet throughout the day.

I met ninety-six-year-old Mrs. Dicks, the financial secretary, who still used a
vintage desktop calculator the size of a small microwave complete with hand crank
and paper roll. She helped to oversee sixteen accounts spread over six banks. ("We
don't want anyone to get their hands on all the money!") It took two senior men
the whole morning and into lunch to count the offering and deposit the money
in the various banks.

I met George, the good-hearted retired missionary to Pakistan who did hospital
visitation and picked the hymns for Sunday.

And I met Bill, the sixty-year-old maintenance man who didn't know how to
maintain anything, but could have been a great pastor.

I learned that the church was universally unpopular in the neighborhood. There
were a number of reasons for this, but mostly because it had demolished historic
homes to create parking lots. These lots allowed the formerly urban congregation
to drive in from their suburban homes, but it created "holes" in the neighborhood
where once proud buildings stood.

The congregation was a strange combination of people. On the one hand we
had the elderly Carl F. H. Henry, the founder of *Christianity Today* magazine
who was recognized by *TIME* magazine as "the thinking man's Billy Graham."
Dr. Henry liked to sit in the pew that was located beneath the weakest part of
the roof. I kept waiting for the plaster ceiling to give way and fall on him. On
the other hand, we had a known fornicator who sang solos from the choir loft
and wore a tasseled Mexican sombrero.

We had Dr. Joe, who clipped his fingernails during the morning service. He
sat near Ed, the retired government worker. Ed wore flag ties most Sundays and
drove only big Cadillacs. He was so pro-American that you'd swear Jesus must
have been born in the Midwest, not the Middle East.

Our front door greeter was missing an index finger, and our back-door greeter,
eighty-year-old Alvin Minetree, wore colorful cummerbunds to match his top
hats and dress up his white suits. He greeted most women with "Here comes a
pretty lady."

This parade of characters gathered each Sunday morning to be drenched in
music, music, music. The organist sported a bouffant hairdo, and played her three
manual Allen organ so loudly the floor shook. The British choir director seemed
to have a guilt complex for being British because she never seemed to run short
of patriotic songs that reminded us of how much God had blessed the USA. We
had a children's choir, solos, and piano duets. But my personal favorite was the

brass ensemble. Every single person who had ever put metal to lips in junior high was called on to climb the attic stairs and dust off their dormant horns. Imagine red-faced trumpet and trombone players blowing "Fairest Lord Jesus" and "Go Tell It on the Mountain" to the delight of the hearing impaired.

The preacher was mostly judged on sermon length. If the benediction was given before noon, he got high marks. This let the seniors beat their way to the Hot Shoppe Cafeteria before the "holy roller" churches let out. And the congregation really liked the children's sermon: It was short, to the point, and the kids were always cute.

As the church administrator, I attended deacon meetings. These were held in the Triple L room and reminded me of 1960s visits to my grandmother's nursing home. Charlie, the very lovable deacon who lived to 103, would arrive early to get the seat that allowed him to rest his head against a pillar. If the meeting went past 8:30 p.m., we would probably lose Charlie to dreamland.

Friendly Frank never liked to make a fuss and didn't much care for people who did.

Eighty-year-old Bland didn't care for the light we had at the back door of the church, but he loved the Sears white metal awning that gave shelter from the rain.

Flag-tie-wearing Ed tried to block the church's support of the local crisis pregnancy center when budget time came around each year because "Abortion is a political issue!"

There were a couple of good, quiet, godly men who usually rallied the group. But few seemed to have the ability to look at God's Word and heed its instruction for giving shape to the church. Inertia had set in years earlier. Uncertainty about the future had frozen the leaders and the congregation. I was told repeatedly that "We are land rich and cash poor," as evidenced in the $300,000 budget which the church struggled to meet. Much of it went to buildings. In short, this was a generation that had spent their entire adult lives witnessing decline, in their city and in their church. And they seemed immobilized by it.

Yet not every late-twentieth-century American inner-city church suffered the fate of this one. Most church growth writers at the time would have said this church had four strikes against it:

1. It was denominationally affiliated (Southern Baptist).
2. It was located in the inner-city (five blocks behind the US Capitol building, which then was not a good neighborhood).
3. The building was old.
4. And there was limited parking.

Yet what became glaringly obvious whenever the deacons or various commit-tees gathered was, there was no group of strong, godly leaders. The few men who could have functioned in that role were too old or too tired from the decades-long slog of church life.

Consequently, the church had little focus and was a magnet for unscrupulous people, wolves posing as sheep. They were sheep without a shepherd. There were many elderly, but no elders.

CHAPTER THREE

ELDERS IN THE NEW TESTAMENT

The danger facing modern congregations is to read into the Scriptures our twenty-first-century ideas about church government. We have added plenty of bells and whistles: directors of mass media, pastors of recreation, Sunday School committees, boards of directors, not to mention all the seminars and books that tell churches "how to do it."

The drive to increase growth and expand ministry has complicated the structure of churches. The consequences have been twofold. First, churches have shifted the privileges and burdens of ministry to the "professional" staff, while bypassing gifted leaders whom God has placed into their memberships. Second, churches have let the call to nurture, equip, and disciple believers to be salt and light in the world get lost in the shuffle of big events and choreographed performances. Both churches and a spiritually needy world suffer as a result. That is why understanding the biblical basis for elders is crucial for establishing vibrant, Christ-centered churches.[1]

No single text in the New Testament provides all the details necessary for structuring a local church. But by combining the various texts addressing leadership, structure, and decision-making, we can construct a framework for church life. The framework may be fleshed out in different ways depending on cultural influences, personalities, pressing needs, and gifts within the church. Nevertheless, several elements are essential to every local church, including the offices of elder and deacon.

---

1 See John Piper, *Brothers, We Are Not Professionals!* (Nashville: Broadman and Holman, 2002).

These two offices were established in New Testament churches during the days of the apostles. After the apostolic age, the earliest churches followed the same pattern of plural elders and deacons, as one can read in the *Didache* (ca. A.D. 80–150).[2] Clement of Rome (A.D. 95) identified "bishops and deacons" as the appointed officers of the church, with no distinction made between bishops and elders.[3] It was not until the time of Ignatius in the early second century that the office of bishop became distinct from the office of elders and inaugurated the historical progression toward the monarchical episcopate.[4] Yet early churches practiced plural elder leadership even during the rise of episcopacy. Over the next centuries, the emphasis given to church structure began to compromise the gospel itself. The Reformation corrected this. Luther and Calvin both made polity secondary to the primary task of preaching the gospel. Later evangelical confessions affirmed the pattern of plural elders and deacons. Elders primarily addressed the spiritual needs of congregations; deacons addressed temporal needs.

THREE TITLES

Elder (Presbuteros)

The term *elder* (*presbuteros*) and its cognates are found sixty-six times in the New Testament.[5] The two dozen uses in the Gospels mostly refer to those men who, by reason of age and status, were involved in the Jewish community's leadership structure. Generally, the Gospels do not portray these elders favorably since they joined the spiritual leaders of the Jewish community in rejecting the Messiah (e.g., Matt. 15:2; 16:21; 21:23; Mark 8:31; Luke 22:52). Elsewhere in the Gospels, the word simply conveys greater age (John 8:9).[6]

However, elders in the New Testament Christian community functioned as rep-

---

2 Simon Kistemaker, *Acts* (New Testament Commentary; Grand Rapids: Baker, 1990), 525, citing *The Apostolic Fathers*, vol. 1, *Did.* 15.1 (Loeb Classical Library).
3 *1 Clem.*, 42.5–7, 44.3; *ANF*, 1:16–17.
4 Ign. *Magn.*, 6.1; *ANF*, 1.61.
5 Benjamin L. Merkle, *The Elder and Overseer: One Office in the Early Church* (Studies in Biblical Literature 57; Hemchand Gossai, gen. ed.; New York: Peter Lang, 2003), 43.
6 The elder permeated everyday life during the New Testament era. For example, ancient Sparta applied the term to those who governed their communities, as well as to decision-makers in academic circles. The Greeks, unlike the Jews, did not necessarily factor age into their usage of the term. Those considered elders in ancient Israel held responsibility for political, military, and even judicial matters. But when the times of kings arose, elders were replaced with the royal bureaucracy. G. Bornkamm, "Presbuteros," in *TDNT*, 6:652–57.

resentatives of the church.[7] Christian elders in Jerusalem, for example, received gifts from the believers in Antioch sent through Paul and Barnabas (Acts 11:30). Later, when Paul and Barnabas circled back to the churches they had established during their first missionary journey, they "appointed elders for them in every church" (14:23). Multiple elders were set apart in each of the infant churches of Asia Minor so that congregations might be nurtured and taught sound doctrine, clearly establishing the pattern of plural eldership. The authority of these first Christian elders came not by virtue of age or length of membership in the church; instead, they received their weighty ministries from the apostolic missionaries.[8] When those missionaries departed, the work of preaching the gospel, strengthening the disciples, and encouraging them in the face of tribulations belonged to the elders (Acts 14:21–22).

Elders also joined the apostles in receiving Paul and Barnabas and hearing their report of their missionary endeavors (15:2, 4). The elders stood with the apostles in addressing the problem of legalistic Judaizers who attempted to subvert young converts (Acts 15:22). Then they joined the apostles in drafting and sending a letter to the new churches, demonstrating the unique authority given to these representatives of the Jerusalem church (Acts 15:23). Elders' authority in doctrinal issues became clear as Paul passed along this decree on his second missionary journey (Acts 16:4). On his third missionary journey, while in Miletus, Paul met with the elders of the church at Ephesus for a final exhortation before his long ordeal of Roman imprisonment (Acts 20:17). In all, church structure may have evolved slowly in the early years, but a plural eldership was part and parcel of church life from the beginning.

It would not, in fact, have been surprising had Luke stopped everything in the process of writing Acts to announce the development of elders. But just as Luke simply describes the beginning of church planting without presenting the apostolic command to do so, so he describes the appointing of elders without mentioning the explicit apostolic command to do so. That is to say, the historical record clearly demonstrates the normative practices of the New Testament church—and plural eldership was at the heart of these practices. The balance of the book of Acts demonstrates that elders were part of the early churches' leadership structure.

The unusual thing, then, about elders in the early church is that they were not unusual. Every example of them in the pages of the New Testament presents them working as a plurality in individual churches (except where a particular elder or overseer is mentioned, e.g., 1 Peter 5:1; 2 John 1; 3 John 1).

---

7   See Merkle, *The Elder and Overseer*, 44–56, for a discussion of the use of *presbuteros* in the Old Testament, synagogue, and ancient culture.
8   G. Bornkamm, "Presbuteros," in *TDNT*, 6:664.

Overseer (Episkopos)

Coupled with title "elder" are the titles "overseer" (bishop) and "pastor." The concept of an overseer (Greek, *episkopos*), like that of an elder, was common during early church times. The Greeks used the term to define an office that had superintending functions, whether in political or religious circles.[9] It conveyed the idea of "to look upon, to consider, to have regard to, something or someone." Hence it implied caring for or watching over others, particularly those in need.[10] Fourth and fifth century B.C. Athens used *episkopoi* as a title for state officials who acted as supervisors in maintaining public order, often by exercising judicial powers.[11]

The Epistles use "overseer" or bishop interchangeably with "elder."[12] Paul, after his ministry in Crete, instructs Titus to "appoint elders in every city" (Titus 1:5; again note the plurality of elders in the single churches in the small cities of Crete). Turning to describe their qualifications, the apostle calls them "overseers" (v. 7; also, 1 Tim. 3:1–7). In his letter to the Philippians, Paul specifically addresses himself to the overseers and deacons (Phil. 1:1). Peter used the verbal form of overseeing *(episkopeø)* as he explained the duties of elders (1 Peter 5:1–3). Luke also used both the terms "elder" and "overseer" to describe the office and function of the Ephesian elders (Acts 20:17, 28). All of these passages assume the establishment of overseers in church leadership. Elders, then, appear to be an essential part of the early church's leadership and ongoing stability.

The leadership of the overseers should mirror that of Christ, whom Peter described as "the Shepherd and Guardian [*episkopon*] of your souls" (1 Peter 2:25). Peter uses the term overseer to speak of the sufficiency of Christ's death on the cross so that believers might "live to righteousness" (1 Peter 2:24). It is through the gospel that believers are now delivered from "continually straying like sheep" (1 Peter 2:24–25). Christ is called the "Guardian of your souls," which implies that he watches over those who are his own in order to preserve them from the effects of sin and to direct them into lives of righteousness. Thus, like Christ, an overseer will watch over the spiritual lives of those under his charge, seeking to protect them from the perils of false teaching and the deceit of sin, so that the church might live as salt and light to the glory of Christ.

---

9   *BDAG*, 379–380.
10 H. Beyer, "Episkopos," in *TDNT*, 6:486.
11 Ibid., 610–11.
12 See Merkle, *The Elder and Overseer*, 1–161, who argues convincingly that the titles *elder* and *overseer* represented the same New Testament office.

Pastor (Poimen)

Although the Greek term *poimen* is translated as "pastor" only once in its noun form, the title joins those of elder and overseer in deepening the hues of this one church office (Eph. 4:11). The word means "shepherd," and is translated thus throughout the Gospels and in two of the Epistles (e.g., Matt. 9:36; 25:32; 26:31; John 10:2, 11–12, 16; Heb. 13:20; 1 Peter 2:25, with most referring to Christ as the Shepherd of his flock). It served as a common epithet among rulers of the ancient east.[13]

Both Psalm 23 and the Good Shepherd motif in John 10 provide rich meaning to the picture of a shepherd who leads, restores, guides, protects, and provides for the sheep, calling each by name and laying down his life for them. Paul couples the terms "pastors and teachers" when he describes the gifts that the ascended Jesus gives to the church (Eph. 4:11), which is better translated, "teaching shepherds" or "pastor-teachers." The nature of the term indicates protecting, governing, guiding, nurturing, and caring for the flock.[14] Christ used the verbal form *(poimainø)* in His post-resurrection charge to Peter, "shepherd My sheep" (John 21:16). The verb also joins "elder" and "overseer" in explaining the function of elders to shepherd God's flock (Acts 20:28; 1 Peter 5:2). Paul also uses it metaphorically when describing the work that he and Barnabas did among the Corinthians (1 Cor. 9:7).

> Elder—the spiritual maturity of the office
> Overseer—leadership and direction for the church
> Pastor—feeding, nurturing, and protecting the flock

While *elder* appears to be the dominant term for the church office dealing with the spiritual needs of the local church, *overseer* and *pastor*, as has been noted, are used synonymously with elder. Each provides a clearer picture of the dignity and function of elders in church life: *elder* emphasizes the spiritual maturity required for this office; *overseer* implies the leadership and direction given to the church; *pastor* suggests feeding, nurturing, and protecting the flock.[15] The diverse cultural background in each New Testament church may have determined which title was applied to this plurality of godly leaders. Although it may not be possible to make

---

13   J. Jeremias, "Poimane," in *TDNT*, 6:486.
14   *BDAG*, 842.
15   Merkle, *The Elder and Overseer*, 156, explains that the term *elder* is more of a description of character whereas *overseer* is more of a description of function.

a clear-cut distinction, it seems that the Jewish Christians preferred *elder*, while the Gentile Christians more often used the title *overseer*, each referring to the same office.[16] The only use of the noun *pastor* is found in Ephesians, yet it can be surmised that each of the churches found this title to be helpful to describe the function of their spiritual leaders.

PLURAL LEADERSHIP

It is difficult to build a scriptural argument against elder plurality in the early church. New Testament scholar Bill Murray points out, "Both the churches at Philippi and Ephesus are said to have multiple 'elders.' These cannot be 'pastors of several churches' in the areas of Philippi or Ephesus." And he explains why: "First, each church is mentioned singularly. Second, elders [*plural*] are mentioned." Then he deduces that there were "multiple elders at each church."[17] Added to this, unless a particular elder is addressed, the term—along with *overseer* and *pastor*—is always used in the plural (e.g., Acts 11:30; 14:23; 15:2, 4, 22–23; 16:4; 20:17, 28; Eph. 4:11; 1 Tim. 5:17; Titus 1:5; James 5:14; 1 Peter 5:1). Theologian Wayne Grudem, after surveying the New Testament texts on elders, concluded similarly:

> First, no passage suggests that any church, no matter how small, had only one elder. The consistent New Testament pattern is a plurality of elders "in every church" (Acts 14:23) and "in every city" (Titus 1:5). Second, we do not see a diversity of forms of government in the New Testament church, but a unified and consistent pattern in which every church had elders governing it and keeping watch over it (Acts 20:28; Heb. 13:17; 1 Peter 5:2–3).[18]

Who were the elders in the early church? It is easy to read our modern concepts of a senior pastor and his church staff into the New Testament pattern. But there were no professional theological schools to produce "pastors" in the first century. The early churches selected men from within their membership to serve as elders. When Paul and Barnabas returned to Lystra, Iconium, and Antioch, "they . . . appointed elders for them in every church" (Acts 14:23). The appoin-

---

16 Ibid.
17 Personal correspondence with Bill Murray, Germantown, Tenn., September 2, 2002.
18 Wayne Grudem, *Systematic Theology: An Introduction to Biblical Doctrine* (Grand Rapids: Zondervan, 1994), 100–120.

tees were not ministerial apprentices or even seasoned pastors. Rather, Paul and Barnabas chose a number of men within each of the churches to serve as elders in their own congregations. There is no evidence in these passages or throughout the New Testament that the office of elder evolved into something like modern full-time ministry service. Rather, it appears that godly men who demonstrated Christian character and leadership qualities were set apart to serve their churches, often, perhaps, while continuing in their normal occupations. Probably not all of them had pronounced preaching gifts, but certainly all of them were "able to teach" (1 Tim. 3:2).[19]

Titus followed this same model of appointing elders while acting as the apostolic representative on the island of Crete. Paul instructed Titus to "appoint elders in every city," then set forth the qualifications necessary for spiritual service in the church (Titus 1:5–9). Missing is any reference to appointing those, in modern jargon, who are "called to preach." I do not deny the call to preach—I believe in it very strongly.[20] But a special gift of preaching is never set forth as a requirement for serving as an elder. He must be "able to teach" and able to "exhort in sound doctrine and to refute those who contradict"; there is no requirement that he be endowed with preaching gifts.[21] Some elders may, but not all need be. Elders must know the doctrines of Holy Scripture and be able to wield "the sword of the Spirit" when teaching or talking with others; but the requirement of pulpit ministry is not laid upon them.

Precisely here do we find the wisdom of the New Testament pattern of plural eldership. No one man possesses all the gifts necessary for leading a congregation. Some men are endowed with strong pulpit gifts, but lack effective pastoral skills. Others excel in pastoral work of visiting and counseling, but are not strong when it comes to pulpit exposition. Some have unusual abilities in organizing and administrating the ministries of the church, but falter in pulpit and counseling skills. Some, to be sure, are multi-gifted and capable of doing different things. But the strain of tending to the entire ministry needs of the church can quickly deplete even the most gifted man.

The dilemma is that every congregation needs to be led by men with all of these skills—pulpit, pastoral, and administrative. Of course, many congregations don't

---

19 See chapter 11 where the subject of leadership development in mission settings, especially among unreached people groups, is addressed.
20 See Tony Sargent, *The Sacred Anointing: The Preaching of Dr. Martyn Lloyd-Jones* (Wheaton, IL: Crossway, 1994), 17–38.
21 See 1 Timothy 3:2, where teaching refers to instruction in biblical doctrines, and Titus 1:9, where the exhortations or urgings are to be grounded in Scripture, as are the refutations.

have the financial resources to hire trained ministers to meet every such need, and so too often they delay in addressing such needs. But the New Testament pattern of elders makes such delays unnecessary. Needs will be met and churches will be strengthened as churches patiently labor to bring together godly, gifted men to serve with equality for the sake of the church's spiritual health and mission. Some of these men will be compensated as full-time or part-time ministers, while others will serve *gratis*.

Leadership by a plurality of godly men who are accountable to one another reduces the temptation for one man to wield excessive authority or to use the church to satisfy his ego. Each man's weaknesses are complemented by the strengths of his fellow elders. Think of Paul's warning to the Ephesian elders (Acts 20:17–38). Paul did not put one man on notice of the dangers awaiting their church, but a group of men. One man might cave in to the pressure of persecution. One man might fall prey to false teachers. One man might be overwhelmed by a variety of problems. In contrast, plural leadership increases the church's ability to stand firmly regardless of impediments to the faith. Mark Dever, senior pastor of Capitol Hill Baptist Church in Washington, DC, and an elder in that congregation, advocates setting apart elders from within the local church. His comments on plurality offer a clear testimony to the effectiveness of this biblical pattern:

> Probably the single most helpful thing to my pastoral ministry among my church has been the recognition of the other elders [most of whom do not receive a salary from the church]. The service of the other elders along with me has had immense benefits. A plurality of elders should aid a church by rounding out the pastor's gifts, making up for some of his defects, supplementing his judgment, and creating support in the congregation for decisions, leaving leaders less exposed to unjust criticism. Such plurality also makes leadership more rooted and permanent, and allows for more mature continuity. It encourages the church to take more responsibility for the spiritual growth of its own members and helps make the church less dependent on its employees. Our own church in Washington has enjoyed these benefits and more because of God's gift to us of elders.[22]

---

22 Mark Dever, *A Display of God's Glory: Basics of Church Structure* (Washington, DC: Center for Church Reform, 2001), 24.

THE SENIOR PASTOR AND ELDER PLURALITY

I am not suggesting that churches replace their pastor and divvy up the load among the elders. It is often preferable, in fact, for some men in every church to apply themselves full-time to the labors of ministry, especially for those who will be involved in the weekly ministry of proclamation. That seems to be the clear intimation of 1 Timothy 5:17: "The elders who rule well are to be considered worthy of double honor, *especially those who work hard at preaching and teaching"* (italics added). The "double honor" refers to remuneration.[23] My own weekly schedule, for instance, is filled with the rigorous study of preparing to teach and preach, counseling, meetings with staff, pastoral visits, and other pastoral responsibilities. With all of this, it would be difficult, if not impossible, to be employed in a secular occupation while also giving adequate attention to my family. Elders do not replace the need for a pastor who labors in the Word and gives overall leadership to the church. Instead, they come alongside him as fellow servants, filling the gaps in the pastor's weaknesses, holding up his arms as he preaches, figuratively speaking, and sharing the burden for meeting pastoral needs in the church.

Some people treat the idea of plural elders as a *third* office in the New Testament to be added to the offices of pastor and deacon. Indeed, John Calvin believed there are four offices: pastor, doctor, elder, and deacon.[24] But the New Testament teaches that a plurality of lay elders belong to the same office as the senior pastor and any other pastoral staff. Benjamin Merkle rightly explains that the limited use of "pastor" in the New Testament emphasizes the dual roles of shepherding and teaching the flock of God, which are the very same roles as elders/overseers. So the "pastor" is not a separate office from overseer/elder. Additionally, the epistles mention no separate set of character qualifications for the pastor because his qualifications are found in the qualities belonging to elders or overseers.[25]

My fellow elders serve to protect me so that I can fulfill my calling and ministry. For instance, my summer schedule in 2002 was unusually packed. I led a mission trip; spent a week out of town, wrote for an online journal; spoke for a week to six hundred kids at a youth camp; participated in a conference; directed our summer

---

23 *LKGNT*, 631.

24 See John Calvin, *Institutes of the Christian Religion* (ed. John T. McNeil; trans. Ford Lewis Battles; Philadelphia: Westminster Press, 1960), 4.3. See also Paul Avis, *The Church in the Theology of the Reformers* (Eugene, OR: Wipf and Stock, 2002 from 1981 Marshall, Morgan, and Scott publication), 109–115.

25 Benjamin L. Merkle, *40 Questions about Elders and Deacons* (Grand Rapids: Kregel Academic & Professional, 2008), 56.

internship program; took a family vacation; and fulfilled normal ministry demands. In the meantime, a friend invited me to lead a mission conference at his church during the fall. I submitted this request to the elders. These men comprise the most supportive group with whom I have ever associated, and they encourage me to participate in ministry beyond our church. But in this case, they knew that I was beyond overloaded. So they told me that accepting this preaching assignment would not be a good decision. As much as I wanted to do the conference, especially on a topic I loved, I accepted their decision as the wisest choice. One of the elders had said to me, "Pastor, we want to protect you *from you*." And he was right on target. In God's providence, I ended up needing the very dates of the missions conference to travel out of town to minister to my father-in-law, who died shortly afterward. Those days will always be etched into my mind as precious time in helping a dying man. The Lord used my fellow elders to keep me on track so that I could best fulfill my ministry and, more importantly, maintain priority in ministering to my own family.

ELDER DUTIES

In some of my discussions with other church leaders on the topic of elders, the question comes up, "Don't elders simply do the job of deacons in Baptist church-es?" It is true that some churches have raised the bar of qualifications for their deacons so that they function as elders, even though their title does not reflect it. It seems that most deacons, however, are treated like a management board. They deal with problems with the water heater, decide on re-striping the parking lot, approve the church youth trip, and so forth.

In fact, these tasks are neither ignoble nor unnecessary. They are quite important. But what we must realize is that, when the leadership group of a church is swamped in the mundane and temporal, they can fail to attend to deeper spiritual needs.

Biblically, therefore, deacons *do* take care of the temporal matters of church life so that elders are free to concentrate upon spiritual matters. Deacons apply much-needed wisdom and energy to the ample physical needs in the church, often using these opportunities to minister also to the spiritual needs of others.

But elders have a different focus. Minneapolis pastor John Piper sums up the functions of elders under two headings: teaching and governing. He observes, "[Elders] are the doctrinal guardians of the flock and the overseers of the life of the church responsible to God for the feeding and care and ministry of the people."[26] Grudem concurs: "Elders, then, had responsibility to rule and to teach

---

26   John Piper, "Biblical Eldership: Shepherd the Flock of God Among You," sec. 6; accessed March

in New Testament churches."[27] While the inclusiveness of these categories seems appropriate, the duties of elders might better be approached in a fourfold manner: doctrine, discipline, direction, and distinction in modeling the Christian life.

Doctrine. The primary biblical qualification that distinguishes elders from deacons is that elders must be apt to teach and able to engage others doctrinally, even those in disagreement (1 Tim. 3:2; Titus 1:9). The elders' attention to doctrine assures the flock that their spiritual leaders will guard them against the "savage wolves" that would attack them to subvert their faith (Acts 20:28–30). But elders are not just guards; they are teachers of truth as well. Shepherding the flock of God requires feeding the church upon the rich truths of God's Word (1 Peter 5:2).

The elders at my church regularly discuss the contents of pulpit and classroom teaching. I freely discuss with them my preaching schedule so that they might offer insight on how I might address "the whole purpose of God" in my pulpit ministry (Acts 20:27). We also work together to plan the ongoing training that our church offers in the broad range of Christian disciplines and ministries, as well as to put together conferences and seminars to profit the church and community. We also develop teaching modules for various church-spon-

> **Four Elder Duties**
> - Doctrine
> - Discipline
> - Direction
> - Distinction

sored venues that include historical and theological studies; topics related to family, evangelism, apologetics, and personal issues; preparation for mission trips; classes on how to study the Bible; and studies on the spiritual disciplines, all recommended and usually taught by our elders. Our elders want our church to grasp every genre of biblical literature and become equipped in the broad facets of spiritual disciplines. Therefore, they help to map out a plan of doctrine for the church.

Discipline. Coupled with doctrine is the matter of discipline. The word conveys the idea of training, admonishing, encouraging, correcting, and, at times, removing someone from church membership. Church discipline has grown out of favor in most circles but it is critical for maintaining healthy congregations.[28] While discipline is the work of the entire church (Matt. 18:15–20; Gal. 6:1–2), the

---

25, 2003; http://www.desiringgod.org/resource-library/seminars/biblical-eldership-part-1a. See also John Piper, *Biblical Eldership* (Minneapolis: Desiring God Ministries, 1999).

27 Grudem, *Systematic Theology*, 153–179.

28 See Mark Dever, *Nine Marks of a Healthy Church*, rev. ed. (Wheaton, IL: Crossway, 2004), 167–194; Jonathan Leeman, *The Church and the Surprising Offense of God's Love: Reintroducing the Doctrines of Church Membership and Discipline* (9Marks; Wheaton, IL: Crossway, 2010).

elders must shoulder the burden to ensure the church's health by leading in its practice. Again, this falls under the role of shepherding as well as keeping watch over the souls of the congregation (Heb. 13:17). If a pastor stands alone in bringing a matter of church discipline to the congregation, opponents will likely skewer him. But the strength of godly leaders within the church, standing together in dealing with such matters, urges the entire church to recognize the seriousness of discipline. Long before my fellow elders and I have presented an individual to the church for the action of dismissal, we have prayed and wept together over the spiritual condition of the person.

I remember a conversation with a fellow pastor in which he bemoaned a couple who attended his church who were divisive and constantly agitating destructive issues. He told me that he was unsure of how to handle the situation, but he understood that some action needed to be taken soon or else he would have larger problems on his hands. Gratefully, this pastor has elders in his church. I suggested that he direct the elders to call in this couple for counsel and warning, so that the elders as a group might bear the burden and not the pastor alone. The elders could decide a course of action to protect the church from division and also protect their pastor from becoming embroiled in controversy.

Direction. Direction involves decision-making, planning, administrating, delegating, and even governing the details of church life. This is where the work of shepherding includes not only feeding but also giving direction to the flock (1 Peter 5:2). Perhaps this work of shepherding and feeding is why the term *overseer* is used interchangeably with *elder,* since the ancient overseers were involved in directing those under their charge. Paul seems to be alluding to the task of direction when exhorting the Thessalonian believers to esteem the leaders who "have charge over you in the Lord and give you instruction" (1 Thess. 5:12–13). To "have charge over" refers specifically to leading and directing the church.[29] Paul also speaks of the elders' "rule" (1 Tim. 5:17), which indicates they will "exercise a position of leadership, *rule, direct, be at the head (of)."*[30] Some have abused this "rule" concept by prying into every facet of their members' lives. But spiritual leaders have no cause to manipulate or control the flock that belongs to a greater Shepherd.[31] Lording one's position and authority in the church is strictly forbidden (1 Peter 5:3). Still, the writer of Hebrews calls these spiritual leaders "the ones leading you," giving the distinct impression of

---

29 *LKGNT,* 602.
30 *BDAG,* 870; italics original.
31 This is clearly stated in Acts 20:28: "Be on guard for yourselves and for all the flock, among which the Holy Spirit has made you overseers, to *shepherd the church of God* which He purchased with His own blood," and in 1 Peter 5:2: "*Shepherd the flock of God* among you" (italics added).

regular direction in ministry (Heb. 13:17). Directing the flock is no stale and stiff business, but calls for regular involvement with and knowledge of the congregation. That's why James instructs the scattered saints to "call for the elders of the church" so that the elders can pray for sick members (James 5:14). Elders must seek to know the needs of the flock, understanding its strengths and weaknesses, while recognizing its spiritual gifts and ministry inclinations.

Distinction. The most daunting responsibility for an elder involves living with distinction, or modeling the Christian life. Elders are to be examples to the flock, which is the reason for immediate public censure when one falls into public sin (1 Tim. 5:19–21). Peter told the elders "to be examples to the flock" (1 Peter 5:3). And the writer of Hebrews reminds struggling believers to reflect upon those who had been leading them and "imitate their faith" (Heb. 13:7).

It is because elders are set up as examples that Paul offers such detailed description for what their character should be like (1 Tim. 3:2–7; Titus 1:6–9). With the exception of "apt to teach" and "not a recent convert," all Christians should be able, in principle, to imitate what an elder is. Instead, elders should model the blamelessness that ought to characterize all who know Christ (1 Tim. 3:2; Titus 1:6).

What difference can elders make in church life? If a congregation has a group of godly spiritual leaders who walk with Christ, who help the body flesh out the details of the Christian life, who attend to the doctrine of the church, who maintain discipline of the members, and who regularly give direction to the church, that church will be better positioned to grow spiritually and do ministry.

REFLECTIONS

- What is the challenge for modern church government in light of God's Word?
- What are three titles used for plural eldership, and how does each shade the meaning of the office?
- How is the plurality of elders taught in the New Testament?
- What are the strengths of plurality in the local church?
- What are the fourfold duties of elders?

CHAPTER FOUR

NOT ACTUALLY A NEW IDEA

"Let me tell you two things you may not like about me if you knew them. Number one, I'm a Calvinist. Number two, I believe elders are biblical and should lead the church."

This was Mark Dever's attempt to provoke the pulpit committee of the Capitol Hill Baptist Church to engage with him theologically. The search was on for a new senior pastor after a tragically short pastorate ended in January of 1993. Dever, the newly minted Cambridge PhD, knew the conversation needed to become more substantial if both parties were to discern whether they were compatible. Several hours of talk over Chinese food had passed, and no one had asked any significant questions about what the young candidate believed. Years later I heard Mark liken Southern Baptists to a man whose car crashed in a head-on collision. The man woke from a coma and only remembered one thing: evangelism. Theology and ecclesiology had seemingly vanished from the Southern Baptist's mind through the trauma.

Over the candidating weekend Mark preached twice, held a churchwide question-and-answer time, and met with various subgroups of the church, along with the staff. On Monday morning, before boarding the plane, two senior members of the church held another meeting with Mark. What did these two godfathers of the church want to talk about? Of all the things they heard over the weekend, only one thing bothered them: Mark's talk about elders.

Why did this topic get stuck in the craw of these men? For five reasons, I suspect. First, it was unfamiliar. They were lifelong Baptists, and mentioning "elders" to most twentieth-century Baptists was like saying "College of Cardinals." It was unfamiliar, maybe even secretive, and therefore deserving of suspicion.

Second, there was a missing history. Richard Nixon had his famous 18.5-minute-gap tape, but that was nothing compared to CHBC. There was a lot of Bible knowledge and a great recollection of (local) church history over the last few decades. But there was a 1,900-year gap in which the history of the church was simply invisible. It was as if no one had said or written anything on the church in between the Apostle Paul and Rick Warren.

Third, it smelled Presbyterian. The logic goes like this: Presbyterians have elders. We're not Presbyterian. Therefore we don't have elders. We are not sure why we are not Presbyterian, but we know we're not.

Fourth, there is inertia. "Don't change anything. Just restore it." That was the impossible, unachievable, unmistakable wisdom by which the church lived. Ironically, one otherwise godly woman who attended CHBC for decades but never joined, was unhelpfully circulating an article among the church staff entitled "Why Churches Don't Change." The congregation had mastered the art of indecision. Words like "bold" and "courageous" were absent from their lexicon.

Fifth, they feared a power grab. This, indeed, was the real culprit. Though they could not explain it, the godfathers were certain that adding elders would reapportion control and give authority to a few, while they had grown comfortable with authority residing, kind of, in no one. At the time, CHBC was layered with a host of committees. There was a Committee of Deacons, Deaconesses, Finance, Buildings, Housing, Missions, Pulpit, Church Council, Flowers (yes, flowers), as well as a Committee on Committees. To many in the church, locating authority in one group of men smelled like trouble.

For Dever the idea of elders was neither new nor foreign. He had been exposed to Baptist churches with faithful elders in the 1980s and had even helped to plant one. In a 1991 letter, he instructed the elders of a young church in Massachusetts what to look for in a pastor, and listed nine different things. Regarding church leadership he wrote the following:

> Seventh, and perhaps most initially difficult in your situation, I would require that the person understand and be convinced of the New Testament practice of having a plurality of elders (see Acts 14:23; the regular practice of Paul referring to a number of elders in any one local church). I am completely convinced of this as the New Testament practice, and as particularly needful in churches both then and now without an apostolic presence.

> That does not mean that the pastor has no distinct role (look up the references to preaching and preachers in a concordance), but he is fun-

damentally part of the eldership. This means that decisions involving the church, yet which do not come to the attention of the whole church, should not fall to the pastor alone, but to the elders as a whole.

While this is cumbersome at points (as I'm sure you know only too well) it has immense benefits in rounding out the pastor's gifts, in giving him good support in the church, and in too many other ways to mention now.

Anyway, this would have to be made quite clear when calling a pastor. If he is a typical Southern Baptist he will assume that the elders are either deacons or there simply to help him do what he wants to do. He may well not have a good appreciation for the fact that you are inviting him fundamentally to be one of the elders, and, among you, the pastor or the primary teaching elder.

I'm convinced that if most pastors understood this idea, they would leap at the idea, given the weight it removes from their shoulders. I'm also worried that many of those who wouldn't, wouldn't do so because of unbiblical understandings of their own role, or, worse, unsanctified self-centeredness.[1]

To assuage fears among the flock, Dever let them know that he could happily pastor for forty years without elders—he would not split the church over it. Yet with or without elders, something had to give. Given the age of the congregation, the giving pattern, and the city demographics, maintaining status quo was not an option. Still, given the congregation's reluctance to change, changing the church would not be easy.

Gratefully, the Capitol Hill Baptist Church did call Dever as the pastor, and in the fall of 1994 he began his ministry among that precious and somewhat recalcitrant remnant. Since my own 90-day temporary job as church administrator had, somehow, grown into several years, he and I did our best to hit the ground running together that fall as pastor and administrator.

Now, twenty years later and with the benefit of hindsight, I can confidently say four things about the prospect of change at CHBC at that point, specifically the change of adopting a plurality of elders. First, change was needed. We had been watching plenty of old church buildings in our neighborhood be sold off, and so

---

1   This letter has been lightly edited.

Our Faith is in Christ, Not Elders!

we were only too aware of what could be coming for us. Some were torn down, others were converted: Grace Baptist Church was renamed Grace Condominiums. To spark some movement, I had formerly written an article for our church's newsletter entitled "Our Five Year Window of Opportunity." That "window" was closing fast.

Second, change would be lonely. Unity of vision was non-existent. And it would continue to elude the church unless it grew to the point where the recalcitrant remnant became a small minority. Fred Catherwood, the son-in-law of D. Martyn Lloyd-Jones and a fellow church member with Mark at his church in Cambridge, England, said to Mark when he left England, "Remember Mark, in five years that church may be yours, but certainly not when you arrive." For a new pastor, an old church is an accumulation of people who have come at different times for different reasons under the ministries of different men. Mark's name might be on the sign, the letterhead, and the bulletins, but he would have to work hard to win their hearts and even harder to shape them into one mind. Without a plurality of elders to help with the work, it would feel lonely.

Third, change would be incremental. To bring about change in a church where there is little understanding and trust, pastors too often resort to politics and manipulation. Undoubtedly many such pastors press for change more quickly than a congregation can handle. But I saw Mark move slowly and carefully. For instance, he:

- addressed the topic of elders in the normal course of week-in, week-out expositional preaching.
- modeled what an elder should be publicly as he led services, and privately as he shepherded his family.
- salted the congregation by giving away good books every Wednesday night at Bible Study and every Sunday night at the church's prayer meeting. (In the 1990s there were only a couple of good booklets on elders, but they got passed around.)
- invited his friend D. A. Carson, when Carson was passing through Washington DC, to give a presentation on elders during the Sunday School hour.

In all of this, there was never a rush or a demand for change.

After a few years, it came time to address the out-of-date church constitution. The rewrite went through multiple layers of individuals and groups, and took two more years. One neighbor quipped, "It took the founding fathers less time to write the US

Constitution!" When it was time to vote on the new document that included elders, there was only one person in opposition. Only one! I think this lack of opposition pointed to God's grace resulting from Mark's incremental, unhurried approach to change. Herb Carlson, a member of CHBC since 1947, observed on Mark's tenth anniversary as pastor, "I don't remember any one day where something changed, but now everything is different!" That's the sign of a good pace.

Did the new constitution read exactly as Dever had hoped? No. Mark and I worked on the initial draft, pointing it in a particular direction, principally to include the offices of both elders and deacons. But after two years of editing by others, the document was better written and off by a few degrees from the original, but nothing fundamental was changed. The lesson: Young pastors too often fight over the leaves instead of the trees and forest, but we should keep our eyes on the bigger picture. We were just happy because we were going in the right direction.

Fourth and finally, change would be worth it. Would you rather pastor alone or have a group of godly, qualified elders to help you as you wrestle through doctrine, discipline, and direction? Can Sara biblically remarry following her divorce? Should Ben be excommunicated for sexual sin? Should we renovate the education wing or give more money to missions? To be a pastor is to bear weight. You bear the weight of faithfully preaching God's Word to God's people. You bear the weight of sheep who sin. You bear the weight of those who mourn. Praise God he designed all that weight to be borne by many, not by one. Ask a pastor who is surrounded, supported, and held up by godly elders, and he will tell you that making the change is worth it.

CHAPTER FIVE

CHARACTER AND CONGREGATIONALISM

Why do we need spiritual leaders known as elders and deacons in our churches? Members often have high education levels, vast experience, and varied abilities. Also, most congregations have less than 100 members. Would it not be easier for one man to lead the church?

In fact, one man cannot care for every need in any ministry. Some churches expect him to, since that is why they hired him. But the living organism known as the local church has far too many needs and opportunities for service and growth for one man to meet. He might excel at preaching, but fall short on ministering to those in crisis. He might maintain regular hours for counseling, but neglect to plan, direct, and equip the church. Often the pastor becomes the brunt of criticism because he fails to wear enough hats to satisfy the needs (and sometimes whims) of the congregation. The church can have unrealistic expectations of the solitary pastor, and the pastor can agonize over feelings of inadequacy for not fulfilling the church's expectations. But there is a better way.

Every situation a church faces calls for attending to the Word of God. In some areas, the Word does not address directly the matter at hand but it has principles worth bringing to bear. In other areas, it gives a clear answer. Certainly, the issue of elders and deacons is such a case.

SURVEYING THE BOOK OF ACTS

By surveying the book of Acts, we see that the official titles of elders and

deacons were not immediately named in the early church. There was no for-
mation committee or announcement that established the offices. Instead, we
see the emergence of what some have termed "deacon prototypes" in "The
Seven" individuals called by the church to care for food distribution in Acts 6,
as well as a prototype of the ministry of elders in "The Twelve" apostles who
labored in the Word and prayer (Acts 6:4). The former group focused upon
the temporal needs of the church, while the latter sought to teach and govern
the church.

The early chapters of Acts refer to the apostles without referring to elders.
Then chapter 11 refers to "the elders" (Acts 11:30). But not until Acts 14:23 are
"elders" formally appointed in the infant church: "When they had appointed
elders for them in every church, having prayed with fasting, they commended
them to the Lord in whom they had believed." These young, small churches of
Asia Minor needed biblical instruction, regular discipline, spiritual leadership,
and models for the faith. So the apostle Paul, wanting to ensure the churches'
continued spiritual growth, appointed elders (plural) in every church (singular).
In Acts 15:2, the elders join the apostles as the spiritual leaders in Jerusalem.
From this point onward, elders become the norm in the book (see Acts 15:4,
6, 22–23; 16:4; 20:17; 21:18). All this offers an excellent pattern.

While there is no mention of deacons in Acts, Paul's letter to the young
church in Philippi treats them as part of the official leadership of the church
along with the plurality of overseers (Phil. 1:1). His first letter to Timothy also
treats deacons as an important part of the spiritual service in Ephesus under
Timothy's pastoral charge (1 Tim. 3:8–13). In the epistles of Paul, Peter, James,
John, the book of Hebrews, and the Revelation, significant passages refer to
spiritual leaders of congregations (see 1 Tim. 3:1–7; Heb. 13:7, 17–19; James
5:14–15; 1 Peter 5:1–5; 3 John 12; Rev. 2–3). No one portion of Scripture relates
everything concerning these spiritual leaders, but taken together these passages
form a marvelous working structure of true, New Testament church life.

WHY ELDERS AND DEACONS?

While deacons are not the subject of this present work, it is helpful to reflect
for a moment upon both offices.

1. *Elders and deacons are the pattern taught in the early church.* The early
   churches serve as role models for the structure and leadership of
   present-day churches. Rather than simply structuring today's churches

in a clever but nonbiblical fashion, churches should adhere to the polity evident in Scripture. This makes sense for evangelicals who believe in the sufficiency of Scripture for life and practice.

2. *Elders and deacons assure congregations that the "whole person" will receive effective ministry.* Responsibilities of elders and deacons certainly overlap at times—deacons will indeed find plenty of spiritually oriented work, while elders will occasionally deal with temporal issues—yet those two offices are distinct in their essential duties.

3. *Scripture does not specify a precise number of elders and deacons to be appointed in the church, but presents the offices in the plural* (two or more). If diverse congregations, like the more mature and larger Jerusalem church as well as the weaker and smaller Lystra church, need elders, then it is apparent that churches of every size and geographical locale do, too. Also, the passing of time does not diminish the spiritual or temporal needs of those making up the church. In short, the New Testament does not treat church location, size, or maturity as relevant to whether a church needs elders and deacons.

4. *Elders and deacons give a church the opportunity to function under God-given authority, which keeps the church headed in the proper direction, builds unity, and increases efficiency in ministry.*

Churches profit spiritually by the effective ministry of elders and deacons. Therefore, churches bear significant responsibility in appointing qualified candidates for the offices.

Why Do We Need Elders and Deacons?

- This is the pattern of the New Testament church.
- The pattern assures congregations of well-rounded, balanced ministry.
- The pattern meets diverse congregational needs through functioning in plurality.
- The pattern strengthens the church's unity and efficiency.

There does not appear to be one way that elders were chosen in the early church. As scholar Daniel Wallace points out, "Much of the instruction given about church order is *ad hoc* rather than of universal principle."[1] So we must understand what is subject to principle and what is flexible. Acts 14 says that Paul and Barnabas "appointed" the first elders in the young churches of Asia Minor (v. 23). However, as commentator Simon Kistemaker notes, "the term *to appoint* actually means to approve by a show of hands in a congregational meeting,"[2] indicating that Paul and Barnabas somehow involved the congregation in their decision. In the earlier case of the deacon prototypes of Acts 6, the language also suggests the congregation was involved in the decision-making process. They were told to "select from among you seven men" (Acts 6:3), meaning they were to inspect or examine men to be selected to this office.[3] The congregation then put forward the names of seven men who met with the apostolic approval. The precise way they did this is not explained.

The same is true in the letter to Titus. In the process of forming the church in Crete, Titus was told to "appoint elders in every city" (Titus 1:5). Did Titus single out the men without the congregation's involvement? Or did he involve them? The ambiguity of the language makes it difficult to say for sure, but the word "appoint," again, suggests it is best to think that Titus received congregational input and, certainly, approval with those he appointed.

When it comes to how churches should select elders and deacons, it is perhaps best to leave the precise details of the process to the individual, autonomous churches. Some flexibility seems to be in order. But at the minimum, congregations should be involved either in nominating faithful men or in affirming men nominated by the existing elders. Certainly nominees should be examined by the elder board, so that they might eliminate anyone not qualified for office. Eliminating candidates is difficult to accomplish at a congregational level because of the intensive and personal nature of examination required.

ELDERS AND CHARACTER

In the Pastoral Epistles, the office of overseer is something that a man might "aspire" to embrace (1 Tim. 3:1). But does he just volunteer to serve as elder? The list of character qualities no doubt means that churches should somehow examine those who aspire to serve as elders; otherwise spiritual wolves would gain ready entrance into church leadership. Elders who fail to uphold the

---

1 Daniel Wallace, "Who Should Run the Church? A Case for the Plurality of Elders," 7; accessed March 25, 2003; http://www.bible.org/docs/soapbox/caseform.htm.
2 Simon Kistemaker, *Acts* (New Testament Commentary; Grand Rapids: Baker, 1990), 525.
3 *BDAG, episkeptomai*, 378.

character and practice necessary for this office should be publicly rebuked before the entire church. They can be accused publicly, but only if there are at least two or three witnesses, lest unfounded charges be leveled against them (1 Tim. 5:19–21).

What qualifies a man for the office of elder in a local church? In my observation, the greatest oversight by churches considering elders—or even churches that have deacons functioning as elders—is a neglect of biblical qualifications. The bar must be raised for these officers to serve their respective churches as they ought. In fact, nothing is more important than examining men in light of the qualifications set forth in 1 Timothy 3 and Titus 1, and then expecting those men to remain faithful in these qualities. In church settings where

> *The bar must be raised for elders and deacons if these officers are to serve their respective churches as they ought.*

shifting to elder leadership might create undue conflict, I would recommend, at the very least, raising the bar for the spiritual qualifications of all leaders. Churches that fill vacant leadership slots without seriously considering the nominees' qualifications set the stage for deeper problems. As Pastor John Piper has expressed, "Spiritual qualifications should never be sacrificed to technical expertise."[4] Gerald Cowen adds, "For the church to have a moral impact on society, the highest standards should be upheld."[5] Appointing public speakers, accountants, legal experts, project managers, banking executives, and advertising gurus does not contribute to spiritual leadership. Individuals who are biblically qualified for either office might have additional technical expertise of these kinds, but such must always be secondary.

---

4 John Piper, "Biblical Eldership: Shepherd the Flock of God among You," sec. 4; accessed March 25, 2003; http://www.desiringgod.org/resource-library/seminars/biblical-eldership-part-1a
5 Gerald Cowen, *Who Rules the Church? Examining Congregational Leadership and Church Government* (Nashville: Broadman and Holman, 2003), 63.

I Timothy 3:1–7

It is a trustworthy statement: if any man aspires to the office of overseer, it is a fine work he desires to do. An overseer, then, must be above reproach, the husband of one wife, temperate, prudent, respectable, hospitable, able to teach, not addicted to wine or pugnacious, but gentle, peaceable, free from the love of money. He must be one who manages his own household well, keeping his children under control with all dignity (but if a man does not know how to manage his own household, how will he take care of the church of God?), and not a new convert, so that he will not become conceited and fall into the condemnation incurred by the devil. And he must have a good reputation with those outside the church, so that he will not fall into reproach and the snare of the devil.

It is worth thinking through these characteristics one at a time.[6] The chief characteristic of an elder is that he is *above reproach*. Paul demands this: "An overseer, then, *must* be above reproach" (emphasis added).[7] The phrase *above reproach* serves as an umbrella under which the balance rests. "It *doesn't* mean that a man has to be perfect," writes John MacArthur. "If so, we would all be disqualified! It means that there must not be any great blot on his life that others might point to."[8] Piper adds, "The word seems to be a general word for living in a way that gives no cause for others to think badly of the church or of the faith or the Lord. . . . The focus here is not a person's relationship to the Lord, but how others see him."[9] A man known as a hothead or a womanizer or a shady business dealer or loose with his tongue has no place in the eldership.

The phrase *husband of one wife* has generated much print over the years. Many commentators offer detailed arguments about its meaning, so there is no need here to work through all the issues regarding this quality. But in brief, the phrase literally means "a one-woman-man," pointing to fidelity and an ongoing devotion in the marriage relationship. In a day of rampant moral failure within church leadership, it is critical that elders set the example for faithfulness and devotion

---

6 See chapter 9 for an example of how a pastor might approach this text expositionally, making appropriate pastoral applications.
7 Italics added where *must* implies a moral necessity.
8 John MacArthur, *Shepherdology: A Master Plan for Church Leadership* (Panorama City, CA: Master's Fellowship, 1989), 72.
9 Piper, "Biblical Eldership," sec. 7.

in their marriages. Is there a reason to question an elder candidate's devotion to his wife? If so, then he should not be placed in a position of leadership.[10]

The word *temperate* refers to the ability of an elder to exercise self-control over his appetites so that they do not dictate his life, whether regarding alcohol (as the original meaning) or the broader desires of the flesh. The elder is thus to be sober-minded in all things.

Prudent implies that an elder's mind remains engaged, that he is able to exercise sound judgment even in difficult times.

Respectable implies that the elder's personal life is well ordered, including in his relationships with others. He does not engage in pretenses, but conscientiously guards his inner life so that his outward conduct might bring honor to Christ and the gospel.

An elder should also be *hospitable*, a word that refers to a love of strangers. His home must be opened to others as a center of ministry beyond the walls of the church building.

The elder's *aptitude to teach* (1 Tim. 3:2; Titus 1:9) is central to his work. Some divide elders into categories of ruling elders and teaching elders, based on 1 Timothy 5:17: "The elders who rule well are to be considered worthy of double honor, especially those who work hard at preaching and teaching." Without question, all the elders should be involved in the ruling or governing of the church. But all of them should also be involved in the teaching ministry of the church. Now, some elders excel in teaching while others excel in governing, but to turn this distinction into two kinds of elder offices seems artificial and beyond the intention of this verse. The necessary balance of teaching and governing keeps the entire group of elders focused on the Scriptures. It also requires elders to be theologically astute, biblically articulate, and ready to instruct individuals or groups as the need arises. An elder who only knows how to "rule" but lacks the biblical precision called for in teaching will likely create disharmony among the elders. Nothing has honed the elders of my church more than making sure that all of us are students of Scripture who are responsible to teach the church.

An elder should *not be addicted to alcohol*. John Piper puts it this way: "Freedom from enslavements should be so highly prized that no bondage is yielded to."[11] In other words, an elder must not "sit long at his wine" or be "a slave to drink," he also must guard other areas of life where he might be tempted to enslavement.[12]

---

10 See Andreas J. Köstenberger, *God, Marriage, and Family* (2nd ed.; Wheaton, IL: Crossway, 2010), 239–248, for a thoughtful survey of the various positions regarding "a one woman man."

11 Piper, "Biblical Eldership," sec. 7.

12 *LKGNT*, 622.

Self-control will also be shown in the elder's temper. Therefore, he should be *not pugnacious but gentle,* which is to say, not a bully but a kind and forbearing man. An elder is *peaceable.* He goes to great lengths to avoid unnecessary conflict in the church.

He is also *free from the love of money,* which reminds us of the temporal nature of material things, and the enslaving power of materialism. Generosity, content- ment, and personal financial discipline serve to cure love of money.

An elder must *manage his own household well, keeping his children under control with all dignity.* Paul explains, "if a man does not know how to manage his own household, how will he take care of the church of God?" In other words, an elder must set the example of spiritual leadership in the home since, John Piper observes,

> The home is a proving ground for ministry. [The elder] should have submissive children. This does not mean perfect, but it does mean well disciplined, so that they do not blatantly and regularly disregard the in- structions of their parents. The children should revere the father *(meta pases semnotetos).* He should be a loving and responsible spiritual leader in the home. His wife should be respected and tenderly loved. Their relationship should be openly admirable.[13]

A man's ability in one realm is not unconnected to his ability in the other. Since spiritual maturity is at the heart of an elder's life, an elder *must not be a new convert.* Why? Paul explains, "so that he will not become conceited and fall into the condemnation incurred by the devil." Nothing seems to puff up an im- mature person more than a title. The eyes of church members are constantly fixed on the elders, seeking exemplary conduct and instruction. Putting a new believer into such a demanding role positions him to slip into the devil's trap of pride.[14]

Since an elder represents his church (and therefore Christ), he must *have a good reputation with those outside the church.* Again, why? Paul answers, "so that he will not fall into reproach and the snare of the devil." This does not mean that the world sets the standard for the church's leaders but, to be sure, the church's leaders must never slip below the world's standards of character, dignity, and propriety (except when the world's standards are contrary to God's Word, as with, for example, contemporary conceptions of tolerance). The high standards of Christian life and character must give the world no cause for accusation of hypocrisy in the church's leaders.

---

13 Piper, "Biblical Eldership," sec. 7.
14 Paul does not lay this same requirement in the epistle to Titus, a matter addressed later in chapter 21. "A new convert" is relative to the context.

Paul's list of character qualities penned to Titus resembles the list given to Timothy, but with some variations.

> ## Titus 1:5–9
>
> For this reason I left you in Crete, that you would set in order what remains and appoint elders in every city as I directed you, namely, if any man is above reproach, the husband of one wife, having children who believe, not accused of dissipation or rebellion. For the overseer must be above reproach as God's steward, not self-willed, not quick-tempered, not addicted to wine, not pugnacious, not fond of sordid gain, but hospitable, loving what is good, sensible, just, devout, self-controlled, holding fast the faithful word which is in accordance with the teaching, so that he will be able both to exhort in sound doctrine and to refute those who contradict.

We might surmise that both epistles offer a sample of what Christian character looks like when taken seriously.

The quality of *above reproach* stands in Titus, as in Timothy, as a sentinel over the balance of the character requirements.

While the language in Titus regarding the family differs slightly from that in Timothy, the intention remains the same. The elder is to set an example by wisely ordering his own home. He must be the *husband of one wife, having children who believe, not accused of dissipation or rebellion.* John Piper provides helpful commentary that explains Paul's meaning regarding the children of elders:

Here, the focus is not just on the relationship of the children to the father, but on their behavior in general. They are not to be guilty of the accusation of "wild living" or uncontrolled behavior. And they are not to be "insubordinate."

Does *pista* mean "believing" (with RSV) or "faithful" in the sense of honest and trustworthy? In favor of the latter would be the use of the word in 1 Timothy 3:11, where women (deaconesses or wives of deacons) are to be *pistas en pasin,* faithful in all things. Other places in the pastoral epistles where the word seems to have this meaning are 1 Timothy 1:12, 15; 3:1; 4:9; 2 Timothy 2:11; 13; Titus 1:9; 3:8. So the idea seems to be of children who are well bred, orderly, generally obedient, responsible, and reliable.[15]

In other words, an elder cannot guarantee that his children are Christians, but he is responsible to see that they are well-behaved while they are under his care.

Paul continues, repeating the need for an elder's being *above reproach*, but now the reason is given that the elder is *God's steward*. The term points to the ongoing responsibility of the elder to manage the affairs of the church. If encumbered by areas of reproach or the need to hide his behavior, then he will not fare well as a manager of a spiritual body.

In Titus, Paul adds that an elder should not be *self-willed*, that is, never so stubborn about his own opinions that he is unteachable, unbending, or considerate only of himself.[16]

Nor should he be *quick-tempered*, or in the habit of firing off his tongue whenever someone contradicts him. Instead, he should be marked by *loving what is good, sensible, just, devout, self-controlled*. His priorities are fixed on the things that matter: relationships, justice, purity, and intense devotion to the Lord. The list is crowned by "self-control," a term meaning "complete self-mastery, which controls all passionate impulses and keeps the will loyal to the will of God."[17]

While Paul tells Timothy that elders must be *able to teach*, he expands on this in Titus, saying that an elder must also hold fast to "the faithful word which is in accordance with the teaching." That is, a man must not only understand biblical doctrine but he must diligently apply it to his life and practice. An elder must be a student of Scripture, faithful in reading and studying Bible doctrine, regular in delving deeply into the Word, thereby setting an example for the congregation. A man's faithfulness in the Word enables him to "be able both to exhort in sound doctrine"—teach, admonish, and instruct whether one-on-one or to groups—"and to refute those who contradict." That is, he readily deals with error and false teaching, and he corrects those who misapply God's Word for selfish or legalistic motives.

> **The most remarkable thing about these characteristics is that there is nothing remarkable about them.**
>
> **—D. A. Carson**

---

15   Piper, "Biblical Eldership," sec. 7.
16   *LKGNT*, 652.
17   Ibid.

In order to avoid self-scrutiny, some people have said that these character qualities are impossible to attain, and that no one fulfills them. But I think it is more accurate to say that Paul is calling upon elders in both of these texts to act like genuine Christians. Other than the ability to teach, none of the characteristics should be unusual among Christians—every believer should seek to be "above reproach." D. A. Carson once observed that "The most remarkable thing about these characteristics is that there is nothing remarkable about them."[18] Living in this way demonstrates that the elder takes seriously the gospel's intent of sanctifying a people for God's own possession (Titus 2:14).

Elders not only lead the congregation, they must also work with each other. The character qualities are therefore critical for plural leadership to live in unity and work together in humility. Alexander Strauch clearly expressed this need:

> When it functions properly, shared leadership requires a greater exercise of humble servanthood than does unitary leadership. In order for an eldership to operate effectively, the elders must show mutual regard for one another, submit themselves one to another, patiently wait upon one another, genuinely consider one another's interests and perspectives, and defer to one another. Eldership, then, enhances brotherly love, humility, mutuality, patience, and loving interdependence—qualities that are to mark the servant church.[19]

A man should demonstrate that he can submit to the elders before being asked to lead with the elders.

It would be wise for any church pursuing a transition to elder leadership, as the leaders teach on the topic, to emphasize the character even more than the function of elders. Functions will vary somewhat from church to church, but the character will not. A holy, humble servant life should always mark the men set apart as elders. Elders, deacons, and other church officers who fail to display the character required of spiritual leaders have done great damage to churches. Therefore, we

The goal of a church should not be to establish plural eldership at any cost, but rather to elevate the standards of spiritual leadership in the church at any cost.

---

18 Stated in a "Henry Forum" given at Capitol Hill Baptist Church.
19 Alexander Strauch, *Biblical Eldership: An Urgent Call to Restore Biblical Church Leadership*, rev. and exp. (Littleton, CO: Lewis and Roth, 1995), 114.

must set forth God's standards, making sure the bar we establish parallels the teaching of Scripture. Even congregations who are unsure of what elders should do are more likely to follow them when they live like Christians—and that, in essence, is what the qualifications describe. In a day when Christian character often seems indistinct from the world, elders should set an example of how to live as faithful disciples. The goal of a church should not be to establish plural eldership at any cost, but to elevate the standards of spiritual leadership in the church at any cost.

PLURALITY IN CONGREGATIONAL FRAMEWORK

In the process of elevating spiritual leadership, churches must pursue biblical patterns, including plural eldership. But some church leaders fear the term *elders*. One Southern Baptist leader stated his stark opposition: "I am not in favor of elder rule in the Southern Baptist church to which I belong, indeed, if the church to which I belong instituted elder rule, I would leave."[20]

During the past two decades a number of Baptist churches have adopted plural eldership in one form or another, but not all have done so smoothly. Churches have split over the issue because people fear that adopting a plural-elder model means jettisoning the cherished Baptist practice of congregationalism. Pastors have even been dismissed from the fellowship of their local associations over eldership.

Growing up in a Southern Baptist church, I observed that the office of elders was foreign to our polity. In the local Church of Christ congregations, on the other hand, the elders seemed to rule so firmly that they appeared to serve at their pleasure. Such a picture of "totalitarian rule" by elders put fear in many a Baptist's mind. In other churches, the elders lacked the spiritual dignity of the office. And in still others, weak elders seemed to lack the passion that ought to characterize spiritual leadership.

None of these pictures of elders comes from the Bible, but they help explain why the office of elders is sometimes feared. Many Baptists fear the loss of congregationalism, while many pastors have feared the loss of authority.

These fears are understandable. But as in any situation that causes fear, stepping back and taking an unbiased look at the facts can alleviate anxiety. I might fear a snake in the path ahead of me. But if I stop to realize that it's not poisonous and that I can easily walk around it, then I do not need to tremble. Facts change my entire outlook. Therefore, let's consider the bigger picture.

---

20 Quoted in Robert Wring, "An Examination of the Practice of Elder Rule in Selected Southern Baptist Churches in the Light of New Testament Teaching" (Ph.D. diss., Mid-America Baptist Theological Seminary, 2002), 96–97.

Plural eldership should not eliminate congregationalism. It is true that some forms of plural eldership completely by-pass the congregation. In the early church, however, the congregation was involved in decisions. Both Jesus and Paul said that the churches hold the final authority on matters of church discipline (Matt. 18:15–17; 1 Cor. 5). The church in Jerusalem selected the deacon-prototypes upon the counsel of the apostles, thus providing a workable pattern for congregational involvement in recommending spiritual and temporal leaders (Acts 6:1–5). After the apostles and elders established the church's position regarding the problem raised by the Judaizers, the congregation became involved by approving the recommendation of sending messengers to the churches of Asia Minor as the official voice of the Jerusalem church. The congregation as a whole was not part of the discussions or debates, but they were later informed, and affirmed the result of the council: "Then it seemed good to the apostles and the elders, with the whole church, to choose men from among them to send to Antioch with Paul and Barnabas" (Acts 15:22). The English phrase "Then it seemed good" was a political term in the Greek world for "voting" or "passing a measure in the assembly."[21]

There is no evidence that the early church voted on every issue. Rather, the plural eldership competently and efficiently handled day-to-day matters. And the church respected and submitted to this leadership, knowing that trustworthy men stood before them by divine design. On occasion, the churches had to be reminded to obey and submit to the plural eldership; but the elders were not despots—the congregation exercised decisive roles in church life (1 Thess. 5:12–13; Heb. 13:17). In other words, congregationalism certainly existed, but not to such a degree that the public assembly literally ran the church.

Absolute congregational government is unwieldy in practice. During my early years of ministry, a seminary president told a group of young, aspiring ministers that if a church _voted_ to call you as pastor then you had best go because that was the will of God. I was shocked by his tone (and I still am) and by his insisting that God's will could be infallibly known through a congregation's vote. It only takes a little reading of church history to refute such an idea. Church votes are affected by human depravity as much as individuals are, and they can hardly assure the revelation of God's mind. Congregations must labor to understand what Scripture teaches rather than assuming that churches speak infallibility whenever they assemble.

A church is not just straightforward democracy, for in churches there is a common recognition of our fallen state, of our tendency to err, and, on the other hand, of the _inerrancy_ of God's Word. So the members of a

---

21 *LKGNT*, 299–300.

church congregation are democratic, perhaps, only in the sense that they work as a congregation to try to understand God's Word.[22]

The eldership should lead the charge in governance and understanding God's Word. As men who are devoted to Scripture and to prayer, elders earn the congregation's trust and enhance their authority as spiritual leaders in the church. The authority of leaders is necessary in a church, as it is in any type of government. While national, state, and local governments serve at the pleasure of their citizens, the citizens depend on their elected officials to give leadership, direction, and protection on a daily basis. Citizens submit to this authority because it gives order to their lives. In a similar way, the congregation that submits to elder leadership can function with greater order and purpose, while the congregation also holds the eldership accountable to exercise faithfully their responsibilities under the Lord Jesus Christ. "The ministry of the church," writes John Piper, "is primarily the work of the members in the activity of worship toward God, nurture toward each other and witness toward the world. Internal structures for church governance are *not* the main ministry of the church, but are the necessary equipping and mobilizing of the saints for the work of ministry."[23] So the congregation at large must focus on mobilizing for ministry rather than spend time worrying over governance. That responsibility is entrusted to the smaller body of the elders. Piper adds, "Governance structures should be lean and efficient to this end, not aiming to include as many people as possible in office-holding, but to free and fit as many people as possible for ministry."[24]

At the root of much opposition to plural eldership are pastors who fear the loss of their authority in the church. Although many Baptist churches claim to exercise congregationalism, their actual structure looks more like a monarchical episcopacy—the solitary rule of one man over the congregation. Early Baptists reacted against monarchical episcopacy in the Church of Rome and the Church of England. Their dissenting voices echoed with other seventeenth-century evangelicals who were alarmed over the abuses perpetrated by the solitary rule of one man over the church. Baptists therefore vested congregations with final authority in matters of church life, but also recognized the need for order that comes only through spiritual leadership. The Philadelphia Confession of Faith (1742) provides a good example of both congregational voice and the spiritual authority of elders:

---

22 Mark Dever, *Nine Marks of a Healthy Church* (Wheaton, IL: Crossway, 2000), 212.
23 Piper, "Biblical Eldership," sec. 4, principle 2.
24 Ibid., sec. 4, principle 3.

[Article] 8. A particular church gathered, and completely organized, according to the mind of Christ, consists of officers and members: and the officers appointed by Christ to be chosen and set apart by the church (so called and gathered) for the peculiar administration of ordinances and execution of power or duty, which He entrusts them with or calls them to, to be continued to the end of the world, are bishops or elders, and deacons.

[Article] 9. The way appointed by Christ for the calling of any person, fitted and gifted by the Holy Spirit, unto office of bishop or elder in the Church is, that he be chosen thereunto by the common suffrage of the Church itself; and solemnly set apart by fasting and prayer, with the imposition of hands of the leadership of the Church, if there be any before constituted therein: and of a deacon, that he be chosen by the like suffrage, and set apart by prayer, and the imposition of hands.[25]

The officers of the church, elders and deacons, are appointed by Christ and chosen by the church. They possess the "execution of power or duty, which He entrusts them with or calls them to" in serving Christ's church. Each elder is "chosen thereunto by the common suffrage"—or voting—"of the Church itself." So the pastor does not lack authority, but rather he shares authority with the plurality of spiritual leaders chosen by the church.

Should this shared authority be feared by a pastor who has been called to serve vocationally in a church? Not if the elders adhere to the biblical requirements for character and practice. Instead, a pastor should welcome this structure as a God-given means for protecting him and enhancing the ministry of the church. Granted, major problems will arise when unqualified men serve as elders. But that is part of the ongoing struggle faced by the church until Christ returns. The pastor must labor to preach, teach, train, and pray until the Lord purifies the church's leadership base, making it possible for the pastor gladly to share authority with a plural eldership.

Another element of the fear-factor involves the concept of "ruling." If ruling means dictatorial control over church members' lives—prying into mundane personal decisions; placing demands on members outside the parameters of church ministry—then such rule should be feared. Indeed, rule of that sort has given bad press to plural eldership and is a distortion of the biblical picture. Elders are never to rule in a "lording" manner; rather they should serve the church in humility,

25 Timothy and Denise George, eds., *John A. Broadus: Baptist Confessions, Covenants, and Catechisms* (Nashville: Broadman and Holman, 1996), 86.

mirroring the shepherd-rule modeled by Christ. Shepherding the flock of God does demand governance, but elders must exercise that governance as those who will give account to the Chief Shepherd (1 Peter 5:2–5; Heb. 13:17).

Plural eldership serves to prevent one man from falling prey to the temptation of dominating a congregation. Shared authority hones the focus and spirituality of the elders. A pastor who is called by a church to full-time employment will certainly hold greater responsibility than the other elders because of the duties entrusted to him. In this case the pastor is first among equals in authority—first by virtue of the church's call and his training and gifts, but equal in that he is not a "Lone Ranger" figure in church leadership. Daniel Wallace explains that "accountability and our sin natures" provide one of the clearest reasons for the shared authority of plural eldership. He continues,

> Each leader knows that he lacks complete balance, that there are things he continues to struggle with. Further, even beyond the sin nature factor is the personality factor. Some pastors are detail men; others are big picture men. Some love music, others have gotten little from music. . . . All of us together contribute to the way the body of Christ works. But a church that follows in lock-step with the personality and foibles of one man will always be imbalanced.

> . . . *Churches that have a pastor as an authority above others (thus, in function, a monarchical episcopate) have a disproportionately high number of moral failures at the top level of leadership.* In other words, it is less likely for a pastor to fall into sin if he is *primus inter parus* ("first among equals" in the sense of his visibility and training, not spirituality) than if he is elevated above the rest of the leadership.[26]

In short, a plurality of elders protects both the pastor and his congregation.

Plural Eldership

* Encourages leaders by shouldering the load of ministry
* Approaches ministry with greater precision
* Curtails tyranny and authoritarianism in the church
* Provides a laboratory for displaying unity in the church

---

26 Wallace, "Who Should Run the Church?" 6; italics original.

Developing plural leadership is demanding. So some might ask, "Why bother?" A plurality offers each elder some measure of encouragement since the body of elders or body of deacons work together on behalf of their particular congregation. Each person works toward the same purpose, and they can lift up one another whenever one faces pressure or needs a word of consolation. Many times I have watched our elders help each other shoulder difficult loads or labor together in prayer.

In my own experience I know what it is to stand alone in a congregation—virtually every pastor knows what I mean. It is difficult and trying to seek after God's Word and find no crowd rushing to join you. But how marvelous and uplifting to have like-minded brothers standing with you. It breathes encouragement into any Christian leader's heart.

A plurality provides the opportunity to do ministry in a more exacting way. Each person in a body of elders or deacons will bring his own gifts and strengths to the overall work, and can apply his gifts to the common good. No one man needs to attempt carrying the load of a congregation.

A plurality, too, curtails attempts at tyranny or dictatorships. Having too much authority and too little accountability corrupts people, especially in the spiritual realm. When someone lacks spiritual maturity, being in leadership can provide opportunities for ego-boosting or power-grabbing. Plural leadership protects against such abuses because the leaders hold one another accountable. Equal authority among the elders checks attempts by one man to dominate the church leadership.

Plurality also serves as a laboratory for proving unity. Any group of people working together for a period of time will have its unity tested. The elders' character, or lack thereof, will surface during times of testing and adversity. Nothing is any sweeter than seeing Christian brothers walk through such times in unity.

REFLECTIONS

- Why do we need both elders and deacons?
- How were elders selected in the early church? Does this offer an example of how elder selection should be conducted in our day?
- What qualifies a man to be an elder? Identify the chief characteristics.
- Why do some church leaders fear plural eldership?

CHAPTER SIX

UNITY IN TRUTH

It was the difference between a train station and a museum. That is how I would describe the contrast between Philadelphia's Tenth Presbyterian Church and the city's First Baptist Church. One was filled with hustle and lives in motion; the other was pretty, still, and deathly quiet. The difference was startling.

It was the mid-1990s, and Mark Dever and I traveled to Philadelphia in search of a model inner-city church to learn from as we worked to rebuild Capitol Hill Baptist Church. At the invitation of James Montgomery Boice—just a few years before his death—we decided to spend the day with this long-time pastor and his staff.

Arriving early, we walked around the city and stumbled upon the First Baptist Church of Philadelphia, which at the time was marking its 300th anniversary. After ringing the doorbell and knocking on the door repeatedly we nearly gave up. Finally an older man opened the door. He looked like he belonged on an Amish farm in Lancaster County rather than in an inner-city Baptist church. Mark, ever the historian, immediately set about learning the history of the church and attempted to discern what the "Amishman"—who identified himself as the pastor—believed. Watching the interchange was like watching two dogs sniff each other, until finally Mark realized that the pastor thought you can believe whatever you want to believe. Sensing a dead end, Mark asked to see the sanctuary.

We were ushered into one of the most finely adorned Protestant sanctuaries I had ever seen. It was immaculately maintained from floor to ceiling and featured massive gold-leaf arches centered over a large, wooden pulpit. The pastor informed us that they had just completed a restoration. Mark asked, "That must have cost a small fortune. You must have a lot of people coming?" The pastor said,

"A couple of dozen." Mark asked, "How did a couple of dozen people afford this?" The pastor told us that the money came from the Andy Warhol Foundation, a foundation supporting the visual arts that Warhol himself funded. (Andy Warhol was a leading figure in the pop-art movement of the '60s and '70s, a homosexual, and a practicing Ruthenian Rite Catholic.)

In short, you could summarize what we saw at First Baptist this way: the Word was not preached, nobody came, and the building was beautiful.

So we made a beeline down 17th Street for Tenth Presbyterian Church, which was founded in 1829. The contrast was striking. The doors were open and the place was teeming with people. "The Catacombs" (the church basement) housed a classical school for inner-city kids. The Alliance of Confessing Evangelicals was pumping out great books and audio. An AIDS program cared for "the least of these." A wide-reaching radio ministry extended the strong expositional pulpit ministry which filled the main hall every Sunday. And the staff was large and welcoming. The building? Though attractive, it was clear by the worn carpet on the stairs and dirty walls along handrails that hoards of people constantly passed through.

You could summarize what we saw at Tenth Presbyterian this way: The Word was preached, people came, and the building was a bit tattered.

What could account for the difference? Not location. Not demographics. Not the age of the church. The two churches shared all these. Yet somewhere in its history, First Baptist Church of Philadelphia succumbed to modernity and embraced a host of compromised theological positions to accommodate it. Somewhere along the line decisions were made at First Baptist that Tenth Presbyterian did not make. Practically speaking, these kinds of decisions are usually made by leaders. At some point the leaders of First Baptist bent and then broke. No doubt it was incremental and perhaps barely noticeable at first. No doubt the explanations for the change included words like "loving," "fair," and "open."

One way to summarize the difference, then, is to say that one church had been carefully guarded by the kind of shepherds that Paul told Titus to appoint, while the other church had not. Paul instructs Titus that an elder holds "fast the faithful word which is in accordance with the teaching, so that he will be able both to exhort in sound doctrine and to refute those who contradict" (Titus 1:9). The elders of Tenth Presbyterian, since 1829, had held to the faithful word and had refuted those who contradicted it. The pastors of First Baptist, if I were to guess based on so many other churches like it, had softened somewhere somehow on a number of their stances.

At the end of our day in Philadelphia the parable of the two churches could not have been clearer: When leaders fearfully accommodate the culture—no life. When elders preach God's Word and guard the sheep with love and truth—life. Faith-filled, God-fearing, Bible-loving, sin-hating, sinner-loving, cultural *drift-resisting* leaders were the key. But how do you find those kind of churchmen to shepherd God's flock?

Unfortunately, at that point in the life of CHBC, Mark Dever bore that burden in an awkward and, hopefully, never-to-be-repeated way. CHBC's new constitution called for the elders to nominate prospective elders to the congregation for affirmation. Given his role as senior pastor, Mark was the only recognized elder at the time, so he had the task of presenting the first slate of candidates. This essentially boiled down to the unpleasant task of evaluating the spiritual state and biblical qualifications of every adult male in the church.

To minimize the loneliness and awkwardness of the task, Dever sent a letter to every member of the church asking them not to nominate—that was his task—but to highlight every man whom they thought matched the description of elders as defined in 1 Timothy 3 and Titus 1. The effect was twofold: First, it got everyone involved in the process. Second, it highlighted for Mark particular men whom the congregation already saw as functioning like elders. As a result, there were at least two men whom Dever had not previously considered who ended up being nominated in that first slate of names.

Two questions remained. First, who should *not* be nominated? Second, who *should* be nominated?[1] The first question was the most painful because there were a few men in the congregation who appeared to be qualified but in fact were not. When interviewed, one man revealed his disagreement with our church's statement of faith over the issue of baptism. That was a problem, especially for a Baptist church. Another man turned out to be an egalitarian, believing that a woman could serve as an elder. The man was a political operative in Washington, DC, so we weren't surprised when he said he wanted to be an elder because "The elder board is where the power will be." Another man rarely attended any meetings of the church other than Sunday mornings. To us this showed a lack of interest as well as a lack of knowledge of the sheep that he would be called to shepherd.

Yet as I said, they all *appeared* to be qualified. All three men described above were leaders, even leaders in their respective fields. They were dynamic teachers. They were the right age—not too young and not too old. And all of them affirmed the gospel.

But the church is not led by businessmen, politicians, or doctors. The church is led by shepherds—shepherds who have sound theological thinking and a history

---

1   Mark Dever and Paul Alexander explore these questions in depth in section 3 of *The Deliberate Church: Building Your Ministry on the Gospel* (Wheaton. IL: Crossway, 2005).

of faithfulness. And often, unsound and unfaithful thinking does not enter the church through direct assaults on the gospel. Unsound thinking, often, creeps into one generation through secondary doctrines, only to subvert the primary doctrines in the next generation, since secondary doctrines, like the doctrine of the church, serve to protect the primary, like the gospel. Therefore, we needed to be vigilant both in what these men believed and in how they lived.

In other words, we were fundamentally looking for men who watched their life and doctrine (1 Tim. 4:16). We did not want truth-men, or love-and-unity-men, but men lovingly united in the truth. We wanted men who were willing to spend themselves for the sake of the flock, seeking to know them, so that they might carefully and individually guide them into a deeper knowledge of God's Word.

Further, we weren't looking for "balance," as some people suggested we should. Some thought the senior pastor's views needed to be rounded off or smoothed out by an opposite point of view. They thought we needed someone who would say "no" to Dever. Certainly you want men who can think for themselves and who are more beholden to God's Word than any man. But trust me when I say that you don't want contrarians as elders. Contrarians gum up the wheels of progress and rob the group of joy in the process (see Hebrews 13:17).

Positively, then, who *should* be nominated? The point isn't whether they say "yes" or "no" to the senior pastor. The point is whether or not the man is committed to the truth of the Scriptures and the good of the church. He always says "yes" to that. Sometimes I like to say that churches should nominate "yes men"? I know, I know. "Yes men" are those who fail to act, who agree just to get along, who don't stand up for anything and take no risks. But the apostle Paul seems to put a premium on "yes men," though of a different kind than what people typically think. Consider the challenge and call of these two verses:

Therefore if there is any encouragement in Christ, if there is any consolation of love, if there is any fellowship of the Spirit, if any affection and compassion, make my joy complete by being of the same mind, maintaining the same love, united in spirit, intent on one purpose (Phil. 2:1–2).

Now I exhort you, brethren, by the name of our Lord Jesus Christ, that you all agree and that there be no divisions among you, but that you be made complete in the same mind and in the same judgment (1 Cor. 1:10).

In both passages, Paul points to submission and unity, but it is not any submission or any unity. It's submission to unity in Christ and to sharing the mind of Christ.

Hollywood films champion the contrarian, the loner, the outcast, the man fighting the machine. We love the idea of a guy who chooses to swim upstream or walk away from the crowd. Hollywood's hero may sell movies, but biblically speaking his character is flawed. He's inclined toward isolation, selfishness, and disunity.

Meanwhile, so many churches in the twentieth century emphasized love and unity, but a love and unity that was strangely and tragically devoid of truth.

In marked contrast to this, we need leaders in the church who will set aside their preferences for the purpose of maintaining unity in truth and love. We need elders who will sacrifice their individual priorities for the sake of the congregation's. We need men who will labor both to understand their brothers and carefully heed the Scriptures rather than stake out an uninformed position and remain unwilling to learn. We need men who love God and the church more than themselves, and so are willing to put what people think of them at stake by confronting error and sin.

When nominating men to serve as elders, you will not satisfy everyone. I remember one woman complaining that she didn't like any of the initial nominees. When we checked to see whose names she had submitted for consideration we discovered she hadn't bothered to turn any in. In short, the idea of elders in the constitution met with near-unanimity, but finding actual nominees nearly broke us. Looking back, one former member tagged the elder nomination process as the beginning of a "*de facto* church split." He was right. A set of elders represents a direction for a church, and the five men who were eventually nominated and affirmed meant the church would be moving in one kind of direction, not another. And this led to a *de facto* church split—albeit a very small one. Those members who did not like the new elders and their direction left the church. Those who did, stayed.

The choice of who was going to shepherd the church was of utmost importance. The wrong leaders would likely lead to more short pastorates by men who would trot out the latest dog and pony tricks and church growth fads. In the long run, it would probably lead to doctrinal compromise. Faithful elders, on the other hand, would restore biblical fidelity and a community marked off by lives that authenticate their confession. Were we going to be First Baptist Philadelphia or Tenth Presbyterian? Were we going to have to sell off the property and become a storage facility for the nearby Library of Congress, or were we going to become a vibrant, truth-speaking community of Christ-followers?

PART TWO

FOUR KEY BIBLICAL TEXTS

CHAPTER SEVEN

A MODEL FOR OUR TIMES

Acts 20:17–31

[17] From Miletus he sent to Ephesus and called to him the elders of the church. [18] And when they had come to him, he said to them, "You yourselves know, from the first day that I set foot in Asia, how I was with you the whole time, [19] serving the Lord with all humility and with tears and with trials which came upon me through the plots of the Jews; [20] how I did not shrink from declaring to you anything that was profitable, and teaching you publicly and from house to house, [21] solemnly testifying to both Jews and Greeks of repentance toward God and faith in our Lord Jesus Christ. [22] And now, behold, bound by the Spirit, I am on my way to Jerusalem, not knowing what will happen to me there, [23] except that the Holy Spirit solemnly testifies to me in every city, saying that bonds and afflictions await me. [24] But I do not consider my life of any account as dear to myself, so that I may finish my course and the ministry which I received from the Lord Jesus, to testify solemnly of the gospel of the grace of God. [25] "And now, behold, I know that all of you, among whom I went about preaching the kingdom, will no longer see my face. [26] Therefore, I testify to you this day that I am innocent of the blood of all men. [27] For I did not shrink from declaring to you the whole purpose of God. [28] Be on guard for yourselves and for all the flock, among which the Holy Spirit has made you overseers, to shepherd the church of God which He purchased with His own blood. [29] I know that after my departure savage wolves will come

in among you, not sparing the flock; [30] and from among your own selves men will arise, speaking perverse things, to draw away the disciples after them. [31] Therefore be on the alert, remembering that night and day for a period of three years I did not cease to admonish each one with tears.

Why appoint elders and deacons as spiritual leaders in the church? Having been brought up in a Baptist church, I attended two Baptist churches during my adolescence, and both were quite traditional. They had senior pastors, deacons, and additional staff members, but elders were at other churches. To my knowledge, everyone with a Baptist background acknowledges the office of deacon without question. But they sometimes balk when it comes to the office of elders, even though the London, Philadelphia, and New Hampshire Confessions, dating from the seventeenth through the nineteenth centuries, identify both offices.[1]

When the church I now pastor in Memphis began studying the biblical teaching on church leadership, including elders, one member abruptly stopped attending. I visited his home and asked about his reason for leaving. Quickly he pointed to the talk about elders. "It's just not Baptist!" he said. I cited historical examples of elders in Baptist churches as well as the biblical teaching, but he would not even investigate the subject.

Yet God's Word always demands thoughtful study, including on the way in which elders guard and lead the church, with deacons coming alongside to serve. The biblical references to elders are commonly equated with the office of vocational pastor or modern-day church staff. But that interpretation means reading our modern practices into the ancient text. Such is precisely what one opponent of elder leadership does when he claims that "all elder/overseers were ministry-oriented and laity-exclusive."[2] While it is true that the pastor is an elder, it is not necessarily the fact that elders are only "paid professionals." And when we neglect to recognize qualified men from the congregation as elders, the church loses some of its greatest leadership assets. In fact, if non-staff leaders are excluded as elders, then multitudes of smaller congregations—many meeting in homes due to prohibitions against public assembling—will lack spiritual leadership altogether. Ultimately, it smacks of arrogance to think that only professionally trained individuals can serve as spiritual leaders.

---

1 *CrChr*, 3:738–40, 747.
2 Robert Wring, "An Examination of the Practice of Elder Rule in Selected Southern Baptist Churches in the Light of New Testament Teaching" (Ph.D. diss., Mid-America Baptist Theological Seminary, 2002), 52.

A more biblical practice of elders strengthens the pastoral ministry of churches. Explaining the benefits of plural elder leadership—staff and non-staff—John MacArthur observes, "Their combined counsel and wisdom helps assure that decisions are not self-willed or self-serving to a single individual (cf. Prov. 11:14)." He asserts, "In fact, one-man leadership is characteristic of cults, not the church."[3]

The apostle Paul understood the great need for godly leaders. On his second missionary journey, Paul came to the famous Asian city of Ephesus, "the chief city of the province," from which he would evangelize Asia Minor (Acts 19:10).[4] Ephesus was an important cultural and economic center in the Roman Empire, yet also an important center for pagan worship that featured the temple of Diana, "one of the Seven wonders of the ancient world."[5] There, Paul preached and a riot ensued. But God gave fruit for his labors so that a church was raised up in the city. The apostle stayed for three years, preaching and teaching the Word. During this period he evidently appointed elders to serve the church.

On his third missionary journey, Paul came near Ephesus, but because he was determined to go to Jerusalem, he did not land in Ephesus. Instead, he sailed past, landing at Miletus. From there, he called the Ephesian elders to meet him. In Acts 20:17–31, Luke records Paul's last encounter with these men, one that breathes with love and passion as the apostle gives his final instructions to the leaders of the Ephesian church. Paul's message points to the unmistakable need for elders to carry on the work of shepherding the church, a need that is evident in all churches. If elders played such a vital role in the cosmopolitan church in Ephesus, do we not have the same need today? Paul's exhortation to the Ephesian elders answers the question, "Why elders?"

Acts 20:17–31

- The Church's Common Need (Acts 20:17, 28–31)
- Shepherds for the Flock (Acts 20:28, 31)
- An Unforgettable Foundation (Acts 20:28)

---

3 John MacArthur, *The Master's Plan for the Church* (Chicago: Moody, 1991), 195.
4 Curtis Vaughan, *Founders Study Guide Commentary: Ephesians* (Cape Coral, FL: Founders Press, 2002), 15.
5 Ibid., 15.

THE CHURCH'S COMMON NEED (ACTS 20:17, 28–31)

The first thing for us to notice in Paul's Acts 20 exhortation is the terms he uses to describe this group of leaders in Ephesus. First, he calls them "the elders of the church" (v. 17). Some have argued that the Ephesian church was divided into house churches, and the elders were simply the individual leaders of the house groups. But that does injustice to the text. "Elders" is plural and "church" is singular.

Second, Paul states that the Holy Spirit "has made you overseers, to shepherd the church of God" (v. 28). *Overseers* is the same term that Paul uses in 1 Timothy 3:1, which the Authorized Version translates as "bishops" and the New American Standard Bible translates as "overseers." In Greek, the term is *episkopos,* while "elder" is how we translate the Greek word *presbuteros.*

Third, Paul uses the word "shepherd" as a verb (v. 28), which refers to feeding and caring for the flock.[6] The Greek word here is *poimainø,* from which the noun "pastor" has its roots, as used in Ephesians 4:11.

The point is that all three of these terms are interchangeable. They do not refer to separate hierarchies or multi-tiered offices in the church, but to the same office or function within the local church. Peter likewise uses these terms interchangeably in 1 Peter 5:1–2.[7]

As we saw in chapter 3, the distinctiveness of the term *elder* points to the character of the man, and was used of men advanced in maturity within the Jewish community. *Overseer* or *bishop* points to his function of spiritual leadership, as these terms were used in the Greek culture for commissioners or administrators of cities. And the term *pastor* emphasizes the man's ministry—the concept of shepherding a flock resonated broadly throughout that part of the world.

Why was there a need for elders to serve in the church? The early church lived under external assault until about the fourth century. For three hundred years, opposition, attacks, and persecution afflicted it, up to the reign of the Roman emperor Constantine. Those attacks came at various intervals in efforts to catch the church off-guard. Emperors Nero, Domitian, Trajan, and Hadrian oversaw legendary periods of persecution. But along with external persecution, corruption in doctrine, personalities, and leadership also brutalized the church[8]: "I know that after my departure savage wolves will come in among you, not sparing the flock" (Acts 20:29).

---

6 *BDAG,* 842, explains that the symbol of a shepherd leading, guiding, and ruling is in mind and in this case, refers to "the administration of a congregation."
7 See chapter 13 for a detailed look at this text.
8 See Justo L. Gonzalez, *The Story of Christianity: The Early Church to Present Day* (Peabody, MA: Prince Press, 2001), 31–108.

As long as Paul was among the Ephesian flock, he could easily recognize the attacks of the adversary and address them. He had the courage and authority to stand against whatever forces attacked the church. But Paul's presence among them was coming to a close. Now they faced fresh opposition without the great apostle deflecting the blows. So Paul charges the Ephesian elders—and all who follow in their pattern—to take on this task of guarding the flock against assaults from without and from within.

Paul uses strong terms to describe the attacks. He calls the perpetrators "savage wolves," depicting the Ephesian church as a flock of helpless sheep (Acts 20:29). Jesus had used the same imagery: "Beware of the false prophets, who come to you in sheep's clothing, but inwardly are ravenous wolves" (Matt. 7:15). Wolves, in this case, would have donned sheep's clothing so that they might subvert the church by subterfuge.

One recurring theme found in the epistles is the warning against false teachers. Some would claim to be "the Christ"; others would have a new revelation; still others would teach a false gospel. And it is a sad fact that false teachers duped many even in the churches of the New Testament. The Ephesian church is among the seven churches of Asia Minor that our Lord addresses in Revelation 2 and 3. Most of those churches had fallen prey to spiritual lethargy, while some had given way to tolerating false teachers. Paul, through his epistles to Timothy, apparently felt the need once again to warn the Ephesian church of false teachers (1 Tim. 4:1–3; 6:3–5; 2 Tim. 3).

When we consider the fact that our Lord as well as Paul, John, Peter, and Jude all warn about false teachers, it ought to alert us that false teaching remains a grave danger. Churches and individual Christians can fall prey to this attack, whether from outside or inside the body. If the church at Ephesus needed men guarding them from false teaching, surely churches in Memphis and Mumbai, Chicago and Cape Town, need the same. In these particular warnings, personality conflicts were far from the apostle's mind. He was concerned about teaching that moved away from Scripture and embraced a distorted faith. He charged the Ephesian elders to "be on guard for yourselves and for all the flock, among which the Holy Spirit has made you overseers, to shepherd the church of God which He purchased with His own blood" (Acts 20:28). The shepherding process demands the ability to recognize wolves. What constitutes a "wolf-theology"?

- Teaching that in any way denies the deity of Christ or the coequality of the Trinity
- Teaching that substitutes anything for the sufficiency of the death of Christ in atoning for sin

- Teaching that denies the need for God's justice to be satisfied in order for sinners to be saved
- Teaching that robs God of glory by insisting that salvation is not totally a work of God's grace
- Teaching that denies the bodily resurrection of Christ
- Teaching that claims to have authoritative revelations that are not contained in the canons of the Old and New Testaments
- Teaching that insists upon some kind of work or self-denial or ascetic practice to improve one's standing before God, rather than simply resting upon the merits of Christ

Is "wolf-theology" taught today? Yes, indeed! I received a note from a pastor friend telling me about the president of a Baptist college in the American south who authored a book denying the authority of Scripture, the virgin birth of Christ, the deity of Christ, the necessity of the cross for atoning for sin, and the need for salvation. Even more distressing is that some Baptist churches have allowed this man in their pulpit simply because he claims to be a Baptist. In such cases, the elders of the church have a responsibility to prevent even dignified-looking wolves from deceiving the flock.

The weight of responsibility for recognizing false teaching, and then acting to remove it, rests with the elders. The elders of the church have the task of constantly scrutinizing "every wind of doctrine" (Eph. 4:14). They should be vigilant in recognizing false teaching, warning the body, and guarding the flock from falling prey (Heb. 13:17).

Paul was concerned not only with the attacks that would come from outside the body, but with the deceit that would arise from within the body: "and from among your own selves men will arise, speaking perverse things, to draw away the disciples after them" (Acts 20:30). Just as there was a Judas among the twelve apostles, there are Judases in the church today. Such persons have self-centered motives for joining the church body. They use the church for personal aggrandizement, to improve their sense of power or their material gain, and to draw disciples away from the truth.

Paul describes their pattern as "speaking perverse things," all with the goal of alienating or drawing away some of the believers from the rest of the church. The word "perverse" captures it well. The Greek term means "to turn aside, to twist, to pervert, to distort."[9] These teachers say things that even children would recognize as immoral. Speaking "perverse things" involved perverting or subtly altering the

---

9 *LKGNT*, 318.

truth. It involved taking that which was true, and then reshaping its meaning or giving it a false application, or manipulating it to say something other than its intended meaning. While the teaching of the "ravenous wolves" comes rather brazenly and is easily recognized, the "speaking" to which Paul refers right here is deceitful and difficult to recognize. It takes discernment to see the subtle shades by which it departs from God's Word. Once a Christian latches on to such distorted ideas of biblical truth, that person is easy prey for alienation from the rest of the church. He or she might view others in the church as unenlightened, and then follow the deceitful teaching to his or her own shame.

A number of years ago, a man and his wife began attending Bible study and services at our church. I had an unusually long visit in their home where the man went into great detail about a particular area of theological interest. He cloaked his doctrine in common biblical language, yet something in his words did not seem balanced. A fellow elder and I happened to be teaching the Bible class that this man attended. One day in class he deftly sought to drive a wedge into the body by a clever denial of the co-eternality of Jesus Christ with the Father. As elders, we sniffed the foul air of false teaching and united against his faulty theology. Seeing this united front, he soon left our church. The flock was protected.

Assaults upon the church body and deceit within the body remind us of a need that we cannot overlook—the need of the church to be protected against false teachers and deceivers. And this is the job of the elders. If elders were needed over nineteen hundred years ago, they are certainly needed today.

SHEPHERDS FOR THE FLOCK (ACTS 20:28, 31)

Acts 20:28 and 31 offer a straightforward outline of the duties of elders. The elders are to guard, to keep watch over, and to shepherd the church. The adversary wants to divide and destroy the church. Sin and false teaching constantly threaten it. Elders must therefore keep watch constantly.

"Be on guard for yourselves and for all the flock," says Paul (Acts 20:28). Being on guard means taking heed or paying attention to what is taught, to the trends in the culture, and to the behavior of the body so that the church might go forth unhindered in its mission. Paul specifically tells the elders to guard over two things:

First, elders must guard their own spiritual lives. Elders must personally and as a group give attention to their own walks with Christ. They should not function as ministerial professionals—men who are good at telling others what to do, but who do not practice what they preach. They are prophets, not professionals, says John Piper: "The mentality of the professional is not the mentality of the prophet. . . .

The more professional we long to be, the more spiritual death we will leave in our wake."[10] As John Stott reminds us, "For they cannot care adequately for others if they neglect the care and culture of their own souls."[11]

In Richard Baxter's classic, *The Reformed Pastor,* the chapter entitled "The Oversight of Ourselves" identifies a number of things elders must guard with regard to themselves. To paraphrase Baxter, we must

1. Take heed to ourselves, lest we should be void of that saving grace of God that we offer to others.
2. Take heed to ourselves, lest we live with those actual sins that we may preach against in others. Let us see that we are not guilty of that which we may daily condemn.
3. Take heed to ourselves that we may not be unfit for the great tasks that we have undertaken to complete. Since we are to teach men the great mysteries of the faith we must not be babes in our knowledge of God's Word and its practice.
4. Take heed to ourselves, lest we exemplify contradictory doctrine. Beware, lest we lay such stumbling blocks before the blind that we occasion their ruin. Beware, lest we undo with our lives, what we say with our tongues. Beware, lest we become the greatest hindrance to the success of our own labors.[12]

Second, elders must be on guard for all the flock. Paul uses pastoral terms to express guarding. It is best illustrated by thinking of a group of shepherds gathered on the back of a Judean mountain with their flock of sheep. The sheep munch on the grass and herbs on the mountainside in carefree fashion, while the shepherds constantly watch for thieves who would rob the flock, for wolves that would devour the flock, and for other dangers that threaten the flock. The job of the shepherd never ends. He constantly watches, constantly checks their health, constantly ensures they are fed and secure. He knows his sheep and recognizes their needs. An elder operates in a similar fashion. He also asks questions of the flock to ascertain their grasp and application of the law and the gospel, and their

10 John Piper, *Brothers, We Are Not Professionals! A Plea to Pastors for Radical Ministry* (Nashville: Broadman and Holman, 2002), 1.
11 John Stott, *The Spirit, the Church, and the World: The Message of Acts* (Downers Grove, IL: InterVarsity Press, 1990), 327.
12 Richard Baxter, *The Reformed Pastor: A Pattern for Personal Growth and Ministry* (Portland, OR: Multnomah, 1982, from 1830 edition), 27–32.

understanding of justification and sanctification. Fred Malone offers some helpful questions in this regard:

- How does Christ's life and redeeming work help you to live as a husband, a wife, a parent, a child, a church member?
- What do you think is God's great goal for your life?
- What does heaven mean to you today?
- What does Christ think and feel about you when you sin?
- Do you think God enjoys you?[13]

The elders who labor at teaching, preaching, instructing, exhorting, and admonishing the flock fulfill this duty. They must at times reprove those who are in sin. They must admonish those who are toying with compromising the faith. They must instruct and exhort the church to walk in sound doctrine. They must recognize error and not be afraid to address it. The nineteenth-century pastor Charles Bridges reminds us that every need in the church body cannot "be fully treated in the pulpit."[14] It requires the individualized attention that can only be given effectively by a plurality of shepherds. Bridges suggests a number of cases that need this kind of special care.

- Shepherding is spiritual work.
- Shepherding is hard work.
- Shepherding is answerable work.

The indolent are slumbering—the self-dependent are falling back—the zealous are under the influence of spiritual pride—the earnest are becoming self-righteous—the regular, formal. Then there is the enquirer, asking for direction—the tempted and perplexed, looking for support—the afflicted, longing for the cheering consolation of the Gospel—the convinced sinner, from the slight healing of his wound, settling in a delusive peace—the professor, "having a name that he lives; but he is dead." These cases cannot, in all their minute and diversified forms, be fully treated in the pulpit.[15]

13 Fred Malone, "Do Personal Work," in *Dear Timothy: Letters on Pastoral Ministry*, ed. Thomas K. Ascol (Cape Coral, FL: Founders Press, 2004), 179.
14 Charles Bridges, *The Christian Ministry: with an Inquiry into the Causes of its Inefficiency* (1830; repr., Carlisle, PA: Banner of Truth, 1991), 344.
15 Ibid.

Elders must be obedient to the Lord even when implementing difficult decisions. Their concern should never be to conform to popular Christianity in order to gain approval. Instead, they should discern biblical Christianity and lead the flock to walk in it without compromise. Elders who aim only for popularity will not care for the flock.

The duty to lead the flock well continues with the command, "Be on *guard . . . to* shepherd the church of God which He purchased with His own blood." Today, we have a rather romantic view of shepherds, especially with Christmas carols referring to them in glowing terms. But when Paul chose this metaphor, he was referring to a job that had no status in society. A shepherd was considered the "low-life" of society. The point for us is clear: the work of shepherding is not for personal fame or reputation, but is to be humble, carried out in loving service as Christ's undershepherd.

Shepherding is spiritual work. J. Oswald Sanders reminds us, "Spiritual ends can be achieved only by spiritual men who employ spiritual methods."[16] Much is made today of church leaders' being people-pleasers. But truly spiritual men focus on pleasing only one person, the Lord God.

Shepherding is hard work. In Bible times, guarding sheep against danger meant mental and emotional strain. Shepherds regularly encountered danger. Remember, David met a bear and a lion while shepherding. Shepherds trudged across mountains and valleys and through rugged terrain in all weather conditions.

Similarly, the work of elders goes on in all conditions and situations. Elders are never off duty when they leave the church building. An elder must attend to his own spiritual life, guarding his own family from spiritual dangers. He must maintain a godly example for the rest of the church. While others rest, he continues to toil through study, prayer, ministry, counseling, visiting, and watching.

Shepherding is answerable work. In the apostle Paul's time, shepherds typically worked for someone else. They had the responsibility of giving an account of each sheep before the owner of the flock. Paul reminds the Ephesian elders of this accountability when he tells them "to shepherd the church of God, which He purchased with His own blood." Elders must be reminded that the church does not belong to us. The church belongs to God through the redemptive price of the blood of Christ. We who serve are merely undershepherds who will one day give an account for our duties (Heb. 13:17).

---

16   J. Oswald Sanders, *Spiritual Leadership* (Chicago: Moody, 1980), 40, quoted in John MacArthur, *Shepherdology: A Master Plan for Church Leadership* (Panorama City, CA: Master's Fellowship, 1989), 134.

John Murray offers a fourfold challenge on what it means to "shepherd the church of God":

1. A shepherd keeps his flock from going astray. In practice this means instruction and warning. . . .
2. A shepherd goes after his sheep when they go astray. In practice this means reproof and correction, in many cases the exercise of ecclesiastical discipline. . . .
3. A shepherd protects his sheep from their enemies. . . . Perhaps there is no more ominous feature of members of the church than the lack of discernment. . . here the elders in tending the flock must cultivate for themselves and inculcate in the members of the church, that sensitivity to truth and right, so that they and the people will be able to detect the voice of the enemy. . . .
4. A shepherd leads his flock to the fold; he pours oil into their wounds and gives them pure water to quench their thirst. I would like to press home the necessity and the blessing of the ministry of consolation.[17]

"Therefore be on the alert, remembering that night and day for a period of three years I did not cease to admonish each one with tears" (Acts 20:31). Elders are involved in spiritual warfare—and the church is a battleground. They are called to be alert constantly. Thus, the Word commands elders to stay awake, be continually watchful for those things that would harm the flock. We face the constant opposition of the adversary, who is an opportunist looking for times when our guards are down and our tolerance to sin is high. It is at those times he strikes. Consequently, elders must stay at their posts, ever vigilant on behalf of the flock of God.

Paul exemplified vigilance, serving among the Ephesians for three years, watching and admonishing them with the compassion of tears (Acts 20:31). It was not just a job. It was a ministry or commission given from the Lord, and he took it seriously. And this is the call to all elders. They must recognize that God has given them a ministry to care for his *own* flock.

It's worth noticing that Paul took the time to "admonish each one." Admonition can range from instructing by biblical precepts and principles to warning someone that they are going the way of sin.[18] The word for *admonishing* means to "lay

---

17 John Murray, *The Collected Writings of John Murray: The Claims of Truth* (Edinburgh: Banner of Truth, 1976), 1:265–66.
18 *BDAG*, 679.

upon the mind" *(noutheton)* or to warn or instruct someone who has gone astray. This is where elders, by precept and practice, should impact the church. When elders live the Christian life so that others see the need to walk daily with Christ, the church is influenced. As they proclaim the truth of God so that others grow in understanding and practicing the Christian faith, the church is influenced. As elders admonish, they show more care for a person's soul than for that person's approval, and the church feels the impact.

AN UNFORGETTABLE FOUNDATION (ACTS 20:28)

One final reminder in this biblical text deserves our attention: "Be on guard for yourselves and for all the flock, *among which the Holy Spirit has made you overseers*" (emphasis added). Paul and his missionary partners may have selected the elders; the congregation may have approved the elders; but the Holy Spirit *made* them overseers. He was the foundation of their authority. The elders' ability to serve the body sprang from the Holy Spirit's distinct calling and work of setting them apart. John Stott therefore concludes of the elder, "So the oversight is his too, or he could not delegate it to others."[19]

This is indeed a mysterious element in the whole work of selecting elders. A congregation seeks to appoint godly men who are confirmed by the qualifications in the Word. The elder board[20] examines the men and presents them to the congregation for approval. Then the whole church sets them apart in a solemn service of installation. Yet behind all of this is the invisible work of the Holy Spirit. He is the one who will ultimately appoint them to this office in the church. John Stott, again, writes,

> This splendid Trinitarian affirmation, that the pastoral oversight of the church belongs to God (Father, Son, and Holy Spirit), should have a profound effect on pastors. It should humble us to remember that the church is not ours, but God's. And it should inspire us to faithfulness.[21]

> I confess that I do not understand all of this working of the Holy Spirit. But I am humbled by the truth that the Holy Spirit, who corporately dwells among the church (Eph. 2:22), works to set men apart for the noble work of eldering. And because the Holy Spirit does this work, the church must

19 Stott, *The Spirit, the Church, and the World*, 329.
20 Sometimes called a *presbytery*, referring to an assembled body of elders.
21 Stott, *The Spirit, the Church, and the World*, 329.

pay heed to the importance of both its own ministry and its response to the elders' leadership.

The Holy Spirit makes these men to be "overseers" not "overlords." They are not given the role of dictators, but of humble, loving servant-leaders in the congregation. They should exercise their duties in dependence on the same Spirit who set them apart, recognizing that their hands cannot do all that needs to be done in the lives of God's people. They must trust the Holy Spirit to work in the secret places of people's minds and hearts to accomplish the divine task before them.

The dangers we face in twenty-first-century America are of the same nature as those faced by our first-century counterparts. The same Lord who directed the apostles to appoint spiritual leaders over the early church directs us to do the same in modern churches. When selecting those leaders, popularity must be laid aside and biblical qualifications emphasized instead. Every man considered by his church to serve as an elder must examine himself in light of God's Word before accepting that appointment.

REFLECTIONS

- In what ways does the church at Ephesus resemble your own church?
- What are the primary responsibilities given to the Ephesian elders?
- What part do the elders' spiritual lives play in the overall effectiveness of their work?
- What does Paul mean by guarding and shepherding the church of God? How are these needs being addressed in your own church setting?

CHAPTER EIGHT

FAILURE, THEN SUCCESS

"**A**ll five nominees failed," said the moderator of the members' meeting. It was the fall of 1998. Mark had nominated five men to serve as elders since the church's brand new constitution called for elders. The members' meeting had gone reasonably well up to that point. No one expected this first slate of elder nominees to fail. But fail they did.

Failed?

But when the new constitution itself was voted on, only one person had opposed it. Plus, we didn't rush the process. We took over two years to prepare the way. Yet there it was: "All five nominees failed."

The constitution required an elder nominee to be affirmed by 75 percent of the congregation, and I was one of the nominees who failed to reach the 75 percent bar. All five of us received between 65 and 73 percent support. Emotions ran high as church members bumped into each other on their way to the exits, some feeling victorious and others feeling discouraged. But mostly there seemed to be a sense of confusion: Now what?

Mark Dever met with me and the other four failed nominees—the men he trusted most to think biblically and wisely—to assess and take counsel. Do we nominate a different set of elders? Do we re-nominate the top two vote-getters? Do we need to go back and change the constitution, lowering the bar to 65 percent? Would any of these ideas split or kill the church? Our new constitution required at least three elders, a majority of whom were not in the employ of the church. How were we supposed to function if we couldn't get anyone elected?

These are the times when expediency and pragmatism come roaring out, and you're tempted to throw treasured theological principles overboard. Praise God that not all temptations gain traction. In our case both the Scriptures and the church's recent history—a poor track record of business-minded programs and ungrounded pastors—combined to drive us to stay the course. We were determined to look to the Bible for guidance.

For us, Acts 20:17–35 captured what we wanted in elders and would drive our response to the failed election. In this passage Paul draws attention to three things in particular.

First, an elder must live among the people. Paul writes, "You yourselves know, from the first day that I set foot in Asia, how I was with you the whole time, serving the Lord with all humility and with tears and with trials which came upon me through the plots of the Jews" (Acts 20:18–19). Throughout his letters, Paul offers his life as a model: "Be imitators of me, just as I also am of Christ" (1 Cor. 11:1). As one person said, "We want elders who smell like sheep, not the golf course." Why? Because one of the ways we learn is by observing the examples of others. Discipleship is equal parts instruction and imitation. Love is theoretical until you see and feel the affection of another. The idea of sacrifice becomes three-dimensional when you see the poor widow put her last two copper coins in the treasury. Therefore we want elders who will model godly lives, which demands proximity.

As an example of how simple this can be, I once agreed to meet a young man at my house and then to walk to a local café for an early morning coffee. I invited him into our kitchen as I gathered my things and kissed my wife and kids goodbye. The young man was in my house for less than three minutes. Outside, he said to me, "You don't know how important that was to see." I said, "See what?" He said, "The way you loved your family." The young man grew up under the poor "leadership" of an abusive, alcoholic father. He had never *seen* tenderness or the simple affection displayed in a kiss on a cheek. The lesson for us? We want elders who will live in full view of a needy, watching world. That is one of the reasons we voted to sell the church-owned parsonage forty minutes away in northern Virginia before Mark Dever ever came to CHBC. We wanted the leaders of the church to live on the mission field of Capitol Hill and among the people known as Capitol Hill Baptist Church.

Second, an elder must teach the people. Whole churches have been built on being "creative" or "cutting edge" and generating new ways to do church. Is this right? God is the Creator and we bring him glory by mimicking him through creating and re-creating, right? Yes. But I think that for elders we actually want men who are generally predictable and imitative, as opposed to creative. When it comes to teaching the Bible especially, we don't want anyone to get creative with the message. Nor are we commanded to entertain. We are told to teach our people God's Word. Full stop. Listen to Paul again: "how I did not shrink from declaring to you anything that was profitable, and teaching you publicly and from house to house" (Acts 20:20). And Paul did not preach his ideas, ideas he imagined would be helpful; he preached the Bible—all of it! "For I did not shrink from declaring to you the whole purpose of God" (v. 27).

Third, an elder is called to protect the people. Paul speaks to spiritual warfare when he says, " I know that after my departure savage wolves will come in among you, not sparing the flock; and from among your own selves men will arise, speaking perverse things, to draw away the disciples after them" (vv. 29–30). The Old Testament is rife with examples of bad shepherds who failed to keep God's law and brought devastating consequences on the people of Israel (e.g., Ezek. 34:1–10). Faithful elders are shepherds who protect God's flock.

This can be done in a couple ways. First, elders can formally protect the flock. One key component of this is giving oversight to your membership practices. Examine everyone coming into the church to be sure they "are in the faith." (2 Cor. 13:5). A careful membership process protects the flock from those who believe and practice false religion. Elders should take the lead here. On the other end of the membership process are those who need to be put out of the church, those who verbally present themselves as Christians and yet whose lives contradict that claim. In Matthew 18:15–17 Jesus tells the church to plead with those who sin in order to bring them to repentance, and, if necessary, to exclude those who fail to repent. Elders protect the flock by faithfully leading them through the sad but loving process of excommunication.

Second, elders can informally protect the flock. Elders normally protect the flock through the regular teaching and preaching of God's Word. That's still rather formal. But a healthy church takes the formal care and protection of the elders and turns to care, reprove, correct, train, and disciple itself (see Eph. 4:15–16). This informal protection happens when the well-taught married couple warns the young woman who is tempted to date outside the faith. It happens when one brother offers to help another brother remain accountable in the fight against sin. And the elders take the lead in this informal protection too, through ministering in personal relationships with church members. Formal and informal protection of the flock should be at the core of the job description of an elder.

With these verses in mind, Dever scrapped his original slate of candidates and nominated five new names. Actually, he didn't. He strongly believed that the first five men he nominated had been living among, teaching, and protecting the flock. So he wrote a four-page document making a variety of arguments for re-nominating the original five candidates, and he presented it to an interested group of about forty church members after a Sunday morning service. Here are some gleanings from it:

- I, the nominator, could be wrong. I certainly do not believe in pastoral inerrancy.
- The constitution could be wrong in the percentage it requires. I have never suggested that the constitution now adopted is inerrant. The Bible nowhere requires 75 percent.
- I am not sure that this congregation was wrong, in that 65 to 73 percent of the congregation present actually *supported* the nominees.
- I think the congregation that overwhelmingly voted to fire Jonathan Edwards was wrong.
- I told this congregation in November of 1993 that, if I came, they needed to know that I worked not ultimately for the congregation, but for God.
- Why do I feel that I should nominate the same five again? Because, after continuing to pray about it, I cannot see any others to nominate at this time…and I cannot see *not* nominating each one of these to the church.
- I am encouraged that the failed nominees resolve to serve the church quite apart from being recognized as elders.
- The humble spirit and manner of the discussion among the failed nominees about what to do only encourages me to nominate them again.
- There is not a coherent alternative vision among those who voted against these five.
- Is it arrogant of me to nominate the same five again? Most of the church agrees with me. I have received much advice to do this. I do not do this lightly at all. My primary consideration: I do not understand this to be a matter of arrogance, but of integrity.
- It is a serious spiritual deficiency in a church either to have leaders who are untrustworthy, or members incapable of trusting.
- In coming to this church, I knew that I would be coming into a trust-poor area.
- Trust is never finally earned; it is given.
- I do see this as a clear referendum on the direction of this church.

What would Mark do if the second vote failed? Prior to the vote Mark wrote, "Finally, if I am unable to nominate men to serve as elders whom a sufficient number of you would recognize, then you would be well within your rights to find another pastor who, you would be presuming, could find those nominees. I would take that as in some measure a release from God."

Yet in November of 1998, the same five candidates were nominated again to serve in the role of elder. This time they were elected by the members, all surpassing the constitutional bar of 75 percent affirmation.

Why did they pass this time? We trust it was God's will, of course. From a human perspective, some were simply persuaded to trust Mark's leadership. Others were persuaded not to count against one man his relatively young age or another his demanding work schedule. And there were some who didn't show up the second time. (The Triple L Club seniors—a big chunk of the initial "no" vote—appeared to give up.)

With that successful vote behind us, our church moved from one shepherd to six.

CHAPTER NINE

ELDERS IN THE LOCAL CHURCH

1 Timothy 3:1–7

[1] It is a trustworthy statement: if any man aspires to the office of overseer, it is a fine work he desires to do. [2] An overseer, then, must be above reproach, the husband of one wife, temperate, prudent, respectable, hospitable, able to teach, [3] not addicted to wine or pugnacious, but gentle, peaceable, free from the love of money. [4] He must be one who manages his own household well, keeping his children under control with all dignity [5] (but if a man does not know how to manage his own household, how will he take care of the church of God?), [6] and not a new convert, so that he will not become conceited and fall into the condemnation incurred by the devil. [7] And he must have a good reputation with those outside the church, so that he will not fall into reproach and the snare of the devil.

The churches of the New Testament maintained a simple form of government. This form gradually took shape in the first decades of Christianity, as Acts and the Epistles reveal, and often it developed in response to some need experienced by a local church. In Acts 6, for instance, a dispute arose over the distribution of food to widows. The apostles responded by proposing that the church put forward "seven men of good reputation, full of the Spirit and of wisdom" (Acts 6:3), whom they would place over this area of service. That way, the apostles could continue leading the church through prayer and the ministry of the Word. This incident gives us a little window into how the churches planted by apostles and missionaries throughout the first-century Roman Empire began to shape their polity or government. Two bodies served in a leadership role: one attending to spiritual needs and the other to temporal needs.

At some point in the early years, the office of elders emerged, as a passing mention in Acts 11:30 suggests. Later, Luke observes that Paul and Barnabas backtracked to the churches planted on their first missionary journey to appoint elders (Acts 14:23). Luke's language—"When they had appointed elders for them in every church"—clearly shows that more than one elder was appointed in every church. Elder plurality in the local church continued throughout the early church and into the next century.

Something happened, however, in the second century that continues to affect the structure of churches today. Ignatius, a bishop in Antioch, wrote a letter to the Magnesians, a people living in modern Turkey, in which he refers to a single bishop in authority over the church.[1] It is the earliest recorded comment that does. With that start, the gradual evolution took place in which a single bishop would preside over the spiritual affairs of a city. Prior to this, the titles bishop (or overseer), elder, and pastor had been used interchangeably, as we have seen. Now, the rule of a single bishop, what has been called a *monarchical episcopacy*, began to take hold. Two major developments followed. First, the bishop of Rome, who would eventually be referred to as the pope, gained primacy over every other bishop. The first pope in the modern usage was Leo the Great in the fifth century.[2] The papacy has continued through the centuries, wherein a single man is entrusted with sovereignty over the Catholic Church. After the Protestant Reformation, the monarchical episcopacy form would transmute into denominations, whether Anglican or in many Pentecostal and charismatic denominations. History clearly reveals the countless tragedies that have resulted from the errors of monarchical episcopacies.[3]

Second, this same *monarchical episcopacy* has been practiced in the modern era in thousands of Baptist and independent churches where a single pastor is recognized as the sole authority over a local church. This form of *monarchical episcopacy* generally lacks the level of authority accorded to the papacy or to

---

1 *Magnesians* 6.1; *ANF*, 1:61, "I exhort you to study to do all things with a divine harmony, while your bishop presides in the place of God, and your presbyters in the place of the assembly of the apostles, along with your deacons, who are most dear to me, and are entrusted with the ministry of Jesus Christ."

2 Justo Gonzalez, *The Story of Christianity* (Peabody, MA: Prince Press, 1984), 1:242–243.

3 For instance, see Justo Gonzalez, *The Story of Christianity*; Bruce Shelley, *Church History in Plain Language* (Nashville: Thomas Nelson, 2008); S. M. Houghton, *Sketches from Church History* (Edinburgh: Banner of Truth, 1980). These works offer ample evidence of the corrupt and unbiblical practices and decisions of the papacy that have shaped the modern Catholic Church.

a bishop in an Episcopalian structure, but it does neglect an important New Testament pattern for the local church: a plurality of godly men leading each congregation.[4]

The sixteenth-century Reformation's return to the authority of Scripture for the doctrine and practice of the church also brought changes into local congregations. As we saw in chapter 1, some recognized four offices in the church. Some recognized elders and deacons but divided elders into teaching elders and ruling elders. And some maintained this same distinction in terms of function while recognizing only the two offices of elder and deacon.

In chapter 1, we also saw that, although not all Baptist churches in early America held to elder plurality, many did. Yet the push westward across the continent meant that a pastor would often serve more than one church with limited male leadership. Out of necessity, he was often the lone elder in the church. Also, Isaac Backus' emphasis on congregationalism and a democratic individualism, as we have seen, meant that he assigned "little real power to the eldership." Church planters influenced by Backus had no authority to appoint additional elders, restricting them to one elder per church.[5]

Thankfully, our day is witnessing a return to elder plurality in Baptist churches. Though not pervasive, it is significant enough that regular anti-elder literature comes out of various circles. In practically every new church that I have heard of in the past ten years, most practice some shape of elder plurality. This return to the biblical practice corrects several significant errors:

1. The failure to appoint qualified men to the biblical offices of elder and deacon.
2. The practice of turning deacons into the spiritual leaders in the church.
3. The practice of putting a single pastor into a position with no support in difficult issues of doctrine, discipline, or leadership.
4. The failure of giving all leadership to one man; *or* to a group of often unqualified men (and women); *or* to no one except the congregation.

---

4 Gonzalez, *The Story*, 242, points out that some scholars believe the early church in Rome was governed by a "collegiate episcopacy," i.e., a group of overseers who served in plurality.
5 Stanley Grenz, *Isaac Backus—Puritan and Baptist, His Place in History, His Thought, and Their Implications for Modern Baptist Theology* (NABPR Dissertation Series, 4; Macon, GA: Mercer University Press, 1983), 278–279. Because of his voluminous writings that influenced nineteenth-century Baptists, later generations "moved beyond Backus" in diminishing the role of elder plurality, as Grenz points out. In my observations, Backus, affected by the Enlightenment and the writing of John Locke, emphasized *individualism* and a strict congregationalism rather than the healthy congregationalism so evident in the New Testament along with elder plurality.

This long introduction sets the stage for us to consider the simplicity of New Testament church leadership. Paul emphasizes character more than function because the character of the false teachers in Ephesus had corrupted and weakened the church.

The local church must give serious attention to the New Testament pattern for spiritual leaders. But what does this involve for modern congregations? This chapter will seek to understand both the character and function of the office of elder.

ASPIRATION TO THE OFFICE OF ELDER

Paul treated the office of the elder as "a fine work" or "a noble task" (ESV). Yet consider Paul's setting for a moment. The churches to whom he wrote were not decades or even centuries old; they did not have a long history of developing godly leaders. Rather, they were often young and fraught with weaknesses due to their background of paganism. At times, they lived with constant opposition. They might have only had a few men among their number. Selecting elders and deacons was not a simple task. Particularly in the areas where persecution grew intense, the elders would have been the first to be persecuted in the waves of pressure upon the churches. To get an idea of the pressure, we might consider the 2011 persecution of the Shouwang church in Beijing, which sought to meet openly in a park after being expelled from their rented meeting place and has been under assault by the government. The leadership remains the primary target of the Chinese police. In the ancient context, such activity makes a man think long and hard before *aspiring* to the office of elder.

Still, Paul opens the discussion of elders in 1 Timothy on the topic of a man's aspirations. "It is a trustworthy statement: if any man aspires to the office of overseer, it is a fine work he desires to do." He uses a doctrinal formula to call special attention this teaching: "it is a trustworthy statement" or a faithful word. In other words, a person can count on it across the board.

With our legitimate concern about egotism and pride, it is easy to shrink from the idea of someone *aspiring* to the office of overseer. Yet Paul's word for aspiring points to the idea of someone stretching out their hand to the office with a genuine desire to serve the people of God. Lest someone aspire to the office for the sake of a title, a quick look at the character qualifications should squash impure motives.

By the same token, I am convinced that if someone must be cajoled into serving as an elder, he has no business accepting the responsibility. Aspiration to the office suggests a passionate desire to serve and shepherd the congregation. For in serving among the elders one is taking care of the church of God (1 Tim. 3:5).

Once again, we see in 1 Timothy 3 that the word *elder* is equivalent to *overseer*, even if writers like Ignatius of Antioch separate them.[6] Paul tells Titus to remain in Crete to "appoint elders in every city," and then in the next sentence refers to the such a man as an "overseer" (Titus 1:5–7). As we have seen, both terms carried important weight in the ancient communities, the former emphasizing the *character* of the dignity and honor befitting such servants, and the latter emphasizing the *functions of* leadership. Paul combines both in the New Testament church usage to explain one office, not to mention the third term *pastor* (see Acts 20:28; cf. 1 Pet. 5:2).[7] With all three we are talking about the same "noble task" worthy of aspiration.

CHARACTER SUITABLE TO THE OFFICE

Paul's goal in listing the character traits in 1 Timothy 3 was not to develop a "super Christian" who soared above ordinary Christians. Rather, he identified those traits that should characterize *Christians*. Aside from "able to teach," there are really no qualities asked of elders that should not be normal for every Christian in the local church.

Is "above reproach," the umbrella characteristic that speaks of unimpeachable conduct, too much to ask of any Christian?

Or is "a one-woman-man"—fidelity and devotedness in marriage—only for spiritual leaders?

Or would we think it strange to ask the typical Christian to be "temperate" or sober-minded; "prudent" or self-controlled; "respectable" or orderly in one's life and duty; and "hospitable" or willing to open one's home to serve others?

Should not every Christian guard against being "addicted to wine" or drunkenness; and being "pugnacious" or a violent bully?

Is it not the norm within the church for believers to be "gentle" or kindly and forbearing; "peaceable" or uncontentious; as well as "free from the love of money"?

Do we not want every Christian father to "manage his own household well?" And do we not expect him to seek to keep "his children under control along with all dignity?" In fact, we believe that all Christian men should be spiritual leaders in their homes, love their wives as Christ loved the church, bring up their children in the nurture and discipline of the Lord, and not provoke their children to anger by heavy-handedness (see Eph. 5:22–6:4). We do not believe that elders

6 See footnote 1 above.
7 See chapter 3 for more detailed explanation.

and deacons alone should lead their families this way, while the rest of us can cast our family cares to the wind.

Should only elders be concerned about having "a good reputation with those outside the church, so that [they] will not fall into reproach and the snare of the devil?" That was a major issue in Ephesus. False teachers had run the church's reputation into the ground. But they, like we, needed elders to steady the listing ship so that both leaders and members live gospel-oriented lives outside the church.

Bible scholar William Mounce argues that the particular qualities that Paul called for among the Ephesian elders and deacons *countered* the lack of Christian character among the false teachers. While the false teachers forbade marriage and maybe even childbearing while also seducing unsuspecting women (1 Tim. 4:3; 2:15; 2 Tim. 3:6), an elder should be "a one woman-man." While they were not self-controlled (2 Tim. 3:3), the elder should be "prudent." While they lacked love for others (1 Tim. 1:5), the elder should be "gentle." In other words, most every trait that Paul requires of elders finds its negative antithesis in something he says about the false teachers. That is one significant reason why Paul's wanted plain, faithful Christian living to characterize those in leadership.[8]

Due to the lack of Christian holiness in our day, some regard these qualities as virtually impossible to attain, reserved only for the Christian elite. Yet nothing could be further from the truth. What Paul wants is for local churches to take Christian living seriously, and this requires appointing leaders who will exemplify Christian behavior. Does this mean that we select only individuals who have perfected these character qualifications? I think not. None of us has perfected any of them. Rather we select individuals whose lives are generally characterized by these qualities.

DUTIES APPROPRIATE FOR THE OFFICE

While 1 Timothy 3 does not outline every aspect of an overseer's duties, it does give us some indication of what he will do on behalf of the church. If we draw from 1 Timothy 5:17 and summarize an elder's responsibilities as "ruling" and "preaching and teaching," we find both ideas in 1 Timothy 3. First, he compares ruling to the loving, wise management that a father exercises over his family. "But if a man does not know how to manage his own household, how will he take care of the church of God?" (v. 5). The word "manage" means "to exercise a

8 Wm. Mounce, *WBC: Pastorals* (WBC 46; Nashville: Nelson, 2000), 156–158.

position of leadership, rule, direct, be at the head of."[9] The same word is used for spiritual leadership in 1 Thessalonians 5:12, where it is translated "have charge over you in the Lord," implying a strong interest in people in order to show care for them.[10] In other words, managing a church does not mean ordering people around but overseeing them (hence the term *episkopos* or overseer), leading in a caring fashion, and working toward their good. As with any kind of managing or governing, decisions have to be made for the good of the church; direction must be set to further the church's mission.

This leadership of governing or managing or ruling should not be done autocratically but within the framework of healthy congregationalism. The elders (and deacons) must be affirmed by the church. For instance, the Jerusalem congregation helped select the seven who served in temporal needs; the ancient *Didache* (AD 80–150) referred to bishops and deacons appointed by the congregation's show of hands;[11] and Reformed and Baptist forefathers have practiced the same.[12] All the while, the elders do lead the church in areas of doctrine, direction, and discipline.

Second, Paul refers in 1 Timothy 3 to the most prominent of the duties for elders—*teaching* and *preaching*. He does not say that an elder is required to preach, but he does require an elder to be "able to teach" (v. 2). Later, he encourages the Ephesian church to remunerate well those elders "who work hard at preaching and teaching" (1 Tim. 5:17). He also told Titus that elders were to "hold fast the faithful word which is in accordance with the teaching, so that he will be able both to exhort in sound doctrine and to refute those who contradict" (Titus 1:9). False teaching had hammered away at the foundation of the Ephesian church, and so there was no room for neglecting doctrinal teaching. Elders were to lead the church primarily through regularly instructing in the Scripture.

Paul does offer a caveat: the elder is "not to be a new convert, so that he will not become conceited and fall into the condemnation incurred by the devil." Due to the attention that comes with leadership and teaching, an elder must guard his heart against the innate tendency toward pride and conceit. Sometimes new converts think more highly of themselves when given positions of leadership. Elders must hold their office with humility, realizing their own sinfulness and weakness and depending upon the redemptive and sustaining work of Christ.

---

9   *BDAG*, 870.
10 Ibid.
11 Simon Kistemaker, *NTC: Acts*, 525, citing *The Apostolic Fathers*, vol. 1, *Did.* 15.1 (Loeb Classical Library).
12 See *CrChr*, 3:725, 739 for examples with the Savoy Declaration of 1658 and London Baptist Confession of 1688 calling for the vote of the church on these offices.

This duty to teach has never been rescinded. Elders must still prioritize teaching the Scriptures. Therefore they must be students of the Word, who practice good study disciplines by working through the biblical text to understand and apply it.

What would happen to the landscape of Christianity if every church had a plurality of godly men leading them, men committed to studying, understanding, teaching, and applying the whole counsel of God? How different, for instance, Southern Baptist life (my own denomination) would be. Right now, only a third of the SBC membership shows up for church on any given Sunday. But with such leaders, integrity could be restored in membership. Churches would more likely take membership seriously if the Word was rightly applied and if the elders' shepherding responsibilities were made a priority.

But let me hasten to add, having elders does not ensure that a church is healthy. First, the church must approve only those men who give evidence of living out the gospel and who are committed to the faithful teaching of the whole counsel of God. Second, the church must recognize the Christ-ordained structure for leadership and teaching in the church, responding to it with faithfulness. Finally, the local church must continually cultivate younger men to serve as future elders, challenging them to be diligent in their Christian discipleship and their study of the Word.

Elders are appointed not for the sake of an office but for the sake of faithfully adorning the gospel of Jesus Christ. A church will best do this by submitting to the pattern given to the New Testament church for its governance.

REFLECTIONS

- How has ancient and more recent history affected the practice of elder plurality in local churches?
- Is aspiration to the office of elder a positive or negative trait? Explain your answer.
- In what ways do the character qualities called for in elders reflect a normal level of Christian practice?
- What value does Paul place on elders teaching in the church? How is this practiced in your church's leadership?

CHAPTER TEN

DISAGREEMENTS AMONG THE BROTHERS

Sitting over burgers in a Capitol Hill restaurant, I said to a fellow elder regarding a third elder, "I am not sure he is qualified."

"You don't think that," my fellow elder and trustworthy friend replied.

"What do you mean?"

He explained, "You are a man of integrity, for which I'm grateful. If you really thought he wasn't qualified, you could not continue to sit at the same table as him. No, I think this is personal."

I knew my friend was right, though I didn't want to admit it. In my flesh, it seemed easier to make the difficulties I had been having with this other elder about his qualifications, which would mean the problem was with *him*, and that I would not have to humble myself to address the bruised relationship.

Let me be transparent with you: friendship does not always come naturally with all of my fellow elders. I love them in Christ, yes. But that does not mean I will be bosom buddies with all of them. The good news is, we can work with people even when friendship does not come naturally, especially if we respect them as men of integrity.

Aside from the reasons Phil has mentioned in his chapter on the necessary attributes of an elder, this is one more reason why it is so critical that all the men sitting around the elders' table meet the qualifications that Paul lays out in 1 Timothy 3 and Titus 1. Eldering work can sometimes feel like charging into enemy fire with your army platoon. You need to be able to trust those men—that they are reliable and will cover your back. When an elder board addresses a tough case of church discipline, or considers a complex case of subtly false teaching, or makes a tough decision that you know will not be well-received by the congregation, you need to know the other men at the table are "above reproach." You need to be able to trust their integrity.

To put it another way, when you are making sacrifices for the gospel, because you love Christ more than anything, you want to know that the life of every other brother leading the church likewise commends the gospel and does not compromise it.

This is why nominating new elders is the one matter for which our own elder board does not allow any dissenting votes. Most matters are able to move through the board with a majority vote. But when it comes to nominating new elders, we require unanimity (with the possibility of up to two abstentions since not everyone may know the man). Why the higher standard on this one issue? Again, because you need to be able to trust the men sitting around the table with you for all the other issues.

So what do you do when you struggle to get along with a fellow elder? First, you have to distinguish whether these struggles are doctrinal, matters of character, or personal. The first two categories, no doubt, are matters of qualification. And typically if a problem falls into one of these two categories, it stands to reason that you will not be the only person who can see it. Several or all of the elders will need to deal with such scenarios.

But it occurs to me that it may be worthwhile to spend the remainder of the chapter reflecting on how to deal with disagreements or disputes between elders when the matter is arguably personal. What do you do then? You should start, of course, by pursuing God in prayer to ward off Satan. Insofar as Satan loves to divide, he often does it between two leaders. And he'll use whatever he can, even simple issues of personality.

Next, pursue the brother to build the relationship. Often, irritation arises out of ignorance. Work to know the brother, and remember that you often don't have all the facts.

Finally, be humble. Even if, in the end, you don't understand why a person is the way he is, God has tolerated far more from you. Also, you can trust that God has given that man to the body, with his particular combination of strengths and weaknesses, to build up the body in ways that you cannot. Study the body passages in 1 Corinthians 12, Romans 12, and elsewhere, and know that God intends good through such differences, even though, in our fallen state, those differences may involve a lack of camaraderie.

Over the years, I've had to practice these very things, as with the brother mentioned above. Indeed, he was doing the same with me. Far more is at stake than my own personal likes, dislikes, and unsanctified turf-wars. The health of the church is at stake, which means that the glory of God itself is at stake (from a human responsibility standpoint).

Often, the personal struggle with another elder can arise as a result of an elder rejecting your ideas at the table. So it's been important for me to separate my ideas from my identity (which is justified in Christ). Thus a rejection of my ideas is not a rejection of me. Along these lines, developing personal relationships outside of the elders' meetings makes the work of eldering easier to do.

No doubt, developing relationships with other elders is difficult to do in a growing church and a busy city. Part of the way our elders address this is, at the beginning of every meeting, we shepherd each other before we shepherd the church. We do this by sharing concerns, confessing, praising, and then praying for one another. Basically, we let one another know what's going on in our lives. We can take up to an hour of the elder's meeting to do this. Beyond this, we try to meet together individually for lunches and dinners from time to time.

Still, even with all this, real differences do arise between elders—between men of integrity whose lives, formally speaking, are above reproach. So how do you know when to back off from pressing your conviction and when to hold your ground?

The short answer, I think, is the clearer an issue is in Scripture, the firmer you hold your ground. On the one hand, I'm not going to yield on the deity of Christ, even if the other twelve elders do. On the other hand, I personally have strong convictions about birth control that are not obvious and clear in Scripture; and these convictions are not shared by all of my fellow elders. On this issue, therefore, I tread more lightly. A situation involving the question of birth control actually came up a while back. I vigorously argued my position biblically and practically. Yet then I had to submit—joyfully—to the other elders who may have been sympathetic to my position but finally voted otherwise.

I remember one occasion in which I took a one year sabbatical from active eldering, and then returned. The brothers asked me what I learned during the break. I realized that the church continued to prosper without my active involvement and opinions as an elder. This caused in me a healthy realization that I should hold my opinions more lightly.

Given the importance of unity and maturity among the elders, there are some traits or characteristics of potential elders that ought to raise yellow flags. The obvious ones include volatility, instability, bad reputation in the community, unruly children, and so on. That brings us back to whether or not the man fulfills the character criteria established by Paul.

But let me point to several less obvious yellow flags. One would be that of a contrarian spirit. You know the sort of guy I mean. If you say "black," he'll say "white." No matter what you say, that's what you get. The spirit that is perpetually looking for the "on the other hand" or waiting for "the other shoe to drop" is not helpful in building up the church. In Acts 6, for instance, Paul instructs the church to appoint deacons not only for their proficiencies, but because these men will bring unity between the Greek-speaking and the Hebrew-speaking widows. How much more should an elder be someone who builds unity and works to resolve rather than to merely offer up an opposing opinion?

Another yellow flag that is commonly overlooked is the question of a man's spiritual fruit in the lives of those around him. To put it positively, this is what drew our attention in 1998, for instance, to a church member named Andy Johnson. He had been quietly discipling other single men on a consistent basis, resulting in real spiritual progress in their lives. To put it negatively, then, no spiritual fruit is a yellow flag, even if the world would recognize the man as being "successful."

Finally, an unsupportive wife is a yellow flag. Eldering done right is a demanding task. It takes time to pray. It takes time to prepare to teach. It takes time to disciple. It takes time to give hospitality. All of these impact the home, and places certain demands on a wife. How does she feel about doing hospitality? How does she feel about losing her husband every other Thursday night to an elders meeting? Does she welcome the unexpected visitor at the door who's in need?

Too often we look toward worldly success to measure a man. We must teach our churches to look for men of the Word—to measure men based on their knowledge of, their submission to, and their ability to proclaim God's Word. I like what Mark Dever says: an elder's "ability to teach" means that when wolves come near the flock, the sheep know that they can trust this shepherd to expose the wolf and, in turn, to protect them. That's the elder's great calling.

CHAPTER ELEVEN

ELDERS AND
CONGREGATION IN CONCERT

Hebrews 13:17–19

[17] Obey your leaders and submit to them, for they keep watch over your souls as those who will give an account. Let them do this with joy and not with grief, for this would be unprofitable for you. [18] Pray for us, for we are sure that we have a good conscience, desiring to conduct ourselves honorably in all things. [19] And I urge you all the more to do this, so that I may be restored to you the sooner.

I have heard many stories of church conflict. Although such conflicts vary, they ultimately root in the leaders' failure to lead and/or the congregation's failure to follow. Sometimes leaders attempt to lead and congregations refuse to follow. On other occasions, willing congregations flounder in spiritual inertia because their leaders fail to lead biblically. In both cases, conflicts ensue.

Church leaders (elders, deacons, pastors, staff, teachers) and congregations must diligently follow the biblical patterns for church life, patterns which includes their relationship with one another. This relationship, after all, sets the tone for Christian growth and development, a lesson made clear in the epistle to the Hebrews.

Hebrews is a massive doctrinal epistle. For depth, richness, clarity, and forcefulness in explaining Christ and the gospel, Hebrews rivals any other portion of Holy Writ. Yet with all of its doctrinal depth, Hebrews remains one of the

123

Bible's most practical books. Its pastoral implications shine throughout the epistle. New Testament commentator Philip E. Hughes, referring to those who satisfy themselves with "an undemanding and superficial association with the Christian faith," explains that the letter to the Hebrews was written "to arouse just such persons from the lethargic state of compromise and complacency into which they had sunk, and to incite them to persevere wholeheartedly in the Christian conflict." He adds, "[Hebrews] is a tonic for the spiritually debilitated."[1] The writer, "clearly a preacher with a pastoral heart,"[2] had no desire to launch into minutiae; rather, he sought to bring a congregation of believers into a steady, focused, and persevering walk with Jesus Christ. "The writer of Hebrews," says Bible scholar Andrew Trotter Jr., "shows that combination of toughness and tenderness that is so crucial in ministry. Even when his warnings are as stringent as any in the NT, he makes sure to encourage those whom he believes are on the right track."[3]

It is not surprising, then, that in an epistle of such strong doctrinal language the pastoral writer would address the critical relationship between the congregation and its leaders. Disjointed relations could render moot the Christ-centered argument of the letter, and which the church's leadership would seek to apply. Since "this author knows his readers intimately,"[4] he leaves no stone unturned in the search for anything that might hinder the application of the doctrine of Christ to their lives. And not following their spiritual leaders would be one such hindrance.

Nothing in Hebrews indicates that the elders and teachers of this church had forsaken their responsibilities. Yet it does seem that, despite their faithfulness, members of the congregation had balked at following them. Accordingly, the writer of Hebrews exhorts the congregation to remember the spiritual leaders who had already passed from the scene and imitate their faith (Heb. 13:7). Then he charges them to follow their current leaders (Heb. 13:17). Both of these exhortations (vv. 7, 17) point to the connection between the doctrine set forth and its application in the daily walk.

Trotter conjectures that the epistle is actually addressed to "a small group of former leaders in the church [who] have encountered difficulties submitting to the current leadership."[5] Perhaps they had suffered under the bloodless persecu-

---

1 Philip Edgcumbe Hughes, *A Commentary on the Epistle to the Hebrews* (Grand Rapids: Eerdmans, 1977), 1.
2 Andrew H. Trotter Jr., *Guides to New Testament Exegesis: Interpreting the Epistle to the Hebrews* (Grand Rapids: Baker, 1997), 45.
3 Ibid.
4 Ibid., 47.
5 Ibid., 37–38.

tions of Claudius in A.D. 49 and the vicious, bloody persecutions of Nero a few years later. Having undergone such trauma, they felt shell-shocked once they surfaced and come back into active church life. The keenness of their doctrine had begun to dull, as had their loyalty to those presently leading the church. So the pastoral writer of Hebrews firmly corrects their theological errors, warns of the dangers of returning to a Jewish legalism, and commands them to follow their leaders in the church.[6]

The string of pointed applications in the last chapter of Hebrews serves to reinforce the point that doctrine is always applicable to daily life. Any congregation's spiritual leaders should major on helping the church to apply God's Word. *As leaders lead the church to apply truth to life, so congregations should follow.* But how does this work out in the ongoing life of the church? Hebrews 13:17–19 answers that question, and we can investigate it under two headings.

Hebrews 13:17–19

- Leaders Who Lead (vv. 17–18)
- Congregations That Follow (vv. 17–19)

LEADERS WHO LEAD (HEB. 13:17–18)

It is true that Hebrews 13:17–18 does not mention the titles *elder, overseer,* or *pastor.* Yet the term used, *leaders,* is a participle that can be translated as "the ones leading you," and seems to point to a plurality of elders.[7] Whether this particular congregation called its "leaders" *elders, overseers,* or *pastors,* they were, in fact, involved in governing, teaching, and shepherding the church—the very functions of plural eldership.

---

6 Ibid., 38.
7 It is worth observing how the term for leaders is used in Luke 22:26, Acts 14:12, and Acts 15:22. See also, *BDAG,* 434. The word *hegeomai,* when used in the present participle, will be translated as "ruler" or "leader," with the context determining the particular type of leader identified. The men accompanying Paul and Barnabas with the Jerusalem Council letter, Judas (called Barsabbas) and Silas, are in Acts 15:22 called, "leading men among the brethren." The same is used of Paul in Acts 14:12, where the participle is used in nominal form, "the leader of the talk," according to *LKGNT,* 296. It seems that the present participle of *hegeomai* took on almost technical meaning with the idea that leadership involved speaking or discoursing of some type. I would argue that this is the usage in Hebrews 13:7, 17, since the implication is that these leaders "spoke the word of God to you" and watched over the souls of the congregation—indicating that *hegeomai* is a distinctly pastoral term that includes teaching, instruction, and preaching.

While today we have no shortage of books, principles, and seminars on leadership, we do have a shortage of godly leaders. Every church needs a plurality of men who will faithfully exemplify the Christian life and clearly explain the Scriptures. What should leaders be doing? Hebrews' answer to that question is by no means exhaustive, but it does direct leaders in how to lead.

Watchfulness

Hebrews 13:17 reminds spiritual leaders that they possess the incredible charge of keeping watch over the church: "For they keep watch over your souls as those who will give an account." The word translated *keep watch* is a strong one,[8] picturing a shepherd who vigilantly and sacrificially watches over his flock. He means to protect them from wolves, and will go without sleep if necessary, straining to discern any cause of trouble. Watchfulness also has a military connotation—that of soldiers guarding their post, keeping vigilant lest the enemy sneak in to cause harm.

The writer of Hebrews also says that these leaders should exercise such watchfulness "over your souls," which is another way of expressing that the leaders' concern is for the whole person, or for "the seat and center of life that transcends the earthly."[9]

Spiritual leaders must be alert and discerning in caring for the church. Their duties chiefly focus on the people who comprise the church rather than on buildings or budgets. What kinds of things are they to watch on behalf of the church (*over* is better translated, "on behalf of")? *First, they are to watch for dangerous doctrines and false teaching.* A clear example of this instruction comes from the apostle Paul's instruction to the Ephesian elders:

> Be on guard for yourselves and for all the flock, among which the Holy Spirit has made you overseers, to shepherd the church of God which He purchased with His own blood. I know that after my departure savage wolves will come in among you, not sparing the flock; and from among your own selves men will arise, speaking perverse things, to draw away the disciples after them. Therefore be on the alert (Acts 20:28–31).

---

8 The Greek word *agrupnousin* means "to be without sleep, to seek after sleep, to be watchful," according to *LKGNT,* 720, and "to be alertly concerned about, look after, care for it," according to *BDAG,* 16.

9 *BDAG, psuche,* 1098–1100.

Spiritual leaders need to keep their fingers on the pulse of doctrine and teaching in a church. More heresies, half-truths, and pseudodoctrines than we can imagine will be passed off as truth.

A few years ago my family attended a Baptist church in Atlanta while visiting with relatives. The pastor read the Scripture and said, "May God bless His Spirit-inspired Word so that it *becomes the Word of God to us today*" (emphasis added). Putting it this way comes right out of the pages of twentieth-century neo-orthodox theology, which denies the full authority of Scripture. But the Bible does not *become* the Word of God; it *is* the Word of God. The congregation was duped by this man's charisma in the pulpit. They needed spiritual leaders who could discern such slick teaching and address it biblically.

Perhaps even more dangerous is the disappearance of theology in evangelical churches. David Wells has pointed out, "No one has abducted theology," as in the abduction of a child. Rather,

> The disappearance is closer to what happens in homes where the children are ignored and, to all intents and purposes, abandoned. They remain in the home, but they have no place in the family. So it is with theology in the church. It remains on the edges of evangelical life, but it has been dislodged from its center.[10]

Watching over a congregation demands attending to the church's theological understanding. Neglecting theology cracks the church's foundation, and ultimately affects its practice. In our day, this neglect is accompanied by the rise of pragmatism, which moves the church away from a biblically centered ministry to a church structure and an individualistic pattern of life that resembles the world more than the New Testament.[11] Wells adds, "It is evangelical *practice* rather than evangelical profession that reveals the change."[12] As evangelicals, we still profess to believe the confessions and creeds of the church, but our practice reveals that we often do not understand the theological implications of what we profess. Spiritual leaders must remain alert and watchful for this kind of neglect.

---

10 David F. Wells, *No Place for Truth: Or Whatever Happened to Evangelical Theology?* (Grand Rapids: Eerdmans, 1993), 106.

11 See my essay, "The Pastor and Church Growth: How to Deal with the Modern Problem of Pragmatism," in *Reforming Pastoral Ministry: Challenges for Ministry in Postmodern Times*, ed. John Armstrong (Wheaton, IL: Crossway, 2001), 263ff.; and John MacArthur Jr., *Ashamed of the Gospel: When the Church Becomes Like the World* (Wheaton. IL: Crossway, 1993).

12 Wells, *No Place for Truth*, 108; author's italics.

Add to this the countless false teachers propagating their doctrine through media, and the cult groups that masquerade as Christian, and spiritual leaders clearly need to be on full-time alert. "Savage wolves" were not just a first-century phenomenon. Marauding packs continue to ravage churches. Spiritual leaders must stand in the breach against such error foisted on the church.

Second, spiritual leaders must keep on the alert for deceitful behavior within the church. Tucked away in the little epistle of 3 John is the warning about Diotrephes, who had grabbed the leadership reigns of a church as something of a dictator. New Testament professor D. Edmund Hiebert describes Diotrephes as "an ambitious, self-seeking, power-hungry individual who aggressively sought to be at the head of things and to rule over others."[13] While he might have masked his motives with orthodox words, he was self-centered and full of pride, seeking to use the church to fulfill his own lust for power. The apostle John exposed his deceitful behavior and called on the church to resist such wickedness (3 John 9–10). He did what church elders should do: they must expose deceitful behavior before it wrecks the church.

Some time ago, I was involved in ministering to a fellow pastor who had a couple of men like Diotrephes in his church. Although he sought to address the problems nobly and biblically, he recognized that the other spiritual leaders of the church failed to expose these deceitful men who grabbed for the reins of power. Asleep on the job, the church's other leaders allowed the wolves to freely ravage the church and undermine the pastor's ministry. The failure of this church to reflect the beauty of Christ in the community must ultimately be traced back to those leaders' abdication of their responsibility to remain alert.

Third, spiritual leaders must keep alert to divisive behaviors. Wouldn't it be wonderful if we could make a wish, and watch all divisiveness in churches blow away? But that is not reality. We will always face that battle in the church of Jesus Christ.

Spiritual leaders must stand firmly against divisiveness. By rebuking, admonishing, and leading the way in exercising church discipline, leaders arrest such rending of the church. "Reject a factious man after a first and second warning, knowing that such a man is perverted and is sinning, being self-condemned," Paul instructed Titus (Titus 3:10–11). None of these things are popular measures in a church. But that is the work of the elders.

P. H. Mell identifies divisive behaviors as one of several "public offenses" in which the sin is "against the Church in its organized capacity."[14] In other

---

13   D. Edmund Hiebert, *The Epistles of John: An Expositional Commentary* (Greenville, SC: Bob Jones University Press, 1991), 336.
14   P. H. Mell, *Corrective Church Discipline with a Development of the Scriptural Principles upon*

words, divisiveness does not merely offend one or two members; it affects the entire body. Spiritual leaders watching over the souls of the church must not hesitate in applying disciplinary measures against offenders. The health and unity of the church is at stake.

Fourth, spiritual leaders must keep alert to the church's spiritual development. This includes positively knowing, teaching, and encouraging spiritual growth in the church. Elders must pay attention to the content of instruction and how members respond. This gives them a better grasp of the church's maturity and ability to discern false teaching.[15]

Accountability

As a pastor and elder in my own congregation, I find no thought more alarming than the one found in this verse: "For they keep watch over your souls *as those who will give an account*" (emphasis added). There is a sense in which church leaders will give an account to two different parties. First, church leaders will give an account for their ministry to their churches. This is an awesome realization. Churches should expect their leaders to be faithful and diligent. As a pastor, I sense this accountability. My own church does not take lightly the work of ministry, and it never should. Churches need to maintain high expectations for their elders' personal walk with Christ, their ministry of the Word, and their example before the body.

Second, this passage in fact points more specifically to a greater day of accountability—the great day of accounting when we all stand before the Lord in judgment. And here the author of Hebrews speaks in unison with the apostles:

- James explains that teachers "will incur a stricter judgment" (James 3:1).
- Peter uses the same word for *accounting* when he speaks of judgment, an accounting that will be given by all men before the eye that sees all and the mind that knows all (1 Peter 4:5).
- Paul refers to this same judgment in the preface to his exhortation "preach the word": "I solemnly charge you in the presence of God and of Christ Jesus, who is to judge the living and the dead...preach the word" (2 Tim. 4:1–2). The words "in the presence of God" convey the idea of

---

which It Is Based (Charleston, SC: Southern Baptist Publication Society, 1860), quoted in Mark Dever, ed., *Polity: Biblical Arguments on How to Conduct Church Life* (Washington, DC: Center for Church Reform, 2001), 423.

15 I'm indebted to my fellow elder, Tom Tollett, in pointing out this implication from the text.

being "in the face of God." Since the relationship of doctrine and practice is tied so closely to the leadership of those in charge of God's flock, the Lord alerts His undershepherds that a time of accounting will take place.

In short, the author to the Hebrews' reference to giving an account is part of a broad New Testament theme. And the accounting of which he speaks faces all the spiritual leaders in the church.

When our day is done, we will give an account for how we discharged our responsibilities. So must live and serve as those who will answer to the Lord of the church for our ministries. "This solemn consideration should affect not only the quality of their leadership," writes commentator Philip Hughes, "but also the quality of the obedience with which the Christian community responds to that leadership."[16] The sobering reality of eternity should never slip beyond the sight of spiritual leaders and their congregations.

Seriousness

Great seriousness, then, accompanies spiritual leadership. There is more to holding the office than wearing the title of *pastor, elder,* or *deacon.* It calls for serving in good conscience and with due diligence.

Evidently, charges had been made against the writer of Hebrews. Perhaps he had been accused of pursuing personal gain or being a poor leader. We can only guess. But we do see his quiet response: "For we are sure that we have a good conscience" (Heb. 13:18), an odd statement unless he was responding to some kind of charge against him. But he sees no need to give a lengthy explanation. His epistle has verified his grasp of God's Word, his love for the gospel, and his passion for this congregation's spiritual growth. So he needed only to affirm, "For we are sure that we have a good conscience," meaning, as Hughes explains, "that his conduct in relation to them can stand the scrutiny both of man and of God."[17] Lest we think that he was boasting he quickly asserts his desire to be honorable in his Christian ethics: "desiring to conduct ourselves honorably in all things." He does not claim to have arrived spiritually; he means to affirm his seriousness in exercising his ministry. Surely he models the conduct still needed by those who lead local churches.

Consider one other note about the seriousness of leadership. In the second sentence of Hebrews 13:17, the writer says, "Let them do this with joy and not with

---

16 Hughes, *Hebrews,* 586.
17 Ibid., 587. *We* is called an epistolary pronoun, which means that *We* served as a substitute for *I.*

grief, for this would be unprofitable for you." Christian leadership is not without emotion. *Joy* and *grief* are two very different terms that can characterize one's emotional response to the demands of church leadership. The phrase, "Let them do this" (a present subjunctive verb that takes on a hortatory sense) commands action on the part of the church.[18] The church was not to respond to the leadership with neutrality; rather, they were to respond so that their leaders might carry out their duties "with joy and not with grief." Joy comes when the leader senses that Christ is being formed in the church (Gal. 4:19), while grief results when leaders see either rebellion against the Word or apathy toward spiritual disciplines.

Conduct

Feeling the weight of accountability and the seriousness of their offices, a church leader cannot help but ask for prayer for his conduct: "Pray for us," the writer says. Why? Because of his "desiring to conduct ourselves honorably in all things" (Heb. 13:18). The writer *desires* honorable conduct, an expression that points to a deep longing. Leaders know that, like their congregations, they are sinners in constant need of grace. They know that they cannot just teach and implore others while neglecting their own conduct. They know that they have weaknesses which the adversary would gladly exploit through multiplied temptations.[19] They know that they grow tired and weary, and at times consider throwing off the yoke of spiritual leadership for lesser accountability. And so, knowing all this, the writer of Hebrews urges the church to pray for him—that his deepest longing of honorable conduct "in all things" might be fulfilled.

When all is said and done, a spiritual leader may not be a great preacher or teacher, may fall short in administrative skills, may falter in his abilities to counsel, and may lack stamina for his duties, *but he must not dishonor the noble office entrusted to him by the church through failing in his conduct.* Other things

---

18 "When one exhorts others to participate with him in any act or condition, the subjunctive is used in the first person plural," known as the hortatory subjective, according to H. E. Dana and Julius Mantey, *A Manual Grammar of the Greek New Testament* (Toronto: Macmillan, 1957), 171.

19 John Owen, *The Works of John Owen: Temptation and Sin* (Carlisle, PA: Banner of Truth Trust, 1991), 6:96, explains temptation as "*any thing, state, way, or condition that, upon any account whatever, hath a force or efficacy to seduce, to draw the mind and heart of a man from its obedience, which God requires of him, into any sin, in any degree of it whatever.*" He further points out that particular temptation is that "which causes or occasions him to sin, or in any thing to go off from his duty, either by *bringing* evil into his heart, or *drawing* out that evil that is in his heart, or any other way diverting him from communion with God, and that constant, equal, universal obedience, in matter and manner, that is required of him."

are important, but the spiritual leader's conduct as a Christian serves as the foundation for the whole of his ministry.

Neglect your conduct and your ministry will be negated. But honor the Lord in your conduct and, even with weaknesses, you will prove to be faithful.

CONGREGATIONS THAT FOLLOW (HEB. 13:17–19)

Faithful leaders must also have faithful congregations, or else their labors will be filled "with grief" rather than with joy. Observers often treat the church as nothing more than a social organization with religious overtones. Even some among local congregations can think of their church only in business and organizational management terms. Yet the Scripture holds a different viewpoint.

The writer of Hebrews exhorts his readers not to forsake their regular assembling together. He views Christians as "brethren," who are united in one family of believers. Each bears responsibility for encouraging one another, and spurring "one another to love and good deeds." Since the church has access into God's presence through "the blood of Jesus," looking to Christ as "a great high priest over the house of God," they should unite and draw near to God as a praying people. They should stand together upon their common confession of Christ, and they should mutually care for one another in fellowship (Heb. 10:19–25). The church "alone enjoys this freedom of access" into God's holy presence as regenerate people.[20] It should hold firmly to its confession of Christ, "first publicly made at their baptism, but also a witness thereafter to be joyfully maintained to the very end of this life."[21] The church cannot exist with "selfish individualism," which is the breeding ground for division.[22] Instead, the individual members must look for ways to incite one another in the practices that characterize true believers.[23] And this certainly cannot take place by absenteeism from the church's gatherings.

In every age, the church's greatest threats come in the areas of "doctrine and life, or belief and behavior," pastor and theologian Philip Ryken explains. "The rebellion of the mind is to deny what God tells us to think (which today takes the form of relativism)."[24] That's why the writer of Hebrews exhorts the church

---

20 Hughes, *Hebrews*, 410.
21 Ibid., 414.
22 Ibid., 415.
23 Rienecker and Rogers explain the word *stimulate* (*paroxusmos*) to mean "irritating, inciting, stimulation," *LKGNT*, 703. It leaves no question concerning the active involvement of each church member in helping to motivate others in the body toward faithful Christian service.
24 Philip Ryken, *City on a Hill: Reclaiming the Biblical Pattern for the Church in the Twenty-first Century* (Chicago: Moody, 2003), 97–98.

to "hold fast the confession of our hope without wavering" (Heb. 10:23). Ryken continues, "The rebellion of the heart is to disobey what God commands us to do (which today takes the form of narcissism)."[25] And that is why church members must be constantly engaged in inciting "one another to love and good deeds." Yet how can this take place in practice? The New Testament clearly shows that "God's plan was to place the church under the care of shepherds."[26] Shepherds lead while the members of the church follow.

Obedience and Submission

Perhaps the most difficult part of this text is found in the opening words of Hebrews 13:17: "Obey your leaders and submit to them, for they keep watch over your souls as those who will give an account." The words *obey* and *submit* conjure thoughts of a wicked slave owner, cracking his whip to bring his slaves under servile obedience. But such a picture is foreign to the meaning of this verse. A closer look at the text reveals the responsibility that God has given to each one in the church.

Spiritual leaders have the responsibility of keeping watch "over your souls," that is, on behalf of your life. God means to protect the church. He does not desire anyone to stumble from false teaching or the enticement to sin or the allurements of the world. Therefore, he warns us of all these things in His Word; and he has given us the holy example of our Lord as well as the apostles and believers throughout the centuries (cf. Heb. 11:1–12:3). But in his great mercy, God has also placed spiritual leaders—elders—in the church and given them the responsibility to deal vigilantly with spiritual hindrances.

When, for instance, a false teaching arises among the churches, the elders are to stand against it for the sake of the flock. Using God's Word, they should expose such error, warn of its danger, and seek to keep the church out of *spiritual harm's way*. It is unfortunate that this ministry by spiritual leaders is often taken too lightly by their congregation or left to the work of a single pastor.

Does the church know the vigilance that is required just to *recognize* false teaching? Do they understand the agony that is involved in dealing with error, often in the face of misunderstanding and opposition? Ryken explains, "Elders and pastors are called to master biblical theology, to spend time studying God's Word and learning the great doctrines of the Christian faith."[27] They risk offending

25 Ibid., 98.
26 Ibid.
27 Ibid., 101.

others while standing for the truth. They are subjected to ridicule by the world and sometimes by the church, all for the sake of the congregation given to their charge.

How should the church respond to those who "keep watch over your souls"? The congregation can obey and submit, or it can stiffen and rebel. There is no middle ground. Apathy is simply quiet rebellion.

If you see the value of spiritual leadership and you recognize that God has placed that leadership in the church for your benefit, then the only response is to obey and submit to your spiritual leaders. To rebel is to commit spiritual anarchy. It is to disobey Jesus.

John Chrysostom, the "Golden-tongued preacher" of the fourth century, wrote, "Anarchy is an evil, the occasion of many calamities, and the source of disorder and confusion"; moreover, "a people that does not obey a ruler [i.e., elder or pastor] is like one that has none, and perhaps even worse."[28] Sadly, many of our churches are characterized by individualism and narcissism, and these instincts surely react poorly to the call to obedience and submission. But whether it is popular or not, the Lord of the church determined that his body works with a plurality of leaders and faithful members who value obedience and submission as a joyful responsibility.

Both *obey* and *submit* are present imperatives, showing constancy on the part of the church. To obey does not mean being a "man-follower" rather than a Christ follower. Rather, we follow our spiritual leaders *only* insofar as they imitate Christ and adhere to the teaching of the Word. We must never obey and submit in areas that clearly conflict with the teaching of Scripture.

Some use these verses to claim *absolute authority*, but such authority belongs only to the Lord. A simple rule of thumb is to use "sanctified common sense" in obeying and submitting to spiritual leaders. These verses command obedience and submission in the realm of the church and the spiritual life. They do not command obedience in personal affairs as relates to finances, business decisions, and even marriage partners. Certainly church elders can offer counsel in these other areas, and may even exhort church members in godly wisdom; but they must not assert control. "They keep watch over your souls," not your bank accounts.[29]

Spiritual leaders bear responsibility for speaking the Word of God to the congregation and giving it an example to follow, and it is in this context that

---

28 J. P. Migne, ed. *Patrologia Graeca*, "Chrysostom," vol. 63 (London: ET, 1893), quoted in Hughes, *Hebrews*, 585–586.

29 By this it is to be inferred that elders are not involved in soliciting bank or investment statements. Elders may, however, find occasions to exhort members regarding giving if negligence in this area has taken place, or regarding wise budgeting if warranted.

the congregation should obey and submit. *Obey* carries the idea of obediently following someone because you trust that person. The implication is that the church hears the elders' teaching of the Word and sees their seriousness in following the teaching of Scripture, so they obediently do likewise. An elder should never adopt an attitude that would suggest, "Do as I say not as I do." Rather, they set the example so that one can confidently say, "Imitate their faith" (Heb. 13:7).

Submission involves recognizing the God-ordained authority established in the church for order and direction. The congregation submits or places itself under the leadership of its spiritual leaders, complying with their direction and teaching. "If obedience applies to the leaders' teaching, then submission relates to their leaders' function."[30] Commentator Raymond Brown offers a needed clarification on what submission means.

> One of the markedly unhealthy aspects of some contemporary teaching is the current "shepherding" fashion and the notion, popularized in some house churches and elsewhere, that every believer is meant to have a spiritual mentor to whom he is fully accountable for every aspect of his life. The spiritual "elder" has to be consulted before making significant purchases, changing one's job and accepting fresh responsibilities. The Scripture does not teach, encourage, or exemplify submission of this sort. It is bad for the one who practises [*sic*] it in that it discourages personal accountability to the Lord God, a mark of true Christian maturity. Furthermore, it minimizes the importance of other deep relationships, especially marriage, through which the will of God can be most naturally discerned.[31]

Our lives are best regulated and governed when we walk in submission to the authorities that God has placed in our lives. In the church, that authority is found in those whom God raises up as spiritual leaders. "Submission to authority is absolutely necessary for the proper ordering of society, and the church of God is no exception. Indeed, submission to authority is often a test of our submission to God."[32] So *obey* and *submit* are not offensive orders, but terms for orderly life in the church.

---

30 Raymond Brown, *The Bible Speaks Today: the Message of Hebrews* (Downers Grove, IL: Inter-Varsity Press, 1982), 264.
31 Ibid., 264–265.
32 Alexander Strauch, *Biblical Eldership: An Urgent Call to Restore Biblical Church Leadership*, rev. and exp. ed. (Littleton, CO: Lewis and Roth, 1995), 160.

Profit or Loss?

Hebrews 13:17 ends with an earnest plea: "Let them do this with joy and not with grief, for this would be unprofitable for you." Elders face weighty responsibilities and demands. They are to lead the congregation in the ways of God. They are to teach and exhort the congregation in the doctrines of God's Word. They are to live exemplary lives, serving as living models of the Christian faith to the congregation. And they are to constantly watch over the souls of the congregation, guarding them from deceit, error, sin, and worldliness. In light of all this, the responsibility of the church is to "let them do this with joy and not with grief."

Elders and pastors should find their greatest delights in carrying out their weighty responsibilities with their church. It should be a joy to lead, teach, set an example, and watch over souls. They should constantly look forward to each day's challenge in spiritual leadership. Pastor John MacArthur writes,

> It is the responsibility of the church to help their leaders rule with joy and satisfaction. One way of doing this is through willing submission to their authority. The joy of our leaders in the Lord should be a motivation for submission. We are not to submit begrudgingly or out of a feeling of compulsion, but willingly, so that our elders and pastors may experience joy in their work with us.[33]

A humble attitude in the members of the congregation is essential for elders to experience joy in their duties. If someone in the congregation is jealous of those in positions of spiritual leadership, the joy of the spiritual leaders will be greatly reduced. Those who are resentful about being under the authority of another create division and strife within the congregation. A world of trouble results when church members rebel against this clear teaching of Scripture.

"Let them do this with joy"—so what is the "this" of the text? It is the all-encompassing work of keeping watch over the congregation's souls. Members contribute to the overall effectiveness of this work by watching their attitudes toward the leaders God has placed over them. "Grief" or "groaning," caused by callousness to the Word and arrogance toward spiritual leadership is unprofitable for the church. Brown adds, "If spiritual leaders have to labour under grim and hostile conditions

---

33 John MacArthur, *MacArthur's New Testament Commentaries: Hebrews* (Chicago: Moody, 1983), 446.

in the local church, then that does not work out to the members' immediate good and certainly not to their ultimate advantage."[34]

But the joy of which Hebrews speaks is not one-sided. Neglecting obedience and submission, the text continues, is "unprofitable for you." The Greek word for *unprofitable* literally means "harmful,"[35] and the plural pronoun *you* refers to the church. The whole church, then, will find it harmful when even a few members rebel against the spiritual leaders of the church.

Why is this so? As the church, we are mysteriously woven together in the bonds of Jesus Christ. Every local church is a unique visible expression of the body of Christ. Every church becomes a family of believers who must learn to live with each other, labor with each other, learn with each other, and face adversities with each other. When one is joyful, all are to be joyful. When one is grieving, all share in that grief. By this same rule, one person's attitude affects the whole church. When someone in the church openly rebels or becomes secretly agitated toward the elders, the whole body, in one way or another, is affected.

Urgency in Prayer

In light of all the responsibilities given to spiritual leaders and the congregation, the pastor who is the author of Hebrews asks his readers to pray for him as well as for the other spiritual leaders in the church. "Pray for us," he implores, so that they might conduct themselves honorably as Christians, elders, and leaders. Then he adds a note of urgency: "And I urge you all the more to do this, so that I may be restored to you the sooner" (Heb. 13:19).

We do not know what hindered the writer from returning to this church. A short time later, he states that Timothy had been released, presumably from prison, and that the writer planned to come with Timothy. Whatever the hindrance, the writer understood that overcoming it would require God's intervention. He needed the prayers of this congregation in order to live honorably before the Lord and to be able to fulfill his responsibilities to the church.

The lesson in all this: not only does the church need spiritual leaders, but spiritual leaders need the church and its prayers. Kent Hughes states this clearly from his years of Christian service.

---

34 Brown, *Hebrews*, 265.
35 *LKGNT*, 720.

How different the modern church would be if the majority of its people prayed for its pastors and lay leadership. There would be supernatural suspensions of business-as-usual worship. There would be times of inexplicable visitations from the Holy Spirit. More laypeople would come to grips with the deeper issues of life. The leadership vacuum would evaporate. There would be more conversions.[36]

As a pastor and elder, my particular needs might be different from those of the other elders and leaders in our church, but all of us need the prayers of God's people who are called South Woods Baptist Church (my own congregation). Their prayers are paramount. Without their faithful praying, our ministry will not succeed. With it, there is no limit to what our gracious God might be pleased to do through our congregation.

So, joining with this first-century writer, I urge you to pray for the leaders of your own congregation. Pray for their Christian walks and discipline. Pray for their roles as husbands and fathers. Pray for their grasp and understanding of the Word. Pray for their preaching and teaching of the Word. Pray for the times of counseling and witnessing, as well as for the times of direction-giving and decision-making. Pray that in the end we might all serve Christ together with joy to his glory alone.

REFLECTIONS

- What does the writer of Hebrews teach concerning what spiritual leaders are to be doing on behalf of the church?
- How are spiritual leaders held accountable?
- How should the church respond to its spiritual leaders?
- In what ways are spiritual leaders dependent on the church?

---

36   R. Kent Hughes, *Preaching the Word: Hebrews, an Anchor for the Soul* (Wheaton, IL: Crossway, 1993), 2:239.

CHAPTER TWELVE

FROM SUSPICION TO TRUST

Our church does not speak of ordaining elders but of "installing" them. My friend Thabiti Anyabwile, however, doesn't care much for the term "installation." He says, "It sounds like you're nailing a peace of furniture in place in the church building. I don't much go for being nailed."

Perhaps a better term would be a "wedding." It is a marriage of sorts between a man and his congregation. At weddings, vows are exchanged—verbal affirmations of a covenant and commitment.

And so, after they were appointed by the church, the five newly elected elders of Capitol Hill Baptist Church made the following vows to the congregation:

1. Do you reaffirm your faith in Jesus Christ as your personal Lord and Savior?
   I do.

2. Do you believe the Scriptures of the Old and New Testaments to be the Word of God, totally trustworthy, fully inspired by the Holy Spirit, the supreme, final, and the only infallible rule of faith and practice?
   I do.

3. Do you sincerely believe the Statement of Faith and Covenant of this church contain the truth taught in the Holy Scripture?
   I do.

4. Do you promise that if at any time you find yourself out of accord with any of the statements in the Statement of Faith and Covenant you will

on your own initiative make known to the pastor and other elders the change which has taken place in your views since your assumption of this vow?
I do.

5. Do you subscribe to the government and discipline of Capitol Hill Baptist Church?
I do.

6. Do you promise to submit to your fellow elders in the Lord?
I do, with God's help.

7. Have you been induced, as far as you know your own heart, to accept the office of elder from love of God and sincere desire to promote His glory in the Gospel of His Son?
I have.

8. Do you promise to be zealous and faithful in promoting the truths of the Gospel and the purity and peace of the Church, whatever persecution or opposition may arise to you on that account?
I do, with God's help.

9. Will you be faithful and diligent in the exercise of all your duties as elder, whether personal or relative, private or public, and will you endeavor by the grace of God to adorn the profession of the Gospel in your manner of life, and to walk with exemplary piety before this congregation?
I will, by the grace of God.

10. Are you now willing to take personal responsibility in the life of this congregation as an elder to oversee the ministry and resources of the church, and to devote yourself to prayer, the ministry of the Word, and the shepherding of God's flock, relying upon the grace of God, in such a way that Capitol Hill Baptist Church, and the entire Church of Jesus Christ will be blessed?
I am, with the help of God.

But it wasn't only the elders who took vows. The congregation, too, had to make commitments, as pointed out in Phil Newton's explanation of Hebrews 13. So the members of CHBC responded with the following pledges:

1. Do you, the members of Capitol Hill Baptist Church, acknowledge and publicly receive these men as elders, as gifts of Christ to this church? **We do.**

2. Will you love them and pray for them in their ministry, and work together with them humbly and cheerfully, that by the grace of God you may accomplish the mission of the church, giving them all due honor and support in their leadership to which the Lord has called them, to the glory and honor of God? **We will.**

Pledging these words, of course, was the easy part.

After the vow-taking was over? At one level we knew that there would be a fight in the heavenly realms. I had often thought that Satan had his thumb on our little church, which partially explain the decades of failed pastorates and declining attendance. A viable witness in a major international crossroads like Washington, D.C. would be a loss for Satan's side. You think I'm exaggerating? We won't finally know till the end of time how it all went down. Nevertheless, I think I am in good company with the Apostle Paul, who seems sensitive to Satan's whereabouts when he speaks in one place of Satan's attempts to take "advantage" of us and, in another place, to "hinder us" (2 Cor. 2:11; 1 Thess. 2:18).

On the human level there seemed a rush of questions that emerged even from the vows we pledged to keep. How exactly will the "government and discipline of Capitol Hill Baptist Church" play out (vow #5)? Is there ever a time when I should *not* submit to my fellow elders in the Lord (vow #6)? The first year of being an elder felt a lot like being entrusted with one's first child. You went through birthing classes with your wife. You scoured every parenting book you could get your hands on. You observed all your close friends who had kids. But then they hand you the baby at the hospital and say "All yours!" Now what?

We new elders had to be patient as we attempted to switch the default setting of many in the congregation—especially the talkative ones—from suspicion to trust. Hardwired into the DNA of a Washington operative, which many of our church members were and are, is the notion that "Sunshine Laws"—euphemistically named transparency requirements—are a good idea because there is a rat hiding in every gift-wrapped box. We had to transform the democratic mindset of "one man one vote" into a mindset that happily unites in following the elders' lead. The sheep needed to trust God, that he would use us new elders to care for them. And they, too, needed to be patient with us as we grew into our new roles. The elders needed to learn what the sheep could and could not bear.

We made a couple of changes that came easily, like changing the name of "business meetings" to "members' meetings." We also moved the bimonthly members' meetings from the Wednesday night Bible study hour, which was attended by nonmembers, to the hour following our Sunday night prayer meeting. Now we take a ten minute break after the evening service and then re-assemble, but only with the members of our church. Why? Because the members' meeting is a family time in which brothers and sisters gather to conduct business of the church, led by the church's fathers, that is, the elders. Nonmembers, those who have not subscribed to the statement of faith and committed to supporting the teaching and mission of the church, should not be in attendance. We also picked the least defensive elder to moderate the members' meetings for when difficult or even accusatory statements were directed at the elders. We needed someone good at absorbing blows and not hitting back.

Even after these changes we struggled to implement our new leadership model. Phil talked in the preceding chapter about how elders and the congregation are to work in concert with each other. Our first year of having elders felt more like contention. Too many members' meetings were filled with tension. Members sometimes accused the elders of railroading something through. I cannot remember one time when a majority of the members went against an elder recommendation, but too often there seemed to be a lack of enthusiasm. There seemed to be an inexplicable cloud over our meetings. Our work did not feel like a joy as it says in Hebrews 13:17.

Memory fades over time and I'm sure there were a number of contributing factors to turning the corner, but I can point to one meeting that helped move the elders and congregation away from so much tension. A portion of every meeting was given to taking in new members, seeing out resigning members, and, occasionally, disciplining unrepentant members. During the time devoted to resignations, there was a very awkward exchange between Mark and a member of the congregation—let's call her Sandy. Mark announced that a woman that we'll call Lynn had resigned. Sandy raised her hand and said, "I just had lunch with Lynn this week and she doesn't want to resign." Mark, also having just met with Lynn that same week, said, "Yes, she does." It quickly devolved into Mark's word against Sandy's.

The situation was complicated by the fact that many in the congregation knew that Lynn didn't trust authority in general and the elders in particular. If Mark pushed for what he knew to be true, it would look like he was pushing someone out of the church who might have caused trouble for him.

This awkward exchange was followed by another case in which the elders recommended that the church excommunicate someone. It was a clear case of serious, outward, and unrepentant sin. The elders had been dealing with the situation for months, but this was the first time the congregation had heard of it. For them, it felt like a hammer to the head because the sinning individual was well-known and well-liked. The elders were calling for immediate removal from membership. As I remember it, we won the vote but lost the congregation's confidence.

By the next day, once we as elders had the chance to think back over the previous night's events, we realized that it is not just *what* we do to lead the congregation, but *how* we do it that is important. We realized that we had to smooth out our processes so that we did not bruise the sheep we were trying to care for. From that day on, for instance, we required all resignations to be submitted in writing. Further, we realized that, even though we were technically right to bring the discipline case to the congregation, we should have given the congregation advance notice. In the same way we as elders need time to process new and startling information, the congregation needs time too. We were unloving to issue an immediate call for discipline.

These days, when someone is in unrepentant sin and in danger of excommunication, we usually place their name on the "Care List." This simply involves announcing the name and situation to the church in accordance with Matthew 18:17 and then encouraging the church to pray for and reach out to the unrepentant member, calling him or her to repentance. Then, at our next regularly scheduled members' meeting, if the situation remains unchanged, the elders lead in disciplining the member by recommending that the congregation exclude him or her.

What's been the result of these seemingly small changes? It was like Satan was thrown out of our members' meetings. We had unwittingly allowed Satan to divide the elders and the congregation. Only afterwards did the relationship between elder patience and congregational trust become painfully obvious.

As the elders matured as a group it became increasingly easier for the congregation to "obey [their] leaders and submit to them" as Hebrews 13:17 says. As the congregation grew in their ability to follow and trust, our work as elders became the joy the author of Hebrews says it should be.

CHAPTER THIRTEEN

SPIRITUAL LEADERS FOR GOD'S FLOCK

I Peter 5:1–5

[1] Therefore, I exhort the elders among you, as your fellow elder and witness of the sufferings of Christ, and a partaker also of the glory that is to be revealed, [2] shepherd the flock of God among you, exercising oversight not under compulsion, but voluntarily, according to the will of God; and not for sordid gain, but with eagerness; [3] nor yet as lording it over those allotted to your charge, but proving to be examples to the flock. [4] And when the Chief Shepherd appears, you will receive the unfading crown of glory. [5] You younger men, likewise, be subject to your elders; and all of you, clothe yourselves with humility toward one another, for GOD IS OPPOSED TO THE PROUD BUT GIVES GRACE TO THE HUMBLE.

A church with strong spiritual leadership, typically, is a church that is stable, united, and healthy. Yet too often churches leave spiritual leadership to chance. They don't evaluate their polity in light of Scripture or require their leaders to meet biblical standards. Instead, they call pastors, hire staff, elect deacons, and carry on doing whatever seems to work best in the moment. Meanwhile, power struggles quietly transpire under the surface. Disunity creeps in. And then, unexpectedly, those struggles come to the surface in a raucous church business meeting. In an effort to quell the commotion, the church quickly makes more staff changes, maybe puts new programs in place. The trouble is, the church is building on unqualified leaders and unwieldy structures. Still, a new crop of even younger leaders is elected to infuse fresh blood into a deathly anemic organism. Sometimes this new infusion gives the body a temporary boost of vitality, but the church never really becomes healthy. Instead, the cycle occurs again and again, and frustration and disappointment are all that remains.

At the heart of a church's development is its spiritual leadership. If the leaders lack the character needed for holy work, the church will lack character, too. Instability will result. Short-term solutions, new programs, and new ideas do not solve long-term problems with character and stability.

There is a better way, a more courageous way: return to the biblical patterns of church structure and life. Only by doing so can a church confidently press onward in a world that is increasingly hostile to biblical Christianity. Developing an elder leadership structure will not solve every problem. But reorienting our churches toward the biblical pattern provides a framework for developing strong and healthy churches.

How do elders fit into the fabric of congregational life? We will investigate this subject by focusing on three questions.

---

1 Peter 5:1–5

- How Are Spiritual Leaders Identified? (vv. 1–2)
- How Do Elders and the Congregation Function? (vv. 2–5)
- Who Holds the Elders Accountable? (v. 4)

HOW ARE SPIRITUAL LEADERS IDENTIFIED? (1 PETER 5:1–2)

The context of 1 Peter 5:1–5 helps us to see the importance of elders in everyday church life. Just before explaining the ministry of elders in these verses, Peter addressed the subject of suffering for the sake of the gospel, calling it "the fiery ordeal among you, which comes upon you for your testing" (1 Peter 4:12; see also vv. 13–19). The seventeenth-century Scottish minister Robert Leighton noted that in the "fiery ordeal" faced by the early Christians, "there is an accession of troubles and hatreds for that holiness of life to which the children of God are called."[1]

Persecution seemed to be the common lot of these believers in Asia Minor.

---

1 Robert Leighton, *An Obedient and Patient Faith: An Exposition of 1 Peter* (1853; repr., Amityville, NY: Calvary Press, 1995), 437.

The early Christians, like the Jews with whom they were sometimes associated, would refuse to participate in the empire's religious practices, such as paying the emperor divine honor. This of course subjected them to Roman intolerance and persecution since Roman officials believed their refusal posed a political threat and would charge them with disloyalty to the government. Peter therefore exhorted the believers to submit to the governing authorities, "that by doing right you may silence the ignorance of foolish men" (1 Peter 2:15; see also vv. 13–14). Yet it was not just Roman officials whom Christians would be tempted to fear. One commentator observed that "Christians faced what was perhaps an even greater threat from the attitudes of the general populace,"[2] possibly because of accusations that Christians lived immoral lives. Also, Christians kept themselves from some of the social engagements that aligned with idolatrous practices, which likely prompted others in the community to accuse them of aloofness. And these accusations led to estrangement and opposition. Peter countered these kinds of difficulties by exhorting his readers to "keep a good conscience so that in the thing in which you are slandered, those who revile your good behavior in Christ will be put to shame" (1 Peter 3:16). Still, believers suffered for the sake of the gospel.[3]

The theme of suffering shows up again in Peter's epistle after the passage dealing with elders (1 Peter 5:1–5), as he deals with suffering caused by the anxieties of life and the attacks of the Devil (1 Peter 5:6–11).

In short, Peter's discussion of elders comes in the middle of his exhortation to persevere during suffering. How are suffering and elders critically related? Believers who face suffering need the nurturing and example that comes from church elders who themselves possess a sense of dignity and dependence on the Lord in the midst of trials. The author of Hebrews perceived the same thing (Heb. 13:7). Elders do not replace the spiritual life of the congregation, but they encourage it through faithfully instructing and applying God's Word to the church. They provide tangible models—"proving to be examples to the flock"—in the face of life's difficulties.

Still, the first question we want to ask of 1 Peter 5:1–5 itself is, how are these spiritual leaders identified by Peter?

By Position

First, Peter identifies the spiritual leaders by their position: they are called elders. Addressing a subgroup of his readers, he says, "Therefore, I exhort

---

2 Paul J. Achtemeier, *1 Peter*, Hermeneia: A Critical and Historical Commentary on the Bible (Minneapolis: Fortress Press, 1996), 23–34.
3 Ibid., 28–29.

the elders among you, as your fellow elder" (v. 1). It is obvious that he is not simply referring to the older men in the congregation since in the next verse he tells them both to *shepherd* and to give *oversight* to God's flock (v. 2). And then he tells them to refrain from using their position to lord it over the ones under their charge (v. 3).[4]

As noted previously, the term *elders*, which was used interchangeably with overseers and pastors (e.g. Acts 20:17–35), was common in Jewish life, referring to leaders in Israel or those blessed of God with advanced years. Due to their maturity they were given responsibilities for leading their communities.[5]

Note also that Peter does not refer to "the elder in each city," as though a single elder/pastor will suffice in each church. Apart from references to one particular elder, as in the case of Peter, New Testament church elders are always spoken of as a plurality. The New Testament does not offer a rule regarding the size of that plurality, but the uniform pattern seems to recommend a plurality. Again, the nineteenth-century Southern Baptist Convention leader, W. B. Johnson, provides some help:

> Whilst a plurality of bishops [elders] is required for each church, the number is not fixed, for the obvious reason, that circumstances must necessarily determine what the number shall be. In a church where more than one cannot be obtained, that one may be appointed upon the principle, that as soon as another can be procured there shall be a plurality.[6]

A plurality provides a greater measure of wisdom and leadership for the congregation, and it adds to the mix of spiritual gifts that serve the body. Together these men can seek the Lord on critical issues facing the congregation. Together they hold one another accountable as examples for the flock.

By Experience

Second, Peter identifies these spiritual leaders through their experience as well as through his own firsthand experience among the elders of Jerusalem.[7] He

---

4 "It is the title of an office rather than a description of seniority." Peter H. Davids, *The First Epistle of Peter*, NICNT (Grand Rapids: Eerdmans, 1990), 175.
5 See chapter 3 for additional discussion on these three interchangeable terms.
6 Johnson, *Gospel Developed*, quoted in Dever, *Polity*, 194.
7 The most obvious example is the Jerusalem Council in Acts 15, but consider also Acts 11:1–18, Peter's testimony before the leaders of the church, as well as Acts 11:19–26, the action of the church leaders in response to the spread of the gospel to Antioch.

understood the pressures these men were enduring in the province of Asia Minor. So he identifies himself as their "fellow elder and witness of the sufferings of Christ, and a partaker also of the glory that is to be revealed" (v. 1). The word *witness* literally means "to testify of something," and Peter joined these men in testifying to the sufferings of Christ, that is, all that Christ endured to redeem sinners. Jesus Christ had redeemed them "with precious blood, as of a lamb unblemished and spotless, the blood of Christ" (1 Peter 1: 19). Peter was also an eyewitness to Christ's glory displayed in the transfiguration and the resurrection (1 Peter 1:3; 2 Peter 1:16–18). Maintaining the centrality of the gospel, Peter assures his fellow elders that they were *partners together in the work of the gospel*.

He also had an eye on the future. These brethren, along with Peter, would share in (literally, fellowship in) the radiant glory of the revelation of Jesus Christ.[8] This was the hope that would anchor their souls in the midst of persecution.

HOW DO ELDERS AND THE CONGREGATION FUNCTION? (1 PETER 5:2–5)

Having identified himself with the elders' position, passion for the gospel, and hope in Christ, Peter moves to their work within congregational life. How should elders function? How should the congregation respond?

Elders' Responsibility

"Shepherd the flock of God among you, exercising oversight," Peter writes (1 Peter 5:2). The words *shepherd* and *exercising oversight* are the synonyms for "pastor" and "elder" in verbal form.[9] These are the same terms (one as a noun, the other as a verb) used by Paul in Acts 20:28 when he said to the Ephesian elders, "Be on guard for yourselves and for all the flock, among which the Holy Spirit has made you overseers, to shepherd the church of God which He purchased with His own blood." Both terms encapsulate the elders' responsibility in the church.

As those who shepherd, elders give pastoral oversight. A shepherd knows his sheep, watches out for dangers, ensures they are well fed and watered, applies healing balm to their wounds, and occasionally disciplines them to return them to the fold. In other words, shepherds watch over the souls of those under their

---

8 *LKGNT*, 765, states that the term *koinonos* means "partner, sharer."
9 Compare the verb *poimainō*, translated as "to shepherd" as used here with the noun *poimen*, which is translated as "pastor" in Ephesians 4:11; also *episkopountes*, "exercising oversight," used as a verb with the noun *episkopos*, translated as "overseer." See *BDAG*, 379–380, 842–843.

charge (Heb. 13:17). They spend time with their flock, understand their needs, and apply God's Word to them with precision. They regularly feed them with the truth of Scripture by unfolding the doctrines of the Word and helping them stand firmly in the faith. John Calvin explained, "Let us bear in mind the definition given of the word [shepherd]; for the flock of Christ cannot be fed except with pure doctrine, which alone is our spiritual food."[10]

As shepherds lead the way for the sheep, so elders lead the way both in spiritual growth and Christian service. They set the example for Christian living, particularly as Peter explains in 1 Peter 2:11–3:16. The English pastor J. H. Jowett wrote, "If a man stand between his brother and spiritual necessity, or between his brother and spiritual peril, he is discharging the office of a day's-man, a mediator, a faithful undershepherd, working loyally under the leadership of the 'chief Bishop and Shepherd of our souls.'"[11]

An elder is also involved in 'exercising oversight,' a term which places the emphasis on the *details* of pastoral care. The early elders were admonished to guard the flock from false teachers. Transient spiritual rogues made their way into communities and threw congregations into disarray. Elders were to ensure that the church maintained solid doctrinal footing and that the members were equipped to resist the influence of false teachers.

Today's elders do the same. When a member of the congregation falls prey to false teaching, the elders should pursue that member like a shepherd going after a lost sheep. Elders should also organize congregational care and the ministry of teaching, which assures the ongoing stability of the church. Well-fed and well-cared-for sheep have less reason to wander from the fold and into danger.[12]

Elders' Disposition

Along with the responsibility of spiritual leadership comes much authority. Elders cannot lead or discipline unless they have some measure of authority. We tend to shy away from any use of the word *authority* in our day, perhaps fearing dictatorial

---

10   John Calvin, *Calvin's Commentaries: Commentaries on the Catholic Epistles,* (repr., Grand Rapids: Baker, 1999), 22:144.

11   J. H. Jowett, *The Epistles of Peter* (1905; repr., Grand Rapids: Kregel, 1993), 96.

12   For additional insight on this work of elders as shepherds, see Richard L. Mayhue, "Watching and Warning," in *Rediscovering Pastoral Ministry: Shaping Contemporary Ministry with Biblical Mandates,* ed. John MacArthur Jr. (Dallas: Word, 1995), 336–50; John MacArthur Jr., "Shepherding the Flock of God," in *The Master's Plan for the Church* (Chicago: Moody, 1991), 169–76; Philip Graham Ryken, "Shepherding God's Flock: Pastoral Care," in *City on a Hill: Reclaiming the Biblical Pattern for the Church in the Twenty-first Century* (Chicago: Moody, 2003), 93–110.

maniacs. No one denies that such egotistical despots exist in church ranks, yet we must never abandon biblical direction because of poor examples. As long as a church insists upon the biblical pattern for its elders, seeking men who possess the disposition that Peter describes, it does not need to fear its elders.

Motivation for service. Some people serve churches because others have talked them into it or because they have been manipulated by guilt until they accept the positions. But consider Peter's words: "exercising oversight not under compulsion but voluntarily, according to the will of God" (1 Peter 5:2). To be under _compulsion_ is to be forced or constrained to do something.[13] Perhaps, for example, a congregation asks a man to serve as an elder, but he declines because he does not believe he has the character to do the job or because he has no desire to serve. Instead of accepting the man's refusal, members keep approaching him, telling him that the church cannot survive without him. Maybe they threaten to leave the church if he does not take the position. If such a man takes the job, he would be serving according to man's will, not God's. All who serve the church must resist fleshly compulsion. Instead, they should serve with a willing heart under a sense of divine direction, thus "according to the will of God."

When a man works voluntarily rather than under constraint, he works harder. He finds joy in what he is doing. He possesses a "staying power" that does not give up when times become difficult. He can deal more readily with discouragement.

The great motivation for serving as elders comes when men seek the Lord and become convinced that it is the will of God for their lives. "Elders had to have courage and to be willing to accept this difficult task," writes commentator Peter Jeffreys concerning the elders of the first century. "They had to want to place themselves in the front line of the battle against Satan. They had to be prepared for all the criticism which sometimes comes the way of church leaders." Moreover, "There were very severe troubles awaiting anyone who took on the office of an elder in those days."[14] Knowing they are centered in God's will gives elders a right perspective on the office together with its demands and pressures.

That said, an elder will be encouraged in the work when the congregation affirms God's will by selecting him to serve as _its_ elder. Also, the council of elders or presbytery affirms God's will by their thorough investigation of the elder candidates. When all this is in place, the peace of the Lord will fill the elder's heart concerning the responsibilities and tasks before him. Now he can serve and face the demands of the office with joy and thankfulness, knowing that he serves by the will of God.

---

13 _LKGNT_, 765.
14 Peter Jeffreys, _Living for Christ in a Pagan World: 1 and 2 Peter Simply Explained_ (Durham, UK: Evangelical Press, 1990), 161–62.

Affection toward service. An elder must be motivated by a zeal for serving Christ. His service is to be "not for sordid gain, but with eagerness" (v. 2). At the time the passage was written, it does appear that some elders were compensated for their service. Paul refers to compensation in 1 Timothy 5:17–18: "The elders who rule well are to be considered worthy of double honor, especially those who work hard at preaching and teaching. For the Scripture says, 'YOU SHALL NOT MUZZLE THE OX WHILE HE IS THRESHING,' and 'The laborer is worthy of his wages.'" Some elders proved to be especially gifted in ministry areas that demanded more time than other ministries. Preaching and teaching, for instance, are especially time-consuming offices. Thus, it seemed fitting for elders who preached and taught to be fairly remunerated so that a man can devote himself to it more fully. Not all elders are compensated, but those who are should not be primarily motivated by the compensation.

Elders must love what they do so that their service is "with eagerness," or full of zeal. *Eagerness* suggests strong enthusiasm for the duties of the office,[15] and might be translated "devoted zeal." Rather than the "sordid gain" of money or fame or power or attention, the elders serve with zealous devotion out of love for Christ and his church. Elders find their greatest satisfaction in acts of service, in what they give rather than in what they get.

Attitude in service. One of the grave dangers attending any sense of authority—whether in government, business, church, or even the home—is a haughty, dictatorial spirit. Peter exhorts, "Nor yet as lording it over those allotted to your charge, but proving to be examples to the flock" (v. 3). No one would dispute that powermongers occasionally creep into churches, desiring to exercise an iron grip on everything. They want to make all the decisions—in finances, sermon content, or church activities. I have heard shocking stories from pastors and church members who have faced these "little dictators." By intimidation, such persons sometimes manage to keep an entire congregation under their sway. That is not Christian leadership.

To discourage such despotic leadership, Peter reminds the elders that they serve at the pleasure of the Chief Shepherd. They are dealing with "the flock of God . . . allotted to your charge" (1 Peter 5:2–3). The terminology paints the picture of the Master parceling out portions of His flock to this shepherd or that shepherd, with the understanding that *they will report to him for the discharge of their duties.* Consequently, they must never lord it over the flock; the flock already has a Lord, Jesus Christ.[16] Instead, they are to prove themselves "to be examples to the flock"

---

15 "The word is extremely strong and expresses enthusiasm and devoted zeal." *LKGNT,* 765.
16 Leighton (*Obedient and Patient Faith,* 469) refers to the Medieval preacher Bernard's com-

(1 Peter 5:3). The word *example* means "a pattern." If a little girl makes paper dolls, she first finds a pattern, then traces around the pattern on her paper to make the dolls. Or when a manufacturer produces an automobile, he utilizes a series of patterns, or dies, to produce the precise parts needed. Peter describes the elders as "Christians with skin on them" who demonstrate how to live the Christian life in all circumstances. That is a weighty responsibility, but much needed in the church.

Congregation's Response

How should the congregation respond to the elders? "You younger men, likewise, be subject to your elders" (1 Peter 5:5). Bible students debate this text, with some suggesting that it refers to men who are younger in age. Others argue that "you younger men" does not refer to "ordinary members of the church, but [to] lower clergy, for example deacons, who are to serve like the elders (thus 'likewise') but also be subject to them."[17]

But the context insists on a different direction. Typically, the elders of the congregation would have been Christian men with more experience. Peter identifies particular members of the congregation as "younger men," who are to subject themselves to the leadership of the elders. Peter Davids comments, "It appears best, therefore, to see the 'younger' here as the youthful people in the church (if Jewish reckoning is involved, anyone under 30 and perhaps even some who were older would be included in this category)."[18] These "younger men" were living under the fire of persecution, yet possibly they burned with passion to spread abroad the gospel. They may have had the tendency to launch into risky actions, which could prove harmful to the whole church and detrimental to the work of the gospel. "Their very readiness for service and commitment," adds Davids, "can make them impatient with the leaders, who either due to pastoral wisdom or the conservatism that often comes with age (the two are not to be equated) are not ready to move as quickly or as radically as they are."[19] Such younger men needed Peter's sage counsel to submit themselves to the elders, and to continue walking with submissive hearts under their God-given authority. But that does not mean that elders were to act as killjoys.

---

ment, "Had I some of that blood poured forth on the cross, how carefully would I carry it! And ought I not be as careful of those souls that it was shed for?"

17 Davids, *The First Epistle of Peter*, 183, identifies some that hold the "younger" to be "a particular class or group in the church that needed to be subject to the official leadership," following the French scholar Spicq. Another scholar, K. H. Schelkle, citing Polycarp, "simply points out that youth often struggle with leadership."

18 Ibid., 184.

19 Ibid.

Humility must clothe both elders and congregation: "And all of you, clothe yourselves with humility toward one another, for God is opposed to the proud, but gives grace to the humble" (1 Peter 5:5). The term *clothe* utilizes a Greek word that referred to a slave tying on an apron over his seamless garment while going about his work. The apron was a sign of the slave's humble position.[20] So Peter reminds all the brethren that humility marks the church as genuine.

Being an elder does not mean that a man is better than others, for "all of you clothe yourselves with humility toward one another." Nor does eldership exclude a man from diligent Christian living, for elders must "prove to be examples to the flock" (1 Peter 5:3). Elders serve not out of constraint or the desire for earthly reward and recognition, but enthusiastically with a sense of God's call to this office.

WHO HOLDS THE ELDERS ACCOUNTABLE? (1 PETER 5:4)

All these exhortations must no doubt be taken seriously since both elders and congregation will stand before the Lord one day. Elders serve "as those who will give an account" (Heb. 13:17). And congregations must recognize that to not submit "would be unprofitable" (v. 17). Both congregation and elders are accountable to the Chief Shepherd.

The Lord's Flock

The church does not belong to the elders, the pastor, or even the members. The church belongs to Christ. That truth must burn in our hearts if we are to accept the biblical teaching for church order and life. Peter calls the church "the flock of God," as though it were a group of sheep that had been entrusted by the Chief Shepherd to a group of shepherds. "In using the imagery of tending God's flock," explains Bible scholar Paul Achtemeier, "the author is drawing on a long Old Testament tradition, in which God is the shepherd of his people Israel, a tradition that may well have taken its origin in the tradition that God led his people out of bondage like a shepherd leads his sheep."[21] The church the elders serve has been "allotted to your charge" (v. 3).

---

20 *LKGNT,* 765.
21 Achtemeier, *1 Peter,* 324–25. He also identifies a number of Old Testament passages showing the shepherd motif: Pss. 23:1–4; 28:9; 74:1; 77:20; 78:52; 79:13; 80:1; 95:7; 100:3; Isa. 40:11; 63:11; Jer. 13:17; 23:1–3; 50:6; Ezek. 34:6, 8, 31; Mic. 7:14. Achtemeier uses "tradition" in the sense of beliefs handed down orally until written.

Jesus Christ laid down his life for the sheep, and he called them out of darkness and into the light of a relationship with himself. The sheep hear the voice of Jesus Christ, not the voice of a stranger; the sheep follow Jesus Christ, not mere men. Jesus Christ gives eternal life to the sheep so that none of them will perish. They are not held in the hands of mere elders, but securely by the Father and the Son (John 10:1–30). Elders merely hold a stewardship before the Chief Shepherd for his sheep.

Service as an Undershepherd

All who serve as elders must remember that they are undershepherds, while Jesus Christ is the Chief Shepherd. One day the Chief Shepherd will appear, and those belonging to him will be gathered for eternity. Those whom he has appointed to serve as undershepherds will give an account for how they have watched over the flock. The reward for service lies beyond this life. "The unfading crown of glory" is the Lord's gift for faithful service. "Lest, then, the faithful servant of Christ should be broken down," encourages Calvin, "there is for him one and only one remedy,—to turn his eyes to the coming of Christ. Thus it will be, that he, who seems to derive no encouragement from men, will assiduously go on in his labours [sic], knowing that a great reward is prepared for him by the Lord."[22]

Scripture teaches that *every* member of the congregation should serve humbly, voluntarily, and zealously, seeking to be an example to others in the body. But the qualities of service, humility, and zeal should be the particular hallmark of those men whom God raises up to serve as elders. The coin of responsibility has two sides: the congregation must acknowledge the men who serve as elders, and the elders must be faithful according to the instructions of God's Word.

REFLECTIONS

- How does the New Testament identify spiritual leaders in the church?
- In what ways do elders and the congregation function together in ministry?
- What should motivate the elders to serve?

---

22 Calvin, *Commentaries*, 22:146.

CHAPTER FOURTEEN

WHAT KIND OF MODEL?

Some pastors have taken the New Testament's admonition to be "models" quite literally. One well-known megachurch pastor has begun to critique pastors' clothing on his website. Skinny jeans? "I'm into the slim pant, but not being super skinny." Ties? A dimple in the knot is required wearing, apparently. "That's the look!" This same pastor sells an exercise video by him and his wife in his church's bookstore entitled "Body by God." I don't think this is what Paul had in mind in 2 Thessalonians 3:9 when he used the word "model" or Peter in 1 Peter 5:3 when he called the elders to be examples to the flock.

In contrast, soon after my conversion God kindly put men in my life as models, as examples that I could imitate. I remember Dennis, for example, who modeled discipline, grace, and restoration in about thirty minutes one hot summer day. How? Dennis was a busy elder with a wife and six kids. I was in my last year of college and had offered to help him do yard work. In the midst of digging a hole together, Dennis disappeared from the backyard. I grew frustrated as time passed. Finally, Dennis returned with all six kids in tow. He leaned in and quietly said, "Sorry, Matt, I had to discipline one of my kids." Having grown up in a home where discipline was too often done in anger and followed by bouts of pouting and estrangement, I stood perplexed as I studied the faces of each child. I was trying to figure out which one had got in trouble, but I couldn't. I quickly tried to remember if I saw Dennis get mad. He hadn't. And I couldn't believe that any child, having just been disciplined, would feel so "restored" that he was immediately and happily joining the rest of the family as opposed to going off and sulking on his own. Anger was absent. Discipline was administered. Grace was given. Restoration was effected. What an example. What a model of godly parenting.

I also remember other elders from those same early years following my conversion. Tom modeled courage as he took the gospel to unbelievers. Terry modeled love for God's Word. Rob modeled praising God with a ready word on his lips and a song in his heart.

You might call this *passive oversight* in contrast to *active oversight*. It is leading by example. The elder doesn't always need to have his mouth or his Bible open, formally instructing a group of people. His example as he lives in true biblical fashion *is* instruction. By his life he is modeling what it means to be a follower of Christ.

But an elder is not called merely to be an example. He is also called to an *active oversight* in which he opens his eyes to watch out for wolves who want to hurt the sheep he's called to protect. He opens his mouth to proclaim the truth of God's Word and thereby shapes the minds and hearts of those same sheep. He opens his heart to the flock, expressing his affections and bearing their burdens (2 Cor. 6:11). He opens his door to practice hospitality (1 Tim. 3:2), letting all who enter smell the aroma of Christ that pervades his home.

This is not the program-driven pastor-manager that is too often held up as the model in our seminaries and church growth books. This is a man who understands himself to be more of a father than an "effective leader" as commonly described in today's business journals. This is a man who knows his people, who loves them and prays for them. He knows, too, that he will give an account for each of them (Heb. 13:17) and therefore is diligent in his care and oversight.

This description of an elder doesn't sound like the authoritative, powerful position we often think of, does it? I often say that eldership is a burden-bearing office by nature. An elder bears the weight of faithfully teaching God's Word to his people and personally reflecting God's character, as well as the weight of knowing the sins of many in the congregation. Praise God that one man doesn't bear this burden alone—by design. God has gifted his church with elders (plural) for this task. And together they watch. Together they instruct. Together they bear these burdens.

At Capitol Hill Baptist Church, the elders gather eight times a year (skipping the summer months and December) for what we call an "issues-centric" elders' meeting. In issues-centric meetings, we give extended time to discuss matters that affect our congregation as a whole, like divorce and remarriage, small groups, adult and children's education, and lay counseling. Additionally, we gather twelve times a year (once every month) for what we call "member-centric" elders' meetings. They typically last three to four hours and follows a version of the following agenda:

- Pray for each elder
- Sing a hymn
- Scripture reading and more prayer
- Review of minutes from previous meeting
- Membership:
  » Discussion and prayer for members whose last name begins with one or two letters of the alphabet (we work through the whole membership over time)
  » Membership additions and resignations
  » Care List: this is an internal list of members—usually about twelve to twenty—who are struggling acutely with matters such as health, marriage, addiction, or sexual sin. More prayer.
- Memos: We typically have two to four memos on matters ranging from missions support to an open deacon position.
- Executive Session: We ask interns, staff, and guests who have been observing our elders' meeting to leave in order to allow conversation among just the elders. Most of this time is used to evaluate and consider prospective elders.

To date, despite the growth and turnover of our church, we've resisted breaking the church into "parishes" where one elder might be assigned fifty members to oversee. Instead we've followed a more organic model where elders proactively cultivate relationships and work hard together to make sure no member goes un-accounted for.

This desire and ability to actively oversee both individuals and the congregation as a whole, coupled with an exemplary life, makes for an ideal elder candidate. We believe God gifts his church with elders, and it is the elders' job to recognize those gifts and put the names of qualified men before the congregation to be affirmed. As mentioned above, the elders of Capitol Hill Baptist spend most of the executive section of our meetings considering potential elders. How?

A retired Navy officer on our elder board gave us some military jargon: we began calling our internal list of men to be considered the "Rack and Stack." For the Rack and Stack, we list all the men whom we think have the potential to serve as an elder sometime in the next few years (rack), and then prioritize them from "most ready" at the top to "least ready" at the bottom (stack). And whoever's names are at the top of the list, having the most points, will be the topic of that night's conversation.

This admittedly crass tool has helped us focus our attention on preparing and testing the men we think are nearest to serving as elders. Sometimes this means giving a man more teaching opportunities in order to test his gifts. Sometimes it means a handful of the elders need to get to know a prospective elder better so they can confidently support his nomination. Sometimes it means investigating a man's theological positions or the state of his family more carefully.

If we feel pretty confident about a candidate's standing, we invite him to fully participate in an elders' meeting, with the exception of voting. In executive session afterward, the entire elder board further screens him with additional questions. In some cases, this process from getting on the list to becoming an elder has taken several years. As elders, we move carefully and deliberately. The reputation of the elders, the church, and Christ are at stake.

What do we often see that disqualifies a man from service?

- He lacks interest in spiritual matters and is consumed with worldly matters.
- He lacks peace and order at home.
- He lacks a wide ministry in the church; he appears to be narrowly tied to his friends.
- He fails to prioritize times when the church gathers, apart from Sunday mornings. (He can't shepherd those he doesn't know.)
- He lacks a spirit of unity and submission. He wrongly sees being a contrarian as service to the church.
- He evidences the rigidity of a young man in his black-and-white counseling.
- He misprioritizes important life decisions, like choosing career over children.

What are some examples of men who have commended themselves for the office?

- Papu pursues those who are drifting toward sin instead of waiting for the next implosion.
- Andy regularly inconveniences himself for the benefit of others and has whole unreached people groups on his heart.
- Andrew smells out particular needs in the congregation and addresses them systematically by finding opportunities to teach the church.
- Deepak absorbs blows from those hurting the most and brings healing and peace to broken relationships.
- David keeps one eye on Scripture in every discussion and seems to flee worldly wisdom.

- Sebastian looks for patterns and biblical principles at stake in our discussions and brings order to potentially chaotic conversations.
- Steve studies to understand the mind of God before speaking to the church.
- Mark prays for the congregation daily.
- Michael draws on all of Scripture to shape the elders' thinking.
- Jamie uses his business training combined with his knowledge of the flock to anticipate future needs.
- Aaron is saddened—even shocked—by sin, lacking guile himself.
- Jonathan strives to believe the best (as love does) and gives others the benefit of the doubt.

Fashion? Let's leave that to the mavens of Madison Avenue. The faithful elder will model the character of Christ in his care and oversight of the church, together with his fellow elders.

PART THREE

FROM THEORY TO PRACTICE

CHAPTER FIFTEEN

THINKING ABOUT TRANSITION TO ELDER LEADERSHIP

What is involved in transitioning to plural eldership? No church or pastor should rush into changing its leadership structure. Careful thought, study, and planning must precede any changes, because implementing drastic changes too quickly might do the church more harm than good.

First, it is important to take a candid look at your church's polity. This entails reviewing the church's constitution, bylaws, and other governing documents, as well as assessing how the church *actually* functions. Many church constitutions, for example, call for congregational rule, but the deacon board or group of trustees or church staff may be the actual ruling authority.

So if you are considering a transition, start by assessing how your church operates and evaluating it in light of God's Word.

On one end of the church polity spectrum lies extreme congregationalism. In this kind of church, the congregation votes on *everything,* resulting in endless discussions, haggling, and posturing—and getting little done. Indeed, for such reasons of efficiency, few churches operate in an absolute congregational mode. But even worse than the pragmatic difficulties are the spiritual dangers. A church that votes on everything is a church that is never taught how to trust authority, which means you will almost surely find a spirit of dissension and suspicion whenever decisions need to be made. Human relationships require, and benefit from, leadership.

In a congregational setting, power often resides in a board of deacons. They are usually nominated at-large, are approved by the congregation, and can serve either limited or unlimited terms. In many churches, deacons are nominated based on popularity or visibility within the church, rather than the basis of the qualifications stated in 1 Timothy 3. Moreover, the deacons—whose biblical role should be one of service to the congregation—are put into the role of ruling the church. In such circumstances, power struggles often emerge between the pastor and the deacons. Rather than working with the pastor, they resort to political manipulation to get their way. Certainly not all deacons or pastors engage in such manipulative behavior, but in over three decades in ministry I've seen far too many who do.

On the other end of the polity spectrum are churches in which the senior pastor has his thumb on everything. He is what W. A. Criswell termed "a benevolent dictator." Such a pastor believes that his leadership is more efficient than a plural eldership, which must work toward consensus. He simply makes a declaration, and everyone is obliged to follow. Of course, he might not be benevolent after all, but a ruthless tyrant, a controlling pastor like Diotrephes, who coveted preeminence in the church and excluded anyone who threatened his position (3 John 9–10). Such a man's unteachable spirit makes him unapproachable and insensitive to pastoral needs. The church seems to exist to further his agenda and feed his ego.

Another much less tyrannical type of polity can be found in some pastor-staff led churches. In these churches, the pastor and staff determine the course of ministry, tap the lay leadership to execute their plans, and assemble the energies of the church into a well-oiled machine. Some even identify the staff as their plurality of elders. Certainly, many of these churches accomplish much—as long as there are no changes in the machinery. However, the machinery may grind to a halt if change does occur, such as a staff member leaving. Further, when conflicts arise between pastor and staff, they are often concealed in order to preserve the appearance of harmony. As a result, highly organized activity may mask unholy lives. Megachurches face the greatest danger at this point because of the enormous pressure on them to exceed past performance, as measured by the previous year's statistics.

There are variations of these models, but common to each is the competition for power and authority that occurs within the leadership. Yet there is a better way: elder leadership. Making the transition to elder leadership within a congregational framework requires deliberate work, faithful prayer, and commitment to the teaching of Scripture.

In 1987, when John Piper led Bethlehem Baptist Church in Minneapolis to change its church polity to an elder plurality, he offered a number of reasons. He spoke of "conforming to the normal New Testament pattern," as well as clarifying the role of their deacons. The deacons were "a hybrid" that existed as a governing board while retaining the name of deacons. Piper also spoke about the "need to provide more thorough care for hurting members and more consistent discipline for delinquent members," and suggested that the confusion in leadership roles might have caused neglect. Piper ended by challenging his church to go beyond staff leadership and put down strong roots of lay leadership.

> We need to develop an ongoing leadership team (elders) where the theological distinctives, the philosophy of ministry and the vision of the future can be rooted more durably than in the paid 'staff.' The church should not be dependent on a few paid staff as the guardians of the vision."[1]

When a church with multiple staff transitions to plural elder leadership, the leaders will hopefully find themselves facing a new level of accountability. Statistical benchmarks will be replaced by the benchmarks of Christian character, faithful obedience, commitment to genuine church unity, diligence in family life, and zeal for equipping the church for ministry. Some program-driven staff members might not be qualified to serve as elders, so staff members should not assume that they will automatically become elders.

I have talked with many pastors who long to share their authority with fellow elders rather than holding it alone. Watching fellow pastors fall into moral or financial failure only strengthens this desire for accountability. Some pastors, however, tightly grip the reins of authority in their churches, shunning accountability by exaggerating their own strength and ability. By refusing to share authority, they set themselves up for a fall.

Pastor Jeff Noblit first considered elder leadership because he feared the temptations of power. Noblit became senior pastor of the Grace Life Church of the Shoals in Muscle Shoals, Alabama—the largest Southern Baptist congregation in the northwest corner of the state—after serving for almost a decade as student minister and associate pastor in the same church. Muscle Shoals is a city of less than 15,000, although the region's population exceeds 100,000. Noblit's predecessor, the church's first pastor, functioned as a single elder. The former pastor was well-liked in both the church and the community, and had been quite successful in his ministry. Moreover, he was *the* authority in the church, with the church's deacons functioning ably in a service role. Although the church occasionally voted on major issues, their affirmation was a formality that served to ratify the pastor's desires.

---

1 John Piper, "Elders, Bishops, and Bethlehem," a sermon at Bethlehem Baptist Church, Minneapolis, MN, 1 March 1987; accessed November 21, 2002; www.soundofgrace.com/piper87/jp870012.htm; page 7.

Shortly after Noblit assumed the role of senior pastor, he faced a major disciplinary crisis in the church that involved removing high-profile members from the membership. Although church discipline had not been practiced in the past, pastor Noblit guided the church through the initial process and gained the respect and admiration of the congregation. The downside came, ironically, when he realized that he had too much authority. He told me that he was afraid of such unrestricted power and that he desired accountability. That led him to move toward elder leadership. Noblit's experience is described in greater detail later in this chapter.

One of the largest hurdles on the path to plural eldership is "governing deacons," that is, deacons who rule the business of the church. When such men lack biblical qualifications for office, they find it difficult to give up their esteemed positions for the sake of a newly formed plural eldership, and it might take years to cultivate change through patient biblical exposition. At other times, deacons only need to be taught the Scriptures and they will gladly conform to the biblical model.

In order to effectively transition from deacon leadership to elder leadership, it is necessary to have both biblical teaching and congregational commitment. Apart from these things, a blunt announcement of a change from deacon leadership to elder leadership, however well-intentioned, will likely meet with resistance from the deacons.

On the other hand, deacons can help to facilitate the change to elder leadership, as one pastor discovered. After serving for many years with the International Mission Board in South America, Chip Faulkner received a call to pastor First Baptist Church of Bethalto, Illinois. The church was still feeling the pains of betrayal and abuse from a former pastor who had held the reins of power tightly. After his departure and Faulkner's arrival, a couple of deacons began to investigate shared leadership. They saw the ugly side of one man holding absolute power in the congregation. So they suggested the possibility of moving toward elder plurality to their fellow deacons.

Pastor Faulkner welcomed this process after he began serving the church. He invited me to travel to Bethalto to speak to his congregation one Wednesday evening on the subject. I questioned the prudence of doing this so early in his tenure, wondering whether a more gradual approach might be wiser. He assured me that the church's past experience made them very open to elder plurality. I was warmly received by the church's members, many of whom asked thoughtful questions. In the following months, Faulkner continued to teach on biblical polity with the present leaders and the congregation. A couple of years later, the church voted to adopt elder plurality within their congregational government. Consequently, they set apart their first slate of elders. After the fact, Pastor Faulkner told me, "I expected our elders to be a blessing, but it is going much better than I ever imagined."

I view Chip Faulkner's experience as an exception. As a general rule, *a pastor who desires plural eldership is wise not to introduce this change until he has established trust with the congregation.* This may take several years of faithfully ministering, and the time comes when he is no longer viewed as an outsider. As the congregation observes him make wise and biblically based decisions in other areas, a transition to biblical eldership becomes more feasible. Trust comes through longevity, faithfulness in pastoral responsibilities, genuine humility, and applying the gospel to all of life. Therefore, I tend to discourage pastors from leading their churches to elder plurality if they don't intend to stay with their flocks. Pastoral ladder-climbers lack the depth and stamina necessary to help a congregation through the transition.

"We've Never Done It This Way Before"

- Plural eldership unites staff and non-staff members in leadership equality.
- Plural eldership refocuses the spotlight in church life.
- Plural eldership provides a new level of efficiency.

"We've never done it this way before!" are the so-called seven last words a pastor might hear from a church. This is an understandable initial reaction from a church, since elder plurality is different than other methods of church leadership, whether benevolent dictatorships, deacon rule, or staff rule. But I would suggest that elder plurality differs positively. So even though "we've never done it this way before," pastors need to help congregations ask themselves why they have not, and examine what biblical foundation, if any, they have for the present church structure. Such risky questions set the stage either for transitioning to elder plurality or exposing an unwillingness to submit to the teaching of Scripture.

First, *elder plurality unites paid staff with non-staff members to lead the congregation.* This assures the congregation that multiple eyes, ears, and hearts will be turned toward members' needs and are committed to leading them spiritually. When pastoral ministry increases, the church usually grows in Christlikeness.

Second, *plural eldership refocuses the spotlight in church life.* Often the church staff, pastor, or deacon chairman receives undue attention from the congregation, and this cripples churches. But elder plurality dismantles crippling power structures, redirecting attention to the glory of Christ. Plurality attacks leaders' inherent temptation to pride, and constantly reminds them that the church exists for the reputation of Christ, not the aggrandizement of men.

In the process of sharing authority, the individuals in leadership will not always get their way in some aspect of church life or ministry. Even in elder plurality, fallible men can make poor decisions, struggle for power, and pursue self-centered desires. Elders must never presume upon their own spiritual lives but must seek to discipline themselves for the purpose of godliness (1 Tim. 4:6–10). Through prayer, discussion, studying the Scriptures, and the illuminating effect of laboring together with other godly men, elders will be able to forge a clearer direction. As a result, the health and effectiveness of the church takes precedence over the plans of one person.

Third, *elder plurality provides a new level of efficiency in church life*. While a single pastor or church staff may make decisions more quickly, they may tend to do so without being sensitive to the overall congregation. Non-staff elders see things that those of us in full-time ministry cannot, even if we in vocational ministry find this difficult to admit. Living most of the week within the walls of ministry may skew a pastor's thinking about the needs of the congregation. I have learned to lean heavily upon the wisdom of our non-staff elders, recognizing that they have unique insights.

During a particularly difficult time for our church financially, our non-staff elders recommended a course of informing and challenging the congregation to rise to a new level in giving. Frankly, I was at a loss on how to best proceed. But these men wisely detailed a plan, without any sort of manipulation or cunning, that helped the church to understand the critical need and how God might be pleased to meet that need. The plan succeeded, thanks to the elders' sensitivity to both the financial need and the congregation's ability under God to meet it.

Such insights often occur during the trying times of ministry. One time I was involved in counseling a couple with marital problems, but I seemed unable to bridge the glaring gap between the husband and wife. One of our non-staff elders joined me in visiting the couple. We both spoke clearly and passionately about marriage and the need for reconciliation. After we left I still felt puzzled about how to deal with them. Their situation weighed heavily on me, feeling as if I was singularly responsible to put their marriage back together. I asked the elder what he thought. He wisely discerned, "There is something they're not telling us that lies beneath the problems. Until they come clean, your counseling will prove futile. You've done what you can. Now we have no choice but to pursue a course of discipline." I realized that this couple's marital problems were not my burden alone, but was shared by my fellow elders and was supported by their insight into marriage and integrity. As it turned out, both the husband and wife had serious, unrepentant issues that eventually required us to remove them from membership. Several years later, after a divorce and much heartbreak, the church restored the now-repentant wife to fellowship.

Establishing elder plurality also requires that we change existing governing documents to reflect the new polity. A church must never begin plural eldership, while ignoring its constitution, bylaws, and policies. If a church fails to update these documents, someone could later appeal to them and disrupt the entire structure. Sharp minds steeped in Scripture and biblical theology must lead the way in reordering governing documents.

Of course, congregational approval of the changes is also necessary. Elder plurality should never be foisted on a church. Instead, a pastor can facilitate a smooth transition in governance by instructing the congregation and engaging their comments and questions,.

CHURCH PROFILES

- Does it really work?
- How can a church transition to elder plurality?

Two questions might come to mind while evaluating this study on plural eldership. First, does it really work? Because of the undue influence of pragmatism in our day, many fail to step out in dependence on God's Word because they fear it "won't work." While pragmatic concerns must never drive our practice, plural eldership does indeed work well in congregational life.[2] And the second question has practical implications: How can we transition to elder plurality? This question will be addressed in the next few chapters. The stories of some churches that have walked through the transition to plural eldership will help put a face to these questions. These churches have not only lived to tell about the transition, but have found elder leadership to be better than expected.

From Pastor's Council to Elders

Jeff Noblit, a committed expositor whom I mentioned earlier in this chapter, began the transition to biblical eldership by preaching for eight weeks through

---

2 For additional considerations on the problems of pragmatism, see my essay, "The Pastor and Church Growth: How to Deal with the Modern Problem of Pragmatism," in *Reforming Pastoral Ministry: Challenges for Ministry in Postmodern Times,* ed. John Armstrong (Wheaton, IL: Crossway, 2001), 263–80.

1 Timothy 3 and Titus 1 on the qualifications and roles of elders. He emphasized the qualifications without being immediately concerned with the specific title. Afterward, thinking that the title "Elder" might overwhelm this Baptist congregation, he led the church to vote to nominate men to serve as a "Pastor's Council." Nevertheless, the qualifications and roles for the Pastor's Council were clearly that of the New Testament elder. Among other responsibilities, the duties of the Pastor's Council included planning for personnel, finance, and long-range goals. After a slate of men were nominated, Noblit screened the nominees, and presented a pared-down list to the church body for affirmation.

Through the transition, the congregation offered strong support and particularly appreciated the new accountability for the pastor and other leaders in the church. The Pastor's Council expected Pastor Noblit to lead, and counted him as "first among equals." Over a period of time the name Pastor's Council was dropped and the title of "Elders" was adopted. Reflecting on all this, Noblit told me that the elder leadership in his church has been "wonderfully effective." He said that they continue to "really strive to make sure that the elders are biblically qualified," and if an elder fails to maintain the type of character and practice needed among elders, he is asked to step down from service.

Preach, Pray, and Depend on the Lord

When Andy Davis accepted the pastorate of First Baptist Church in Durham, NC, he knew that leading the church toward biblical reformation would be difficult. But he had no idea how difficult things would actually be. When he arrived in 1998, he found five "points of power." First, the pastor and staff had responsibility for particular ministries. Second, the deacons were to assist the pastor with the church's mission, which some did, though others held power and money in the church with a tight fist. Third, the same deacons exercising power also controlled various church committees that kept their grip on church ministries. Fourth, a church council, comprised of a broad spectrum of committee chairs, met monthly and exercised control on policies governing church life. Fifth, the church body supposedly held the final voice of authority, but they typically followed the lead of a few key players who controlled the finances and other policies.

Observing that a number of deacons lacked the qualities described in 1 Timothy 3, and that these were the deacons who maintained a tight grip on power, Pastor Davis began to teach on the meaning of biblical authority in the church. One significant issue to address was the topic of gender and authority in the church. Deacons were serving in authority over the congregation rather than in a service role as taught in the New Testament, and a campaign arose to place a particular woman onto the deacon board. Given the deacons' current role in the church, Davis recognized that this amounted to a rejection of Scripture's teaching regarding spiritual authority since Paul says that elder-like authority in the church should belong to men (1 Tim. 2:12). A number of people in the church reacted viscerally to Davis' teaching. At one point, a woman prayed in a specially called prayer meeting, "God, help us learn that we are a modern people and we don't need to do everything it says in the Bible!" That woman's prayer actually exposed the root problem in the church: Some of the key leaders did not care what the Bible taught. They were out to shape the church according to their desires, not Christ's desires.

Three years into the pastorate, Pastor Davis proposed changing the church's bylaws regarding deacons to make the position more biblical. The opposition mounted a response, and Davis could feel the weight of hatred against him as he preached the Sunday prior to the Wednesday vote. In fact, on that particular Sunday morning the controversy left him feeling physically weak, barely able to walk. Before he went home to try to recover before the evening service, a godly church member recommended that he read Psalm 37. Davis took the counsel and found the psalm to be a balm from heaven. He explains what happened through meditating on it:

> That time of meditation and prayer over Psalm 37 changed my perspective in less than an hour. I knew immediately what would happen at that climactic Wednesday night vote: The plots and schemes of the powerful men who opposed my by-law change would succeed in the short term, but the church would be healthy in the long term. We would lose the battle, but would win the war.[3]

As expected, the church was packed for the business meeting. Davis had never seen a quarter of the people who showed up. The opposition won the vote 172 to 125, and believed that it would be a deathblow to Davis' ministry. But just the opposite happened. He returned to the pulpit the following Sunday and continued his series in Romans with a joyful resolution that God had called him to serve this church and that the best days lay ahead.

---

3   This quote and the entire story discussed in this section are from Andrew Davis, "The Reform of First Baptist Church of Durham," *9Marks Journal*, Nov/Dec 2011, vol. 8, no. 6; accessed November 18, 2011; http://www.9marks.org/journal/reform-first-baptist-church-durham.

The church began to see an amazing response to the preaching of God's Word, and new members were regularly added. A year after the failed bylaw change, Davis put the same proposal forward again, but this time the result was reversed: 170 to 120 voted in favor of following biblical authority. Those who had lost their control over the church left, while new people joined with a view to embrace biblical authority and follow Jesus as Lord. A new era began.

Pastor Davis' reflections of what took place after the change in church polity gives a unique perspective on why he moved to embrace elder plurality:

That was in 2002. Over the next few years, my own personal influence at FBC rose to a potentially unhealthy level. Many of the people who remained and were strongly active in the church were extremely supportive of me, my preaching, and my leadership. They wanted to do anything they could to bless me and my family. At first, that was very encouraging, and in many ways it still is. But I began to realize that FBC could never reach the heights of biblical fruitfulness with my own gifts and limitations dominating the leadership and direction of the church. Those next few years were characterized by licking wounds, enjoying good worship services, and growing steadily. But I knew a significant change was needed in our polity. At one point, a lay leader in the church said to me, "Andy, you have unparalleled influence in the church. . . . Be careful what you do with it!"

So I traded in that "unparalleled influence" for a new, biblical polity: a plurality of elders. For over a year, a select group of deacons and other lay leaders and I met to craft a new constitution and by-laws with a plurality of elders at the center of the church leadership structure. We then did a great deal of teaching on the topic, and had three different "town meeting" type question and answer sessions with the whole church. We moved very slowly and deliberately, and by the time the third one occurred, it felt like the people were saying, "Enough already! We agree! We are ready to vote."

When the vote came to change the entire government structure of FBC, it was approved at well over ninety percent. Next came votes approving five individual lay elders, and they were all approved at ninety-five percent or higher. On a shelf in my office, I have the ballots of the elders' election side by side with the blue ballots from the failed by-law change from 2001. They are tangible reminders to me of the amazing journey of church reform that Christ has worked at FBC.[4]

Pastor Davis' story points to a crucial question for those considering transitioning to elder plurality: does the church accept and follow biblical authority? The faithful exposition of Scripture, regular prayer, and depending upon God enables a church to move toward elder plurality, and it won't without these essential disciplines.

My Own Story

Developing church polity from the ground up is part of church planting. In 1987, I began work as the founding pastor of South Woods Baptist Church in suburban Memphis, Tennessee. The church formally constituted in January 1988. Since South Woods had no congregational history or traditions to protect, establishing polity worked differently than in the other churches just described. Leadership definitely rested on my shoulders from the beginning, but I soon formed a "steering committee" to help guide this new flock through the sometimes murky waters of developing a viable church. The steering committee helped with decision-making, and provided both short-term and long-range planning. Soon we realized that our loosely structured polity might lead to problems in the future, so we formed a "Pastor's Council," which served as an interim step toward a permanent church structure. The Pastor's Council consisted of seven men who seemed to understand the spiritual state of the congregation. The council and I began a lengthy study of the biblical texts addressing church leadership, structure, decision-making, and any passages that might shape church polity. We tried to approach church structure with as little bias as possible so that we might better grapple with the biblical direction for the church. All of us were long-time Southern Baptists, so we were all familiar with issues of pastoral authority, deacon leadership, congregationalism, and the diverse ways in which these worked out in autonomous congregations. Each man understood some of the problems common to the structure of Baptist churches, problems that we desired to avoid if possible. Our journey through Scripture continued for about a year and a half, and we kept copious notes on our studies and drew conclusions together. That laid the groundwork for elder leadership.

We also knew that we must do more than simply inform the congregation of the proposed structure—the people needed a chance to learn just as we had. So

---

4 Ibid.

I began a three-month series of expositions on Sunday evenings that addressed each of the biblical texts that our Pastor's Council had studied. I sought not only to explain the texts, but also to apply them to our own situation. The studies were often interspersed with question and answer sessions. These sessions helped our members work through the difficulties of confronting tradition with biblical truth. After completing this study, the congregation voted unanimously to adopt elder leadership. Although the vote was unanimous, during the process a couple of families left because of disagreement over elder leadership. Lastly, the change was codified in a new "Policy and Procedure Manual," which served as our bylaws.

I found establishing plural eldership to be the most important step in strengthening my ministry and ensuring stability in our church. Not every step has gone smoothly. The initial group of elders, for the most part, lacked the maturity needed to walk through some of the demands of pastoral leadership. Still, the congregation respected the elders, and this was instrumental for the elders to be able to enhance the church's ministry. As the congregation matured, the Lord raised up other men to replace the initial elders so that today we have an outstanding body of elders leading our church. I am privileged to work side-by-side with these men in directing the ministry of our church and training the body for ministry. We pray together, teach together, share together our joys and burdens, and hold one another accountable. The blending of different personalities, gifts, strengths, and even weaknesses continues to hone us as spiritual leaders. The trust that has developed between our eldership and the congregation has become a precious treasure to guard. I often remind our elders that nothing can do greater harm to our church than for this trust to be broken by carelessness in our spiritual lives or duties.

REFLECTIONS

- Describe your own church's polity.
- In what ways does your church conform to *or* conflict with plural eldership?
- How can plural eldership change the dynamics in a local church?
- What are some key considerations in transitioning to plural eldership?

CHAPTER SIXTEEN

EVOLUTION, NOT REVOLUTION

The pulpit committee member told me, "We just want someone to preach God's Word and love us."

"No you don't," I replied.

"What did you say?" someone else asked, thinking he must have misheard me.

"I said, 'No you don't.' I know you think that's all you want. But you actually want a lot more. You want all the things you like to stay the same, and all the things you don't like to be changed by the new pastor. And that 'preach God's Word and love us' part? You want God's Word preached in a certain way, and you want to be loved in a certain way."

This exchange took place over coffee. Six pulpit committee members were interviewing me about a friend who was a candidate to be the next pastor of their church. I wasn't deliberately *trying* to be a stick in the eye (that comes naturally). I was trying to help them examine what a transition to the next pastor would feel like.

Pulpit committees, not unlike people engaged to be married, inexplicably avoid looking at the warts and see only an imagined halo behind their intended's head. I wanted this group of godly, well-intentioned men and women to go in with their eyes open. All transitions are hard, especially if the new guy is following a long-tenured and popular pastor ("Will he ever measure up?"), or is following yet another failed pastor in a long string of them ("Will the congregation ever really trust him?").

The advice that follows is intended to help those of you who have set about refashioning the structure of your church's leadership, whether you are a new pastor or a seasoned veteran. Specifically, I'd encourage you to consider various groups as you begin your transition.

THE CONGREGATION

First, consider the congregation. If you are moving the leadership or polity in a new direction, such as establishing a plurality of elders, prepare yourself now for the likelihood that people will leave your church. People will always leave for different reasons, but some will certainly leave over significant changes in the leadership structure. If you make it a prerequisite that you will not make any changes that cause anyone to leave, you will never make necessary changes.

When you see people leaving, it will help if you note why they are leaving. We rarely see everyone leaving for the same reason. Immediately after my church's polity changes, we saw less than a half dozen who left, but they all left for very different reasons. In other words, those who left would have been unable to unite to plant another church.

Prepare yourself, too, for the unflattering words you will hear as people leave. But don't assume they represent the majority. I learned as a young man that, in the church, unhappy people talk and happy people don't. I sat through too many committee meetings and congregational gatherings before I figured out that a majority of people will be polite and accommodating as they listened to angry rants, but then they will vote down the few who sucked up all the microphone time.

Remember, also, that the biblical polity structures that you put in place will help build the healthy church you envision. You are building for people you have yet to meet. The future members won't know what you did to help them, but they will most certainly be the beneficiaries of your wisdom, obedience, and perseverance.

THE STAFF

Second, consider the staff. The church staff can make or break a transition to biblical polity. Why? Too many church staff see themselves as the de facto leaders of the church. They do all the work. They have all the information. They know all the people. They have access to the purse strings. But most church staff meet few, if any, of the biblical qualifications for church leaders spelled out in 1 Timothy and Titus. I have seen gossipy secretaries spread rumors faster than Facebook and business managers put a stranglehold on finances.

Therefore, a successful transition to an elder/deacon structure may require replacing some staff members. At a minimum, it demands understanding who the true leaders of the church are. I remember Mark Dever occasionally stopping church staff meetings shortly after we elected elders, saying, "This subject belongs with the elders. We're not going to discuss it here." It is vital for every staff person to understand that they are there to carry out the direction of the elders, not set the direction of the church.

THE DEACONS

Third, consider the deacons. If your church is transitioning from a pastor/deacon board model to an elders/deacons model, the transition for the old deacon board may be very difficult. These men formerly had at least some of the authority that now has been granted to the elders. Further, the deacons are likely transitioning from a deliberative body that met once a month to individuals who work throughout the week to oversee physical needs of the body. Written job descriptions may be helpful to ensure everyone knows what is expected and to cut down on turf wars.

In our experience, older deacons lost some of that authority to younger and more biblically robust men who were now serving as elders. In such situations it is very important to honor those older deacons—even if they didn't do everything right—for their years of service.

THE ELDERS

Fourth, consider the elders themselves. When Capitol Hill Baptist Church appointed our first slate of elders, friction unexpectedly arose between the staff elders and the non-staff elders. At the heart of the problem was access to information. Staff elders spent a good part of their week together and naturally vetted the issues, while the non-staff elders were busy with their jobs. In early elders' meetings, when the two groups came together, the non-staff elders found themselves pushed to make decisions when they didn't even know beforehand what was on the agenda, let alone have time to pray and think through the decisions.

We rectified this by requiring memorandums for each agenda item to be written beforehand. The elder chairman would ensure these memos would be assembled and distributed to all the elders approximately one week prior to each elders' meeting. This extra administrative step proved a huge aid to the non-staff elders and helped unite the elders. It also had the further benefit of forcing long-winded brothers to succinctly write their thoughts in memo form.

In the eyes of the congregation, a newly-minted elder board will likely prove immediately fruitful if they give themselves to member care. The elders can pretty easily give oversight to a new member class, membership interviews, members' meetings, and the teaching of the church. If a young elder board proves faithful in these areas, they will naturally accrue authority.

THE SENIOR PASTOR

Finally, the most difficult transition to elders may be for the senior pastor. He moves from being the top of a pyramid to one among many. He exchanges the position of "having the last word" to being "first among equals." So, senior pastor as you make the transition, consider the following:

Share Authority

As senior pastor, you are called by God to entrust yourself to other elders who are gifts given to the church by Jesus for edifying and strengthening the body (Eph. 4:11–12). But you might say, "These men aren't as theologically educated or experienced as I am." True, but if they meet the qualifications and have been appointed to this role by the church, then they are sufficiently educated and experienced. You might say that if they are good enough for Jesus, they should be good enough for you. So trust them. Submit to them. Trust that the Holy Spirit will move through them for the good of the church. Share your authority and model what it is to be under authority.

Share Your Pulpit

In addition, share your pulpit and other teaching opportunities, and pray for the Lord to further develop the other elders' teaching gifts. You have to be willing to give men the opportunity to try, fail, be critiqued, and try again. In order to serve as an elder a man must be able to teach (1 Tim. 3:2), but that doesn't mean he has no room to grow. Consider how much richer your church will be if there are multiple men who are able to faithfully preach God's Word rather than just one.

First Year

If you are the senior pastor, you should consider chairing the early elders' meetings so that you can ensure that the work of elders, not deacons, consumes your meeting time together. Administrative matters have a way of creeping onto the agenda of every elder meeting.

Discipline yourself from the beginning to schedule prayer, Scripture reading, member care, and theological discussion. Prioritize these areas over budgets and buildings. If you hardwire good practices into your meetings, in time you can yield the chairman's position in order to free yourself up and make room for other elders' leadership.

First Word

If you are the senior pastor, consider letting every elder speak on a matter before you do. If the senior pastor speaks first, it will stifle conversation. Better for the senior pastor to listen to the other elders work out a situation, get educated in the process, and only intervene if they've come to a conclusion that is theologically wrong or pastorally insensitive.

EVOLUTION, NOT REVOLUTION

Dick Lucas is an evangelical Anglican best known for his thirty-seven years as rector of St. Helen's Bishopsgate Church in London. As his ministry as rector came to a close in 1998 he said to his successor William Taylor, "William, think evolution, not revolution." Note how Rev. Lucas assumed change was coming. Despite nearly four decades of labor, which by any standard was a massive success, Lucas did not try to freeze the ministry in place. He assumed change would come, and merely addressed the *rate* of change.

So consider your transition to a biblical polity. Consider what your congregation can bear. Then think evolution.

CHAPTER SEVENTEEN

Can It Be Done?

Making the Transition to Elder Leadership

A pastor of a large Southern Baptist church contacted me. He wanted to discuss transitioning from a pastor-and-staff leadership to an elder-led church polity. He said, "I need to decide if this is a hill worth dying on." He understood that in the traditional Southern Baptist setting there might be a concerted reaction against transitioning to an elder-led church.

He's not alone. Many pastors and church leaders contemplate the same concern as they begin to understand the biblical teaching of church leadership. Some rush into the process without laying the proper groundwork and end up with major church conflict that often culminates in the pastor being dismissed from leadership. How, then, does one begin the transition?

Begin slowly. This is not a process to be completed overnight. Forms of leadership, patterns of decision-making, and ingrained habits of church life rarely change quickly. So if you begin this process, move slowly and do what you can to see it through to the end.

Brief pastorates fail to build the trust necessary to shift a church to a biblical polity. It takes time for a congregation to embrace a pastor's faithful teaching concerning the nature of the church, the believer's relationship to the church, the authority and responsibilities of leaders, the unity of the body, and other doctrines related to a New Testament church. Foundational to teaching on ecclesiology are the inspiration of Scripture, the doctrine of God, the person and work of Christ, soteriology, and the person and work of the Holy Spirit. Faithful exposition of

God's Word will give a pastor the opportunity to deal with each of these doctrines as he works his way year-by-year through books of the Bible. *Only when a church begins to think biblically will elder leadership seem plausible.*

The following process is recommended for establishing elder leadership in congregations. This approach can be adapted to individual settings, but note that completing the process will likely take at least eighteen months to three years—perhaps longer. I divide the process into three phases.

Evaluation Phase	Presentation Phase	Implementation Phase
• Assess • Study • Probe • Summarize	• Exposition • Discussion • Qualifications	• Pray • Screen • Install Elders • Involve • Review

EVALUATION PHASE

First comes the evaluation phase. In it you want to assess your current polity, study the Bible's teaching on church leadership, probe how well your other leaders' understanding of the issues are developing, and summarize your new position in a brief, accessible document.

Assess

First, assess your current polity. Who are the leaders in your congregation? What titles do they have? What roles do they play? For example, your church might have any combination of, deacons, stewards, trustees, board members, church council, teachers, small-group leaders, committee chairmen, and staff members. Take the time to evaluate each current leader's role, character, and gifting. What kinds of standards are already in place for these leadership roles? How many truly demonstrate godly leadership? Who appears to enjoy the title and recognition but does not exhibit dependable servant leadership? Who is teachable? Who demonstrates the heart to pay the price of servant leadership? Who has the ear of the congregation? Ask tough and probing questions, and reflect carefully on and evaluate the answers that emerge.

The pastor will constantly need to seek the Lord throughout the transition process, but especially during the initial stages when he lays groundwork for elders.
He will need to size up the current leaders' understanding of basic doctrine, grasp
of spiritual authority, commitment to servant leadership, and determination to
obey the Lord of the church at all costs. The pastor will need to direct his teaching,
preaching, and training to fill the gaps in these areas. To accomplish this, it will
be necessary to teach some leaders in a one-on-one or small-group setting. Other
leaders will respond well to the pastor's pulpit expositions. It should be recognized
that some leaders will, of course, balk at any change in leadership structure. The
pastor must labor to be gentle with those in opposition and yet stand faithfully
upon the truth of God's Word.

I recommend that a pastor narrow the leadership core of the church to a
manageable group and invite them to join him for a thorough study of every
biblical passage addressing leadership, decision-making, church structure,
and all that falls under the realm of church polity. At such a time the pastor
will need to lead the group in properly interpreting each text in its historical,
grammatical, and theological context. The pastor might need to begin with basic
principles of hermeneutics. I don't recommend using study guides or books on
elders at the outset. That should come later. Rather, open the Word of God and
allow the leadership core to see what Scripture sets forth for the church. Basic
exegetical tools, Bible dictionaries, concordances, and commentaries can be
helpful during this round table dialogue. Ask questions of the texts. Maintain
copious notes for later use. With an openness to obey the Word of God, face
the passages that stand in clear opposition to the church's current polity. Give
assignments to those involved so that they are forced to dig into the Word on
their own in order to report their discoveries at the next meeting. Be open with
each other, and avoid defensive posturing. Keep the goal in mind: leading the
church to be biblical.

The pastor may become quite vulnerable during this study since he is leading
the church to consider major changes in structure. If the church leaders are
more concerned about holding their positions than obeying the revelation of
Scripture, the pastor may be in for rocky times. Still, he must take the high road,
emphasizing his desire to obey the Lord and to lead the church to obedience.
The pastor must be patient yet firm, realizing that a heavy-handed insistence
on his interpretation may prove counter-productive. During this time, the pastor and others who lead the study must model the godly leadership described
throughout the New Testament. Expect the Lord to turn hearts, and give him
time to do so.

Study

The second step in the evaluation phase is a more in-depth study. First, look at some of the Old Testament passages that deal with leadership in general. There are plenty of examples of both good and bad leadership but keep in mind that the national structures of Israel do not equate to church structures. Comparing and contrasting King Saul and King David's leadership can be helpful. Looking at the leadership principles in Joshua, Ezra, and Nehemiah might also help the study group to grapple with qualities necessary to lead a congregation. None of these examples, however, will adequately explain the New Testament church polity.[1]

Template for Studying Selected Texts from Acts

- Problem
- Solution
- Process

Next, move to the New Testament, studying every passage related to leaders, leadership practices, leadership requirements, church structure, decision-making, crises requiring decision in church life, and church conflicts. Many scholars discourage using the book of Acts as the basis for doctrine, but the best examples of church decision-making and leadership will be found there. Acts, in fact, offers illustrations of what the epistles state in principle. At minimum, the study group will need to consider Acts 1:12–26; 6:1–7; 11:1–18; 11:19–26; 13:1–3; 14:21–23; 15:1–41; 20:17–38; and 21:17–26. For consistency of interpretation, various passages should be analyzed in a threefold manner: *problem, solution, process*. Applying this analysis especially helps to understand how the early Christians arrived at decisions that affected church life and how leaders functioned in relationship to the congregation. The study group should also consider other texts, such as Matthew 18:15–20; 1 Corinthians 5:1–13; Ephesians 4:11–16; 1 Timothy 3:1–16; Titus 1:5–9; Hebrews 13:7, 17–19; and 1 Peter 5:1–5.

Pay close attention to the historical and cultural backgrounds of each text. Some of the passages might deal with specific problems that required an unrepeatable process to resolve. Make the distinction in your study, but learn from the

---

1 I found Gene Getz, *Sharpening the Focus of the Church* (Wheaton, IL: Victor, 1984), to be helpful in identifying many passages for study. Gene Getz, *Elders and Leaders: God's Plan for Leading the Church* (Chicago: Moody, 2003), identifies additional texts for study.

principles unfolded. Notice the trends established that provide lasting patterns for all churches. Do thorough work on word studies, grasping the use of words common in the first century that may have different implications today. Keep detailed notes of the discussions during each meeting, making them available to study-group members. Given the nature of this kind of study, it may be useful to limit the discussion to group members so that premature conclusions do not get spread throughout the church. Until the leaders are able to share their conclusions with the congregation, it may suffice to periodically notify the congregation that church leaders are doing a thorough study of Scripture regarding church polity.

Probe

Third, probe your current leaders' developing understanding of, and attitude toward, biblical teaching on church polity. The more your leadership group can be involved in the intensive study, the better chance they will embrace the biblical pattern for church polity. Leaders need to know that they are part of something vital to the future of their church. For this reason, it is important that the pastor not do all the study and then just dump information into the group members' laps. Rather, give assignments and set expectations for study within the group. Help them understand how to use exegetical tools in their study: point them to commentaries, theological works, and word studies that might help them grapple with their assigned text. In the process, you will be discipling them.

I worked through this same process with a leadership group. Although at the beginning some were opposed to elders in Baptist life, as they worked through Scripture on their own, they arrived at a new and better conclusion. Seeing for themselves what Scripture taught gave them a sense of ownership and determination to see the process through.

That said, the pastor must always do his homework first. There is no guarantee that someone assigned a text will know how to study and interpret it. So the pastor must be prepared to ask questions, make observations, and gently guide the group to the clear sense of the biblical texts. A good way to do this is to prepare probing questions for each text, such as the following:

- Why was there conflict in the early Jerusalem church as recorded in Acts 6:1–7?
- What kind of guidance did the apostles give to the church?
- What was the church's responsibility in addressing the conflict?
- What priorities does the text give to each type of church leader?

- What were the issues that caused the early church's structure to emerge?
- Are the same kinds of needs present in our own church setting?
- How well does our church conform to this early church model?

Throughout the study the pastor will need to reinforce the importance of understanding and obeying the Word of God. We often make much of the Bible's inerrancy, but do we strive to believe and obey the inerrant Word? Are we willing to follow the Word of God regardless of what tradition or popular trends may demand? The critical issue in the whole process is whether or not we will submit to what God says.

Summarize

Finally, summarize your study group's findings, both throughout the process and at the end. My own process of carrying a leadership group through a study like this took a year and a half. We did not necessarily meet each week. But we did persist. All the while we recorded our findings and ultimately developed a brief summary for the congregation.

I wouldn't advise you to hand the congregation a long document regarding your study, since most people will not take the time to read it. Try to narrow your thoughts into a one- or two-page summary, and perhaps prepare a lengthier document for those who desire to study the findings in detail. Stand together as a leadership group on what you have done. Give ample scriptural citations so that those who are interested can investigate God's Word on their own. Above all, bring the force of your argument on church polity back to the one place of final authority: the Word of God.

Your short summary will serve as a primer to stimulate questions and develop guidance for more detailed study. It will also become a proving ground for the church's commitment to Scripture. You might also consider reading Benjamin Merkle's excellent book, *40 Questions about Elders and Deacons* (Kregel, 2008), as a useful tool in thinking through pertinent issues.

The next step will be critical in helping the congregation grapple with the teaching of God's Word.

PRESENTATION PHASE

After evaluation comes presentation, in which you preach the relevant passages to the church, lead them in discussing how they apply to your congregation, and publicly establish the qualifications for the office of elder.

Exposition

First, preach Scripture to the church. Biblical exposition is always the best way to lead change. Rather than stringing a group of verses together to prove one's point, the faithful expositor will open a text of Scripture and unfold it so that the congregation can understand the passage's message in its context. It will be helpful to preach through the texts that the leadership group wrestled through. I did this over a three-month period on Sunday evenings, and afterward often opened the floor for dialogue. I announced ahead of time that our leadership had worked through these texts, and that I now wanted to set forth our understanding of them for the whole church. The leadership team was also available to answer questions.

One or two weeks will not lay groundwork for transition, so take whatever time is needed to deal thoroughly with each text. Realize that in many settings church members have never heard the word "polity," and think that "elders" belong only to Presbyterians. Since Scripture interprets Scripture, the pastor will need to show the connections between the series of texts he lays before the church.

Some pastors may find that covering a short series in Acts, a break, and another series in the Epistles will allow the congregation time to absorb more fully the biblical teaching. Studies of 1 Timothy 3 and Titus 1, addressing qualifications, show those elders as representations of the gospel in the community. Exposition provides the best means for unfolding the contexts surrounding the passages and helping the congregation to understand how the early church's structure developed in the crucible of congregational life.

Discussion

Next, foster open discussion among the congregation as a whole. The leadership group's summary document may help to facilitate discussion after the sermon series, though each pastor will have to determine what is best in his setting. I would not advise you to proceed to the discussion phase if the sermon series was not well-attended and well-received. In that case, the church might not be ready, and forcing a discussion might result in needless conflict. So, assuming all has gone well, ask the congregation to read the summary document and the biblical texts it discusses. Invite members to bring their questions into a congregational forum.

Bring the church body together for a time of discussing the leadership group's conclusions, as well as the content of the sermons. Openness and honesty about the differences between what the Word teaches and what the church currently practices will help to bridge the understanding gap. Always go back to the Scripture as authority for changes, being careful not to make personal attacks on former leaders. Answer as many questions as possible, holding multiple dialogue sessions if needed.

After the pastor and study-group members have answered the congregation's questions, ask the church to adopt the biblical structure for the church's own polity. Making such a decision could involve amending or removing the church's current constitution, or bylaws, or policy manual, or other governing documents. Some people, especially older members, consider church constitutions to be sacred property, so tampering with them may cause ire. You are blessed if you have older members in leadership who can speak appreciatively of the past, while supporting obedience for the future. The pastor and other leaders need to show humility and patience in creating change, realizing that some still might not follow.

The pastor and leadership study group will need to develop the church's new governing document based on the group's understanding of Scripture. This new document will need the congregation's approval. At no time should the congregation receive the impression that this document is being crammed down their throats. Give members time to digest what the new document means and how it will change the church's life. Granted, some details of governance may be vague or unknown. But candor about uncertainties will give the congregation confidence that the leadership's uppermost desire is to follow the Word of God and to trust that the Lord of the church will bless obedience.

Qualifications

Nothing is more critical in transitioning to elder leadership than setting forth the biblical qualifications for church leaders. If the congregation understands the requirements for being an elder, members will have greater respect for the elder body. It is ironic that, in their rush to transition to biblical elder leadership, some churches underemphasize or overlook the biblical qualifications for individual elders. If the church transitions to elder leadership but then installs men who lack biblical qualifications, greater problems may result. So be diligent to instruct the church properly on this point.

Setting forth the biblical qualifications (1 Tim. 3; Titus 1; 1 Pet. 5) can be done, first, through pulpit expositions. Sunday morning is preferable at this point because the largest portion of members will be present. Sunday school is another strong venue for teaching on the subject. Printed material may also be helpful. The aim is for the entire church to know what is expected in elders, and in deacons as well. Knowledge about the biblical qualifications for eldership not only helps the congregation hold the elders accountable, it also may deter wrongly motivated or otherwise disqualified men from pursuing eldership.

When you begin this teaching, some men presently serving as leaders may not meet the biblical qualifications. Unless pride has been checked in their lives, such men may revolt against the intense biblical standards. Take their complaints back to the Word of God as the final arbiter of church disputes. The church's mettle will be tested at just this point.

How many elders should you seek to appoint? Setting an arbitrary number of elders for any church is inadvisable because much depends on the spiritual maturity of the congregation. Some churches begin by establishing a ratio system—one elder for every certain number of members. Whatever number or ratio is established, quality must be emphasized over quantity. It is far better to begin with a smaller group of well-qualified elders than to fill a quota with unqualified men. After the church has matured, the elders might recommend setting a certain number of elders, limiting their term of service, and establishing a rotation system for the sake of keeping them engaged in the work. Above all, hold forth the biblical standards for church leaders.

IMPLEMENTATION PHASE

After the presentation phase you can move to implementation. At this stage you want to pray as a church, screen your potential elders, install your new elders, involve them in the full range of church life, and review biblical teaching on eldership.

Pray

Before selecting elders, call the church body to prayer. Selecting a group of men to serve the church as spiritual leaders is a major step that will impact the whole life of the church. Church members must understand the seriousness of such a decision and their own part in it, and collectively seeking the Lord's guidance will reinforce this. The church must also be aware that the adversary will attempt to scuttle their plans to follow the teaching of Scripture. Be vigilant, then, in calling upon the Lord of the church to direct each step and decision.

Selecting qualified men to serve as elders is so important that the process should never be rushed. If the pastor and leadership group determine that the church currently has no men who are qualified for eldership, then teaching, developing, training, and praying must continue until the church can appoint qualified elders.

Screen

In narrowing the field of elder candidates, each church must establish a plan that works best for it. In some cases the senior pastor might choose the initial group of elder candidates and then take them through the screening process, much the same way that Paul and Barnabas may have appointed elders during their first missionary journey (Acts 14:23). Once the elder body is established, these elders may take the lead in nominating subsequent elders.[2]

Mark Dever utilizes a quadrant to help evaluate elder candidates.

(1) Central Christian Concerns	(2) Distinctive Theological Concerns
(4) Love for the Congregation	(3) Distinctive Cultural Concerns

(1) The top left box signifies *central Christian concerns,* which includes such things as a faithful Christian testimony, the ability to articulate the gospel, a stable walk with Christ, consistent Christian character, and a strong family life. The notable characteristics listed in 1 Timothy 3 and Titus 1 apply.

(2) If the man demonstrates faithfulness in this area, then *distinctive theological concerns* must be considered (Acts 20:28–31). This top-right quadrant aims at the candidate's position toward the church's doctrinal statement as well as his grasp of the faith. Can he biblically articulate the church's position on baptism or worship or evangelism or church government?

(3) Having shown understanding and ability to dialogue theologically, the bottom-right quadrant evaluates *distinctive cultural concerns* that are presently

---

2 This is the most plausible method for beginning elder leadership in any type of missionary setting. Assuming that the congregation is young and not well-versed in Scripture, the missionary will need to carefully evaluate potential candidates for elder, and then invest as much time as possible in training them before turning the reins of leadership over to the elders on behalf of the church. Maintaining contact with the elders to "coach" them through the early years of leadership could prove invaluable to the church's future. See chapter 21 for a more detailed approach.

affecting the church: the role of women in the church, for example, or the effects of the church-growth movement on the church (Titus 1:9).

(4) The final quadrant concerns whether the elder candidate's understanding of the gospel and theology translates into a *love for the congregation* (1 Pet. 5:2–3). Is there evidence that he genuinely loves the body of Christ and desires to serve and minister to the church?[3]

In other churches, members of the congregation nominate the initial group of elders for consideration and screening. The senior pastor, being an elder, must take the leadership at this point. He may ask two or three other godly men to assist him in this process, or even utilize elders from another church to hold him accountable during the process of screening.

Since our church was accustomed to congregationalism, after preaching on the biblical qualifications for elders, I asked the congregation to nominate men whom they believed were qualified to serve as elders. I provided a simple form that asked if the nominator had read and agreed to the biblical standards for elders in 1 Timothy 3 and Titus 1, and if the nominator believed that the nominee qualified on this basis. Then the nominator was asked to write a brief explanation of why he or she nominated a particular man to the office of elder. (We do the same for deacon.) This explanation sheds light on whether the nomination is based on the popularity of the nominee or on his servant-heartedness.

After allowing two weeks for nominations, the pastor—and anyone chosen beforehand to assist—will narrow the field of nominees. Once an elder board is established, they will embrace this responsibility. Some nominees will be excluded due to circumstances in the nominee's life known to the pastor. Family concerns, personal habits, or problems in other areas may disqualify the nominee. The pastor will then remove disqualified nominees from consideration without making their nominations public.

The congregation needs to understand the sensitivity involved in screening candidates, and the need for complete confidentiality. Once the initial list is narrowed, the pastor will contact each nominee personally to ascertain his willingness to undergo the elder screening process and to serve if approved. Holding forth biblical standards seems to significantly narrow the field of nominations. Even some of those who initially accept nomination may subsequently withdraw themselves after considering the seriousness of the office. My own church's practice is to keep the names of the nominees private so that there is no public embarrassment if a nominee is disqualified.

---

3 Mark Dever, senior pastor of Capitol Hill Baptist Church, Washington, DC, telephone conversation, February 3, 2004.

Those who agree to be nominated are then asked to complete a thorough doctrinal questionnaire.[4] The nominee will write about his conversion and personal walk with Christ, explaining also his views on the gospel, the church, and the role of elders. He will need to study the church's doctrinal statement and completely affirm it or identify any areas of disagreement. The nominee will also need to evaluate himself in light of the biblical qualifications for elders, addressing his family life and his relationship to his wife and children. He will also explain why, if selected, he should serve as an elder and how he will seek to lead the congregation.

The written questionnaire must be taken seriously, for it asks the nominee to put what he believes in writing. It will also reveal whether or not he as a church leader can articulate the Christian faith and basic ecclesiology. Such a questionnaire might raise concerns about the nominee that need to be investigated. Or it might be the means of disqualifying him for service due to frank admissions about his walk with Christ or lack of understanding Christian doctrine.

As a word of caution and encouragement, let me suggest making the most of the screening process. Although some candidates may not currently qualify to serve as elders, more discipline or training may help them qualify in the future. Therefore, nurture the spiritual development of men who show promise for future service as elders.

After satisfying the initial screening and questionnaire requirements, a nominee should meet with the council of elders. Initially, a pastor may need to call upon the aid of pastors of likeminded churches to help question the candidates. But once elders are established, the examining council will consist of a church's own elders. An examination council will need to read each nominee's questionnaire responses and pose questions related to the nominee's assurance of faith, personal spiritual disciplines, understanding of doctrine, and views on the church. The rigor of the examination council will help prepare the nominee to serve as an elder, in which he will be called upon to answer the church's questions about doctrine and church life. The examination phase should never be a mere formality. Some issue might, in fact, be raised that will uncover questions about a man's family life or walk with Christ or views of the church. It should be possible to disqualify a man at any point during the screening process.

Once nominees have passed the initial screening, questionnaire, and examination council, they are publicly identified to the church. The final line of screening involves the church. In my church, we then give the congregation a two-week period to contest the nomination. Church members are asked to put in writing

---

4   See the Appendix for a sample questionnaire.

any concerns and give these to the pastor, who will accompany the church member in discussing the concern with the nominee. If the concern proves inconsequential, the nomination stands. If the concern is warranted, then the nominee will be asked to withdraw his name from further consideration until the concern is resolved. After the two-week waiting period, the church is asked to approve each elder nominee by vote or affirmation.

Leaders should hold the line on biblical standards throughout the entire process. The church will grow to respect them as they faithfully adhere to Scripture. Even after elders are established, the biblical standards must be reviewed regularly.

Install Elders

Once your congregation has recognized its first elders, the elders should be formally installed. The installation process gives both the elders and the congregation a chance to affirm God's hand upon the leaders and the people. Installation implies that a man has been recognized as qualified for this biblical office and set apart for faithful service.

The installation process should also be used to challenge the church to pray for the elders, hold them accountable, and follow their leadership. The elder himself should be challenged to faithfully teach the Word, give wise direction to the church, shepherd the flock of God, and set an example for all to follow. The installation service provides a unique opportunity for showing the biblical foundation for the church's polity and how it affects the church. Consider utilizing vows for the new elders similar to those that Matt mentions in chapter 12.

Involve

New elders will need to be trained in how they are to function in regular church life. Training can take place during a special weekend retreat or even during the ongoing elders' meetings. Since the office of elder might be new to many in the congregation—including the new elders themselves—we should not presume that new elders will fully understand the task before them. Training is essential.

Elders should be involved in the full range of church life. Those who demonstrate pulpit gifts will be called upon to preach. Others will excel at pastoral care, administration, or leading worship. All will be involved in various areas of teaching. Some will be gifted in counseling and might need to take the lead in this area of church life. Those especially gifted in evangelism might be at the forefront of that part of church ministry. Since elders shepherd the flock of God, all will need to consciously engage in discipling the church body. When it comes to solving problems, there is no better group in the church than the elders.

As men serve together as elders, they will get a better feel for one another's gifts, strengths, and weaknesses. All will not teach equally well or be equally gifted in counseling or administration, so those whose gifts suit them for particular tasks may need to be directed to the areas where they can contribute most effectively.

Review

At least once a year the pastor should plan to teach in some way about the ministry of elders. The congregation—both new and longstanding members—needs to be reminded of the scriptural basis of elder leadership. Similarly, the elders themselves need to be publically challenged and held accountable to God's standards for them.

REFLECTIONS

- What steps can you take to assess your church's present leadership?
- Do you recognize any men presently serving the church who appear to have the necessary qualifications to serve as elders?
- How can you communicate the need for plural eldership in your church?
- Identify a workable process in your own setting for selecting and screening elder candidates.

CHAPTER EIGHTEEN

TEMPTED TO AVOID CHANGE?

The title of the chapter you just read is "Can It Be Done?" The answer is "Yes!" This entire book has been an exercise in answering that question biblically and practically.

But I want to quickly add that it does not absolutely have to be done. Elders aren't essential in order to have a true church that rightly preaches the Word and rightly administers the sacraments. Your soul can be well cared for by just one pastor. You can preach (or hear) sound sermons for thirty years without elders. Furthermore, you can visit the sick, marry, bury, and do everything else a church does and never have elders.

You can also sit on a beach under a blazing hot sun without sunblock. And you can swim in the ocean without the protection of a lifeguard. I've done both and was neither burned nor crushed against the rocks. But I don't recommend it. You do either enough times and odds are that at some point your fried hide will be cast onto the jetty.

My point is this: In good times, when everyone is happy and healthy, a church's particular polity doesn't much come into play. But when bad times hit, it seems polity is the only thing that matters. Have you ever noticed how constitutional experts come out of the woodwork when problems flare up? You know you're in trouble when you see your congregants carrying two books into church: The Bible and *Robert's Rules of Order*. I was an observer at one congregational meeting where a man who was publicly challenged about whether or not his position was biblical blurted out, "We're not a people of the Bible. We're a people of the constitution."

I can drive around my city and see how unbiblical polity has hurt or even killed church after church. One local Episcopal church had its property confiscated by the bishop—a leader who long ago abandoned any notion of biblical authority—because the church could no longer live with the positions the bishop took or submit to her authority. Another local church caused an internet sensation and eventually split over what ecclesiastical authority existed outside the local congregation. But most churches I drive by sit largely empty, abandoned because those who gained authority were in fact biblically unqualified and no mechanism was in place to remove them. In other words, their polity was broken. So congregation after congregation did the only thing they could do: they voted with their feet and walked out.

TEMPTED TO AVOID CHANGE?

Not too long ago I had an appliance repairman in my home who told me to never get rid of the twenty-five-year-old washer and dryer I had. I assumed enough years would go by and I'd go out and buy the same brand again, given how well it performed. But he told me how the company had built its reputation on great quality but long ago had switched to cheap parts. In other words, they were trading on a reputation that was no longer deserved. I think a lot of church leaders trade on things that are not designed to bear the weight that biblical polity is designed to bear. As a result, they avoid making the necessary correctives toward proper church governance. There are two things in particular I have in mind.

First, too many churches and leaders trade on tradition. Leaders especially have wrongly assumed that tradition will see their congregations through difficult times. That may have been true in a culturally homogenous, static society in which traditions were passed down from generation to generation. (Once a Lutheran, always a Lutheran?) But for the rising generation today, loyalty to time-honored traditions lasts about as long as a website page view. We don't have to wait to see the result of this strategy. The empty buildings that once bustled with lively congregations are living monuments to the failure of tradition as a sufficient support for difficult times.

Second, churches and leaders trade on personality. Churches are often founded by charismatic personalities. As the church grows, authority accrues to the winsome, larger-than-life leader. With each passing year the leader's word can increasingly transform into law. The man can be a dictator, but if he's a benevolent, kind, cheerful, godly, humble dictator, it seems to work. But what happens if another equally-sized personality challenges him? Or what happens when he grows old, a transition needs to occur, and the next guy is not nearly as charming? In the end I think you'll find that a winning personality is a poor substitute for good polity.

Iain Murray once told me the exercise philosophy of Dr. Martyn Lloyd-Jones: "Why run when you can walk and why walk when you can sit?" Was Lloyd-Jones just being funny? In the biography version of the story it is hard to tell. Lloyd-Jones was a brilliant doctor, but we all have our blind spots. Let's say we all adopted his philosophy. We'd also have to keep in mind that the average person loses five to eight percent of his or her muscle mass every decade with the onset of middle age. Can we sit? Yes. Are there consequences? Yes.

I am not telling you that change will be easy. I am not telling you there won't be unintended consequences. I am telling you that making no changes is not a neutral and therefore safe position. Inattention, like inactivity, will likely have negative consequences.

So consider your church's polity. Consider the changes that would have to take place. Consider your hesitations. Pray. Seek counsel. And move ahead in God's timing.

CHAPTER NINETEEN

PUTTING IT ALL TOGETHER

I'm accountable only to God," one pastor declared in response to those who questioned him. Another pastor stated that the church's elders, who had asked about his plans, had a responsibility to follow *his* vision for the church—without questions.

Many, if not most, pastors would rightly condemn these brazen displays of autocratic authority. Yet the issue of authority regularly surfaces within congregations. Who holds authority within the church? In plural elder leadership within a congregational setting, the final authority in church matters resides in the congregation, yet elders are not without authority. In order to exercise oversight the way Scripture commands, elders must exercise authority within the congregation.

CONGREGATIONALISM, ELDERS, AND AUTHORITY

What kind of authority do elders hold within a congregational polity? To correctly answer that question, it is crucial to understand biblical teaching rather than simply follow tradition. A church might decide to take every decision affecting the church to the floor of a business meeting: from carpeting the nursery, to hiring a secretary, to ordering a case of florescent bulbs, to assisting someone in need. But such congregational decisions will often be ill-informed. Can churches function like this? Certainly they can, albeit at a snail's pace. More often, this kind of congregationalism offends various groups within the church and cripples the church's ministry.

That said, one has to overlook a number of New Testament passages to conclude that the congregation has no authority regarding church matters. In cases of discipline, the church body is the final arbiter (Matt. 18:15–20). While the elders might be involved in working through many of the details, the church decides whether to remove a member who has rejected biblical standards for Christian living or doctrine. In 1 Corinthians 5, Paul instructs the Corinthian church to stop tolerating a member's immoral behavior, but to discipline the immoral member. The church then appears to have taken the action (yet perhaps with too much severity), at least if this is the action Paul refers to in 2 Corinthians (see 2 Cor. 2:5–11). In another instance of congregational authority, the church selected qualified men to assist the apostles with food distribution (Acts 6:1–6). It appears, too, that Peter reported to the apostles *and* to the church about carrying the gospel to the Gentiles, so that the whole group found satisfaction in his report (Acts 11:1–18). The church at Jerusalem sent Barnabas to investigate the spread of the gospel to Antioch, showing something of the church's involvement in missionary work (Acts 11:22; cf. 13:1–3 which holds similar implications). While the issues at the Jerusalem Council were first addressed to "the apostles and the elders" (Acts 15:6), the entire church got involved in the final decision that called for messengers to send a letter of acceptance and instruction for Gentile believers (Acts 15:22).

From these examples we can conclude that the New Testament church was not a passive entity, watching apostles and elders from the sidelines. Members exercised authority through involvement in decision-making that affected the future of the church.

Having noted this, there is no doubt that a group of men led the church. For example, the apostles called for congregational action (Acts 6:2); the apostles and elders "came together to look into this matter" of uncircumcised Gentiles being converted (Acts 15:6); Paul instructed the elders of Ephesus to exercise spiritual oversight over that church (Acts 20:17–35); and so on. Congregationalism does not function well without effective leadership. And for leadership to be effective it must carry some level of authority.

Since Peter called for elders to shepherd the flock of God but to not lord this authority over them, it is obvious that authority was involved (1 Peter 5:2–3). Shepherds do not normally offer suggestions to sheep. The church members are called upon to obey their leaders, even submit to them, because of their work of spiritual care (Heb. 13:17). Paul exhorts the Thessalonian church to "appreciate those who diligently labor among you, and have charge over you in the Lord and give you instruction" (1 Thess. 5:12). To "have charge over" clearly implies authority to lead the church. The church reciprocates with affection and esteem so that the leaders "are not to be regarded simply as the cold voice of authority."[1] The church needs leaders with authority in order to give the church direction, to exhort where needed, to correct and restore those who have gone astray, and to model the servant-leadership of Christ among the flock.

Because authority is delegated to the church's spiritual leaders, plural eldership demonstrates the wisdom of the Lord. "A plurality of elders is necessary because of the tendency of those in authority to play God."[2] The pastor who claims he is accountable only to God is in "dangerous territory,"[3] and stands to make decisive errors in judgment that can affect his ministry and that of the church. Such a pastor resists plural eldership because he does not want to be held accountable to anyone. Any pastor who has no regular, personal accountability for his time, actions, and lifestyle can easily be deceived by his own sinful heart. Certainly he is accountable to the church for his actions, yet such accounting is often too vague to do any good. As theology professor John Hammett wisely pointed out to me, "To be accountable to the church is to be accountable to no one." In other words, accountability to "the church" can be too broad. It can lack the systematic interaction necessary to keep those in authority on track. So elder plurality holds each man—including the senior pastor—accountable to one another. Discussion of each man's spiritual development during elders' meetings or elders' retreats provides an atmosphere in which those in authority examine the ways they are tempted to misuse authority. Accountability of this sort helps to foster the wise use of authority.

SENIOR PASTOR, ELDERS, AND AUTHORITY

I am thankful to have men around me who will not hesitate to exhort me, inquire about my priorities and schedule, or recommend that I take time off for refreshing. If I think that I'm slipping in the use of authority delegated to me as senior pastor, or struggle over how I've handled a situation in the church, I seek counsel from my fellow elders who help me to see multiple sides of an issue.[4] So

---

1 Leon Morris, *The First and Second Epistles to the Thessalonians*, rev. ed., NICNT (Grand Rapids: Eerdmans, 1991), 167.
2 Ray Steadman, quoted by Jim Henry, "Pastoral Reflections on Baptist Polity in the Local Church," address given at the "Issues in Baptist Polity Conference," New Orleans Baptist Theological Seminary, February 5, 2004.
3 Quotation from Paige Patterson in response to the author's question about how single pastoral authority lacks accountability, "Panel Discussion: Issues in Baptist Polity," New Orleans Baptist Theological Seminary, February 6, 2004.
4 Merkle, *40 Questions*, 57, disagrees with the use of "senior pastor" as a title since it is not found in Scripture and may give the idea of a third church office. While I agree with his sentiment and hold to the view of two church offices, the use of the senior pastor designation remains

while I have ample authority within our church as an elder who holds the position of the senior pastor, I gladly share that authority lest my own weaknesses lead me to abuse or neglect this authority.

Sometimes pastors ask how it is possible to function as a senior pastor with elders who share pastoral authority and responsibility. Having had it both ways, I am convinced that the shared authority and responsibility in plural eldership works much better for the church as well as for me. Since every issue of church life no longer rests on my shoulders alone, I can concentrate on areas where I have the most to offer the church while my fellow elders do the same. When I have to make tough decisions affecting others within the church, I do not face these decisions alone, but I have godly men to pray for me and counsel me through the decisions. Times of decision are times of danger for men serving in a single pastoral authority position. Some issues cannot be thrown into open congregational discussion: initial disciplinary matters, for example, or problems with Sunday school teachers, or restructuring ministries. But as elders meet in private, they are able to openly discuss each issue, search the Scriptures for answers, and plead with God together in prayer. A senior pastor can then give more confident leadership to his church, knowing that decisions were made through the counsel of wise men.

I have been called to preach and love doing it. Because of my calling, I have more opportunities to address the congregation, and thus have a unique platform from which to exercise authority in the church. As the church's senior pastor, I am in a position to speak, to lead, and to bring about change within the church. Although my authority is sometimes more noticeable due to my position, it is not above that of the other elders. Not all elders have this calling to preach full-time, yet all of us share in the authority of leading and giving oversight to the church. Some do so more behind the scenes, while others—such as the senior pastor—present more visibly the authority vested in plural elders. Mark Dever has expressed this well in an essay delivered at the 2004 *Issues in Baptist Polity* Conference in New Orleans.[5]

> The elder that we usually refer to as "the" pastor—the person like me—is, these days, the one who is generally set apart to fill the pulpit on Sunday. He is the one who marries and buries. He will often be paid—either part-time or fully. If the church is larger, he may be the one who hires and fires,

---

helpful in many cultural settings. The fact that these titles are interchangeable demonstrates that the biblical writers were not focused on one designation for the elder role.

5 For more information on conference papers see "Issues in Baptist Polity," Part 2; http://www. baptistcenter.com/Journal-for-Baptist-Theology-and-Ministry.html; Spring 2005.

and who sets the direction for the church as a whole. In our congregation in Washington, I am recognized as an elder by virtue of my call as the senior pastor of the church. Anyone whom we hire to work in ministry will either be called an assistant, or a pastor. The title pastor is reserved for those whom the congregation recognizes as an elder.

Among these elders, I have only one vote. Because of the leadership responsibility I have as the main public teacher, there is undoubtedly a special degree of authority that attaches to my voice in elders' meetings, but the other brothers probably have by now a pretty good assessment of where I am most concerned and most helpful, and where I have less to contribute. In an eldership, though formal authority between the members is equal, there will always be those who garner special regard in one area or another.[6]

So what is the role of the senior pastor in a plural eldership? First, he is often devoted full-time to the work of ministry. If so, he spends major time in study, prayer, preparation, proclamation, and teaching. He often will have pursued formal theological training, which equipped him for the responsibilities of senior pastor.

Second, he is needed as a leader among the elders since he devotes his full labors and energies to the ministry. Quite practically, he is in the best position to lead, initiate policy, create changes, direct ministries, and give attention to the needs of the church body. He lives each day for this purpose, while the other elders might have other vocations such as sales or medicine or construction design, as in my church. The senior pastor's fellow elders support him as they recognize the priority of preaching for New Testament ministry (1 Cor. 1–3). They also seek to sharpen and hone the senior pastor's skills and understanding of the Word through ongoing interaction.

Third, the distinct call to preach is not an equivalent to the office of elder. A church might have preachers who are not elders and elders who are not preachers, since the call to preach or ability to fill the pulpit is not required of elders. "There is no hint that all preachers must be presbyters [elders] or that all presbyters must be preachers."[7] Instead, the need to consistently, carefully feed the flock of God must not be undermined by routinely passing around pulpit responsibilities.

---

6 Mark Dever, "Baptist Elders: Contradictory, or Consistent?" www.9marks.org/partner/Article_Display_Page/0,,PTID314526|CHID598016|CIID1, 15.

7 Donald MacLeod, "Presbyter and Preachers," Monthly Record of the Free Church of Scotland, June 1983, 124.

Finally, although the senior pastor has the major platform for addressing the church, he does so with the knowledge that his fellow elders stand with him in the work of ministry. A rogue pastor who would seek to speak *ex cathedra* as though he alone knows the will of God for the church will find plural eldership restrictive. While elders should appropriately encourage and commend the senior pastor in his labors, they should also kindly remind him of his own fallibility so that he does not think more highly of himself than he ought (Phil. 2:2–3; Rom. 12:3–5).

TWO OFFICES OR THREE?

One of the strongest objections to this vision of plural eldership comes from those who insist that non-preaching elders constitute a third office in the church, instead of the dual offices of pastor/elder/overseer and deacon. Obviously, through the centuries some have created three offices by artificially dividing the office of elder between "teaching elders" and "ruling elders." But Gerald Cowen states, "There is no such thing in the New Testament as an elder who only rules and does not teach."[8] Yet Cowen goes on to caricature plural eldership as a third office in the church and thus not scriptural. He goes so far as to identify the "pastor-elder-bishop" as only the preaching pastor, writing, "No allowances are made for different kinds of elders with different qualifications. There is not one kind that is called of God to pastor and teach and another that is not."[9] In other words, if a man is not called to serve as preaching pastor of a church, he has no business being an elder. Interestingly, Cowen admits, "It is true that whenever the term *elder* or *bishop* is used in the New Testament it is used in the plural, which would mean that the general practice of the churches in New Testament times was to have at least two elders."[10] Yet since the New Testament does not set a precise number of "pastor-elders a church should have," Cowen bypasses plural eldership in favor of one leader called "the pastor,"[11] seemingly ignoring his own exegesis of the biblical texts.

Many of those making the strongest objections to plural elders will acknowledge that a church can have multiple pastors. Indeed, they might happily admit a pastor of education, pastor of worship, pastor of students, pastor of children, pastor of administration, pastor of missions, pastor of evangelism, and even pastor of

8 Gerald Cowen, *Who Rules the Church?: Examining Congregational Leadership and Church Government* (Nashville: Broadman & Holman, 2003), 39.
9 Ibid., 82.
10 Ibid., 14.
11 Ibid., 14–16.

recreation. Certainly, not all of these pastors desire to be in the pulpit or are gifted to preach. Yet they are called pastors or associate pastors by the church. They do not fit the model of preaching pastor, but are still called "pastors"—plural. They are involved whenever the church needs an examination council to set apart men to the ministry or diaconate. They are expected to fulfill the qualifications noted in 1 Timothy 3 and Titus 1 for overseers and elders. But they have different gifts, different ministries, and different strengths that contribute to the total ministry of the church.

Cannot that same logic be applied to the plural eldership of both staff and *non-staff* members of the elders? While an elder might not be called or gifted to preach, he might be especially gifted at leading or organizing or administrating along with teaching. He contributes to the church in a different way than the senior pastor, offering strengths that the senior pastor might lack. Since there is no New Testament requirement that an elder must preach, then we have to conclude that if a man possesses the other character qualities noted and is a capable teacher, then he may well be a good candidate to share in leading the church.

CHURCH STAFF MEMBERS AS ELDERS

Some churches deliberately have only full-time staff as elders, and all their staff members are elders. In this way the church is able to function with a plurality of elders. But to exclude non-staff members from the eldership weakens the leadership group and deprives them of some of the most capable Christian servants in the church. It also places all leadership in the paid staff. However, when staff elders leave for other ministries or are removed from their positions, their departures can weaken and destabilize the eldership. On the other hand, a blend of staff and non-staff elders provides more continuity in the church's leadership. Such a blend also helps the elders evaluate each issue from a variety of angles.

But there's a second issue here: Should every staff member automatically serve as an elder? Not necessarily. For one, administrative staff often function like paid deacons; they need to be godly and gifted in their ministry, but the qualifications for their job don't necessarily match the qualifications for eldership. Further, some pastoral staff, such as pastoral assistants or youth workers, might be on their way to being elders but are not yet fully qualified. They might be too young to offer the wise counsel necessary, or still unproven through the crucible of difficult times, and thus lacking the insights of life experience that are so valuable in an elder.

During my college days I served as a staff member in two churches. At nineteen and twenty years old—and on staff—I was definitely not mature enough to exercise the authority of eldership. I did, however, have the ability to serve as a staff member, contributing to the overall work of ministry. But in decisions regarding doctrine and discipline, men who had longer track records of applying the Word of God to their lives were needed to lead the churches.

It appears best to have a balance between staff and non-staff elders, if at all possible. In this way, the staff cannot be charged with "stacking the deck" on important votes, especially financial matters that affect the staff. If approved by the rest of the elders, it may be beneficial for staff members to sit in on elders' meetings, to contribute when necessary, and to learn from the elders' interaction. For a staff member to hold the title *elder,* though, should not be a given and is not necessary for every staff role. If being an elder does become "everything" to a staff member, he may not be ready to handle the mature responsibilities of eldership.

ELDERS AND DEACONS

Elders cannot do everything that needs to be accomplished in the church. Deacons serve in partnership with elders as the second of the two offices of the church, serving physical needs. Each church must work out its own details of how elders and deacons function, but at minimum, these two offices should seek to complement each other rather than to compete. Their duties might occasionally overlap, and in such times they should communicate well with each other, realizing that their service together meets the leadership needs in the church.

A strong deacon body lays the groundwork for effective elders, allowing elders to focus on their particular responsibilities while focusing on necessary but often mundane tasks. We have found that giving each deacon a task or area of tasks helps to facilitate the work with greater efficiency. Rather than focusing on meetings and decisions, the deacons oversee an area of church life, such as security, finance, or buildings.

If a church chooses to have committees, then the elders and deacons might take part in the committees of the church, perhaps even having one elder or deacon assigned to each committee. Our elders nominate all committee members and decide which committees are needed each year in order to adequately serve the church. With few exceptions, each committee has at least one elder or deacon. Since these individuals are most aware of the direction of the church, they help the committees to remain focused on how to best utilize the gifts of the church, thus maintaining continuity in the overall work of the church.

ELDERS' MEETINGS

Our elders meet on a monthly basis, but also maintain regular contact with each other through email and phone conversations. We serve together, but we are also friends who pray for each other and hold each other accountable in our Christian walks. Meetings are planned to best utilize our time together and to consider the most necessary areas of church needs. A typical agenda from one of our elders' meetings might be as follows.

- Scripture reading and prayer
- Review contacts with members, identifying needs or additional contacts needed
- Study and present research on a doctrinal issue
- Discuss a potential church discipline issue
- Work on committee selections
- Discuss replacing teachers for upcoming Bible classes
- Plan small group and Sunday School studies
- Discuss potential church planting opportunities
- Discuss upcoming mission-trip needs and how to best involve the congregation
- Discuss ongoing pastoral internships; review an application for our internship
- Discuss evangelistic outreach ideas for summer and fall

Sometimes we do not complete the agenda, in which cases we might meet an additional time or carry on the discussion via email. When we bring on new elders we add training to the agenda in order to introduce the new elders to their ministry. We have found that a two- to three-hour period is not always enough to pray, discuss church family needs, deal with issues of discipline, and make plans for the church. So we might plan a retreat in order to concentrate time on pressing matters or the larger planning issues of the church. In our times together we've learned to value openness, forthrightness, gentleness, and humility.

ELDER AND CONGREGATIONAL MEETINGS

In Baptist church life, business meetings often bring carnage. I have rarely met a Baptist pastor or long-time church member who does not have war stories to tell about members' meetings. But this should never be the case when the

Spirit-indwelt, regularly disciplined, regenerate membership of a local church assembles to discuss membership issues.

Further, the elders should handle much of the business that would otherwise be discussed by the congregation, who, for the most part, might be uninformed. If a church trusts its elders as men of God who serve for the good of the church, the majority of issues that concern the local church need not be discussed in members' meetings. Certainly the members should be consulted on major issues, such as calling an associate pastor, buying property, building a new facility, or changing the church structure. But elders and deacons work together to address the regular business of church life—elders concentrating on the spiritual, and deacons concentrating on the temporal—so that the church body can concentrate on the work of ministry.

Each church will need to develop a timeframe suitable for congregational meetings. However often a church decides to hold meetings, some type of monthly communication from the elders and deacons, keeping the congregation up-to-date on the latest changes, decisions, and needs, might solidify the church's harmony. Some churches have found that every-other-month, quarterly, or bi-yearly meetings work well. Others opt for a yearly congregational meeting that considers the church budget and recommendations for the year ahead. If a church has been accustomed to business meetings that wade through endless details, then a pastor would be wise to slowly taper this kind of tradition rather than abruptly end it.

At times, of course, the congregation should be called to corporate action. Accepting new members and dismissing from membership those who have moved or requested a membership transfer calls for brief congregational meetings. In considering disciplinary matters, my church has followed the practice of addressing them during the church's monthly gathering at the Lord's Supper. Such timing seems appropriate considering the sanctity of the service as a *church* ordinance that acknowledges the person and work of Christ and the effect of his work upon the entire church body. One of the privileges of church membership is admission to the Lord's Table, so it is fitting that the church would exclude someone from the Table in conjunction with celebrating the Table.

ELDERS' TERMS OF SERVICE AND DISMISSAL

The polity framework sketched in the New Testament does not give every detail; rather, it leaves some things to the wisdom of the local churches. For example, while the New Testament affirms plural eldership, it does not prescribe a set number of elders for each church or how long each elder is to serve. It would be inadvisable, for example, to establish a rotating system of elders unless the size and maturity of the church ensures an adequate number of elders to maintain plurality. Rotation has its pluses, in that more men will be able to serve the church, the elder body will maintain more diversity, and "fresh troops" will be provided for the demanding work of eldering. But rotation assumes that each year mature, qualified men will be ready to join the elder body.

A disadvantage to rotation is that wise, mature leaders who understand the church's needs rotate out of active service. That can be a great loss to the church. Further, rotation establishes a quota to fill, even if the church lacks qualified men to serve. Filling spots with unqualified men will certainly weaken the effectiveness of the entire elder body.

Perhaps a better way to address term length—particularly in churches that have previously grown accustomed to a rotating deacon body—is to begin with elders serving an unspecified length, with the caveat that a review of rotation and tenure will take place three or five years after beginning plural elder leadership. Elders' tenure can be reviewed as part of reexamining the church's governing documents (constitution, bylaws, polity manual, etc.).

The only New Testament passage addressing the removal of elders relates to discipline: "Do not receive an accusation against an elder except on the basis of two or three witnesses" (1 Tim. 5:19). Since elders are open to congregational scrutiny, and at times baseless accusations, Paul adopts the Old Testament practice of requiring two or three witnesses to substantiate an accusation of serious offense (Deut. 19:15). John Calvin wrote, "None are more exposed to slanders and insults than godly teachers. They may perform their duties correctly and conscientiously, yet 'they never avoid a thousand criticisms.'"[12] Paul does not specify what type of sin falls into this category, but it can be assumed that it is serious enough to call into question the elder's capacity to continue serving the church. Paul says further, "Those who continue in sin, rebuke in the presence of all, so that the rest also will be fearful of sinning" (1 Tim. 5:20). If an accused elder continues in sin, the church must take action to reestablish the testimony of the elders and the church. Since one of the four primary responsibilities of elders is to model the Christian life, breaking this trust by continual sin requires a public rebuke of the elder before the congregation. The term for 'rebuke' implies that the charges of sin have been clearly substantiated and that the elder has been found guilty. Although the text does not give details, there is little doubt that the convicted elder is removed from office in the same way that a church member would be

---

12 John Calvin, *The Epistles of Paul to Timothy and Titus* (1548–50 reprint, London: Oliver and Boyd, 1964), 263, quoted and expanded upon in John Stott, *Guard the Truth: The Message of 1 Timothy and Titus* (Downers Grove, IL: InterVarsity, 1966), 138.

censured and removed from active membership. It would make no sense for him to continue serving after such public rebuke of his sin. As seminary president Albert Mohler has stated, "Clearly, leadership carries a higher burden, and the sins of an elder cause an even greater injury to the church. The public rebuke is necessary, for the elder sins against the entire congregation."[13]

ELDERS: NOW, LATER, OR NEVER

Now that we have investigated the biblical teaching on plural eldership and offered recommendations for establishing elder leadership in churches, the final hurdle is determining the appropriate response. Some who study the subject of elders declare that they will *never* consider it for their church polity. Some traditions are deeply ingrained and some interpretations of New Testament polity differ from what has been presented here. In such cases, consider the following exhortation: Whatever type of leadership structure you embrace, by all means determine to raise the standards for leaders to match the biblical requirements. The failure to meet those requirements is the greatest deficiency in church leadership. A lack of godly men—men who are saturated in the Scriptures, wise through the application of God's Word to daily life, and faithful in spiritual disciplines—leaves any leadership structure deficient. So if plural elder leadership does not match your views of polity, at least give major attention to elevating your church's standards to mirror the biblical demands on spiritual leaders.

Perhaps while reading this book you have determined to begin moving toward plural elder leadership in your own church, and you are ready to do it *now!* Not so fast, please. Remember to lay the groundwork. Radical changes in church polity might not find a welcome reception, so proceed judiciously. Chapter 17 offers a model for bringing about the change in congregational thinking and implementing the transition to elder leadership. Study it carefully, adapt it to your own setting, and by God's grace, move forward.

Some of you may find plural elder leadership appealing, yet your tenure at your church has been brief, and you don't want that tenure to quickly end. So you are pondering the idea of making a change in your church structure *later*. If that is you, get started *now*. Focus on faithfully teaching Scripture to your church, because more important than changing your polity is developing a congregation that studies and applies the Word to daily life. Set your focus, by God's grace, on

---

13 R. Albert Mohler, "Church Discipline: The Missing Mark," in *Polity: Biblical Arguments on How to Conduct Church Life*, Mark Dever, ed. (Washington, DC: Center for Church Reform, 2001), 53.

developing just such a church. The polity change will follow in due time, because a congregation that loves the Word of God and desires to follow whatever the Lord has spoken will be open to plural eldership. Keep challenging your church to study the Scriptures thoroughly, to ask questions of the biblical texts, and to think biblically.

Changing church polity to align with the teaching of the New Testament can be a fascinating journey. At times you'll be like Daniel Boone as you hack your way through the underbrush that has covered the clear paths of God's revelation. On other occasions you might feel as though you are in a hot air balloon, rising to great heights in the church's grasp of Scripture, only to suddenly sink as you strive for the changes demanded in the Word. Stay on the journey, knowing that the Lord of the church will one day call you to report on how faithfully you discharged your duties to his flock. And maybe along the journey, you will know the joy of leading your church to embrace plural elder leadership. Then, a new phase of the journey begins.

REFLECTIONS

- Think about the subject of authority in the church. How would you characterize the authority of the congregation and the authority of the elders? In what ways does this authority differ?
- How can the senior pastor function with elders who share equal authority?
- How do the elders and deacons cooperate in service for the good of the church?
- What is your response to this study of plural elder leadership? In what ways does this challenge your previous thoughts about church polity?

CHAPTER TWENTY

WHAT YOU WILL FEEL

In the 2011 film *The Iron Lady,* Margaret Thatcher, played by Meryl Streep, is asked by her doctor how she's feeling. Thatcher replies, "What? What am I 'bound to be feeling?' People don't think anymore. They feel.... One of the great problems of our age is that we are governed by people who care more about feelings than they do about thoughts and ideas. Thoughts and ideas. That interests me. Ask me what I'm thinking."

This book has been about thinking. Thinking about what the Bible says about church government. Thinking about your denomination's or church's polity. Thinking about how best to bring about reform. Thinking and knowing are primary. Thatcher's character is right.

YOU WILL FEEL...

But I would be remiss if I didn't say anything about feelings. An elder does not merely think his way through his calling and tasks; he feels. And the range of emotions may be surprising. Take comfort and courage from the list that follows.

Proud

Being called to serve as an elder among a respected body of elders may initially cause you to feel proud. "I finally made it!" I suspect this will give way soon after the work begins. Yet elders will face an ongoing temptation to pride, not just in the same way all Christians do, but in a way that is heightened by their office. Paul had this in mind when he wrote that an elder must not be "a new convert, so that he will not become conceited and fall into the condemnation incurred by the devil" (1 Tim. 3:6).

Energized

Sitting "at the gate" with godly men who know their theology and have seemingly unending pastoral wisdom is eye-opening and invigorating. Even though this is rightly energizing, it's probably good, when you become an elder, to close your mouth and simply listen for the first few months. Take it all in. Learn.

Shocked

With a simple vote of the congregation, you are now an elder, and so you begin attending elders' meetings. But now, for the first time, you are hearing about members of your congregation that you had no idea struggled with such heinous sin. As a non-elder you thought your church was a holy community. As an elder you discover layers of sin that would make your grandmother blush. When you're shocked by sin, channel that concern into prayer for the sheep.

Perplexed

The complexity of people's sin can be unnerving. And while Scripture is sufficient to enable us to live in a way that pleases God, figuring out how to apply Scripture to particularly messy situations can be far from easy.

An example: A husband commits adultery. He repents. His wife decides not to take him back. Should either be disciplined? Can they divorce and both remain as members in good standing? What role does the church play? How hard should the elders press for reconciliation?

This is where a plurality of elders is crucial. Time and again you'll discover that wisdom comes as you work together to resolve the sticking points.

Divided

Being out of sorts with the elders or with any individual elder feels a lot like being out of sorts with one's spouse. Above all, the elders are to be united, right? They are to model submission and lead with one voice, aren't they? Yet, at times, there will be theological disagreement or even personal compatibility problems between men. So do all you can to make peace.

Unappreciated

Like your children who have no idea of the sacrifices you make for them, the sheep you've been charged to protect, instruct, love, and discipline will undoubtedly leave you feeling unappreciated. Read and re-read 1 Corinthians 13 and consider what it means to love the sheep. Consider what burdens the apostle Paul bore for the churches, and imitate his affection for God's people.

Misunderstood

Even the most carefully crafted words can be misconstrued. An elder has to know that his well-intentioned words will at times be wrongly received. Patience, forbearance, and a ready willingness to explain things again will foster understanding and preserve unity.

Judged

The feeling of being judged will come on you in waves as angry people leave your church over a theological position you hold or a policy decision you made. Labor to believe the best about others. If they go, wish them well, pray for them, and speak kindly about them. And remember that God alone is Judge.

Like Quitting

At some point, whether due to discord among your fellow elders or fatigue from bearing more than perhaps you ought, you will feel like quitting. Before you quit, get counsel from your fellow elders. Don't make a rash decision. Hebrews 10:36 says, " For you have need of endurance, so that when you have done the will of God, you may receive what was promised." Knowing your need for endurance as you take on the mantle of elder will help you persevere.

Out of Balance

"How do you balance home, work and church?" That's probably the question I get asked the most from fellow elders in my church and other churches. But think of any number of biblical characters and ask yourself if their lives looked balanced. Abraham? Noah? Moses? Jesus? Paul?

In short, I think we can be tempted to value balance like we value comfort—a bit too strongly. "Balanced" people probably don't go into overseas missions, let alone stay up all night with a sick member in the hospital. "Balanced" people don't give their money away, let alone get up early to pray with and disciple a younger man.

If you take on the responsibility of being an elder, you and your family need to know that life will, at times, be out of balance. You will, at times, be heavily weighted toward things at church. The key is making sure that that is not the default setting. If you have a busy day, week, or month at church, make sure your family is fully informed and then swing things back the other way the following day, week, or month.

But ultimately we are called to faithfulness—at home, work and church—not balance.

Joyful

When you give yourself to the Lord's work in unity with fellow elders, it is a delight. Laboring with brothers in prayer and counsel and then seeing the Lord bring the desired fruit in a repentant sinner's heart is simply a joy. What better work is there than to calibrate your church's curriculum, ensure the preaching is sound, build a loving community, and then have unbelievers enter your body, smell the aroma of Christ, and respond in faith?

Content

Bearing a burden by oneself is excruciating. Rest and contentment can be found in sharing that burden with godly brothers as they wait with you for resolution on any number of matters with which the elders are wrestling.

United

Psalm 133:1 says, "Behold, how good and how pleasant it is for brothers to dwell together in unity!" In the same way that a child prospers when his mother and father are in agreement, a church will prosper when brother elders are united for their good. It is a sweet feeling to be united with godly men in a godly cause.

Wiser

If he's honest, every elder will tell you that he can have his mind changed several times in the course of a discussion. Hearing brother after brother unpack his thoughts and apply various parts of Scripture to a particular problem will do this. In this process wisdom is gained. That gained wisdom will trickle out in an elder's teaching in the church as well as in his example at home.

Loved and Respected

A congregation that is well-shepherded will reciprocate with love and respect. They may not agree with every decision, but they will lovingly defer to the elders because they have benefited from the elders' faithful oversight time and again.

Like You Made a Difference

I love how Isaiah describes the collaborative effort between man and God in Isaiah 26:12 when he writes, "LORD, You will establish peace for us, since You have also performed for us all our works." Elders above all people should recognize God's providential and regenerating work in their midst. But that's not to ignore God's use of human instruments. As you see some brought from death to life, as you hear baptismal testimonies, as you see marriages restored, or young couples leave home to take the gospel to an unreached people group, you will know your work made a difference.

JOY AND REWARD AHEAD

Margaret Thatcher had another memorable quote: "If my critics saw me walking over the Thames they would say it was because I couldn't swim." In other words, some people will always find something to criticize. But consider what the Lord Jesus Christ endured "for the joy set before him" (Heb. 12:2). There is joy and reward ahead for those who serve faithfully, despite what critics, detractors, and, sometimes, even your own emotions may say.

CHAPTER TWENTY-ONE

LEADERSHIP DEVELOPMENT
IN HARD PLACES

Missionaries, New Churches, and Elders

Near the end of the twentieth century, the East African nation of Rwanda bore the title of the most evangelized and Christianized country on the continent. Around ninety percent of the country had been baptized as Christians. Much of the Christian influence resulted from the widespread East African Revival that began in Rwanda in 1927 and then spread to different denominations and neighboring countries.[1]

Yet in 1994 conflict arose between the minority Tutsi and the majority Hutu people groups, the former having been exiled by the latter but who were now trying to regain governmental control. Ultimately, the conflict led to the slaughter of almost one million people in a nation of less than nine million. At a mission gathering, James Engel expressed what some nationals in Rwanda were feeling: "In all of your zeal for evangelism, you brought us Christ but never taught us how to live."[2] A graduate of the Rwanda Institute of Evangelical Theology explained the standard practice

---

1 Patrick Johnstone, *Operation World: The Day-by-Day Guide to Praying for the World* (Grand Rapids: Zondervan, 1993), 472; Glenn Kendall, "Rwanda," *Evangelical Dictionary of World Missions*, A. Scott Moreau, ed (Grand Rapids: Baker Books, 2000), 842–843.
2 James Engel, "Beyond the Numbers Game," *Christianity Today*, August 7, 2000, 54 in David Sills, *Reaching and Teaching: A Call to Great Commission Obedience* (Chicago: Moody Press, 2010), 55.

among Rwandan churches: "We used the Bible, but we didn't really *think biblically*, or always *teach the Bible accurately.*"[3] John Robb and James Hill observed that most in the Rwandan church were nominal Christians due to the church's failure "to do the work of discipling of these multitudes."[4] A third-generation missionary to Rwanda, Meg Guillebaud, witnessed firsthand the ungodliness in leaders as well as the shallow teaching, with the "result Christians were not being discipled."[5] She further pointed to a pervasive syncretism that weakened Christian influence in this highly evangelized country.[6] Though Rwanda was once lauded for effective evangelism, the 1994 genocide blighted nationals' confidence in the church since so many professing Christians perpetrated the killings.[7]

What difference would it have made if the Rwandan church had learned to think biblically because their leaders had faithfully taught them the Word of God and discipled them in the faith, just as Jesus had commanded? The rapid growth of the Rwandan church left a leadership gap that might have changed if the last charge of the Great Commission ("teaching them to observe all that I commanded you") had received as much attention as the first ("Go therefore and make disciples, baptizing them"; Matt. 28:19–20). The Great Commission demands ongoing teaching and training.[8]

Rwanda had official freedom of religion during the days of revival, but what about other places on the globe where open gospel proclamation is prohibited and believers regularly face persecution? What will keep new believers from reverting to their former religion or from syncretizing Christian worship with pagan superstitions? Missionaries face the significant challenge of identifying and developing leaders in the "hard places" of the globe—areas of rapidly developing churches and areas of persecution. While the same need confronts church planters in heavily churched areas, the issues are vastly different where few mature Christians exist.[9] The desire

---

3 Alexis Nemeyimana, African Inland Mission On-Field Media. *So We Do Not Lose Heart*, video from AIM International Online, MPEG; accessed September 20, 2009; in Sills, *Reaching and Teaching*, 162; italics Sills; http://www.aimint.org/usa/videos/so_we_do_not_lose_heart.html.
4 John Robb and James Hill, *The Peace-Making Power of Prayer: Equipping Christians to Transform the World* (Nashville: Broadman & Holman, 2000), 178–179.
5 Meg Guillebaud, *Rwanda: The Land God Forgot? Revival, Genocide, and Hope* (Grand Rapids: Kregel, 2002), 285.
6 Ibid., 287.
7 Kendall, "Rwanda," 843.
8 Sills, *Reaching*, 55, citing Paul Washer, "Gospel 101," *HeartCry Magazine* 54 (Sept–Nov 2007): 6.
9 Bruce Riley Ashford, "A Theologically-Driven Missiology," in Chuck Lawless and Adam Greenway, eds., *Great Commission Resurgence: Fulfilling God's Mandate in Our Time* (Nashville: B&H, 2010), 202–203, identifies two missiological issues related to Church Planting Movements (CPMs). The first raises questions about the theology and methodology in CPMs; the second, the focus of this chapter, looks at "the question of how soon a believer might be recognized as an elder." This situation arises in both CPMs and persecution settings, so this chapter will consider the overall leadership need in both.

to make disciples must also include plans to teach and train them. This chapter's thesis is that new churches in hard places must identify and develop shepherding leaders (elders) who will teach, model, and train the church toward spiritual maturity. Leadership development is particularly challenging where Church Planting Movements (CPMs) have left multiple leaderless churches and where persecution makes leadership development seem improbable. In this chapter we will explore why and how missionaries must prioritize developing leaders and appointing elders in new churches in hard places. Further, I will draw from the Pastoral Epistles to investigate how soon a convert can serve as an elder, and then conclude with a plan for leadership development in hard places.

A MISSIOLOGICAL QUANDARY

As missions professor Bruce Ashford has pointed out, Southern Baptists "have long been praying for and working towards the birth of CPMs among the unreached people groups of the world, and indeed, even in our own country."[10] Some of the reported CPMs are in regions known for the persecution of Christians. Yet he rightly warns that, since our goal is "the increase of God's glory and kingdom," nothing should supplant the priority of God's glory, particularly by reductionist methods that lack biblical fidelity. "For this reason, we are concerned not only with rapidity, but also with the purity of the gospel and the health of the church." So neither an "inordinate emphasis on rapidity" nor a doctrinal purity with no concern for multiplication is acceptable.[11]

Yet if God is pleased to rapidly multiply the church, such positive news may ironically perplex church planters and missionaries. Quickly growing churches need quickly maturing leaders to shepherd them. Therefore, missionaries face the question of how soon a convert with leadership potential might be recognized as an elder.[12] Does one's age and length of experience as a believer figure into leadership appointment? How will churches in persecution-prone regions with only young believers press on toward maturity?

The problem is more acute where persecution is common. A missionary may need to limit his time with new churches so that his presence does not endanger them. Yet failing to establish some semblance of leadership for the newly birthed churches is a gross dereliction of duty. "The challenge of creative access countries," missiologist David Sills reminds us, "does not preclude fulfilling the

---

10 Ibid., 202.
11 Ibid., 202–203.
12 Ibid., 203.

biblical commands to teach them to observe everything Christ commanded us."[13] The missionary must establish an appropriate plan for shepherding new churches, even if it seems inadequate. Specifically, he faces three challenges: (1) carefully training and appointing leaders who demonstrate the type of character called for in 1 Timothy 3 and Titus 1; (2) quickly implementing a leadership structure that will outlast his personal ministry among them; and (3) commending the church to the Lord who is able to protect them. This was the pattern that Paul and Barnabas followed during their first missionary journey (Acts 14:23). Mission leader Daniel Sinclair calls this the "one consistent ending point" used by the apostles and their partners in church planting.[14] They labored to establish a leadership team that would shepherd new churches.

Each local church needs indigenous leadership, and in most congregations "that should consist of a plurality of elders."[15] That is the ideal to which every congregation should aspire. Yet circumstances may require creativity within biblical bounds to establish an initial leadership framework that will suffice until the ideal can be reached. Missionaries will need to guard against imposing a Western church model in either CPMs or persecution settings. As Edward Dayton and David Fraser correctly state, he "must allow the true essentials of the church to have controlling power over the accidental features of organization, institution, and tradition," distinguishing "between the exemplary and the mandatory in Scripture."[16] In the midst of laying the groundwork for ongoing teaching and leadership in new churches, Scripture must be kept central. This is paramount, even as missionaries consider questions of contextualization.

AN ECCLESIOLOGICAL NECESSITY: THE RATIONALE FOR SHEPHERD LEADERS

The New Testament requires qualified leaders for sustaining the health of local congregations.[17] This is indeed an essential mark of a healthy church.[18] Leaders— whether called elders, pastors, or overseers—must give attention to teaching,

13 Sills, *Reaching and Teaching*, 68.
14 Daniel Sinclair, *A Vision of the Possible: Pioneer Church Planting in Teams* (Colorado Springs: Authentic Publishing, 2005), 219.
15 Gary Corwin, "Church Planting 101," *Evangelical Missions Quarterly* (April 2005, 41:2), 142.
16 Edward R. Dayton and David A. Fraser, *Planning Strategies for World Evangelization*, rev ed (Grand Rapids: Eerdmans, 1990), 242.
17 See examples in Acts 1:15–26; 2:42–47; 4:32–35; 5:1–11; 6:1–7; 11:19–26; 14:21–23; 20:17–35; 1 Thess. 5:12–13; 1 Tim. 3:1, 5; 5:17; 2 Tim. 1:6–8; 4:1–5; Titus 1:5–9; Heb. 13:7, 17; James 5:14–15; 1 Peter 5:1–4.
18 Mark Dever, *Nine Marks of a Healthy Church*, exp. ed. (Wheaton. IL: Crossway, 2004), 218–243.

modeling, training, exhorting, disciplining, and correcting. Nineteenth-century Presbyterian David Dickson explained, "The eldership, *under some form or other*, is absolutely necessary for a healthy and useful church."[19] He goes on to show how Wesleyans adopted a form of eldership with class leaders, Baptists and Congregationalists with deacons, and Episcopalians with a formally sanctioned lay agency.[20] In other words, the name or title is not as important as the character and function of the leader. Pastor-theologian Philip Ryken regards elder leadership as essential to protecting God's investment in the church. He asserts, "God's plan was to place the church under the care of shepherds."[21] Daniel Sinclair concurs, pointing out that in his extensive observations of pioneer mission work, the churches that fail to establish elder plurality inevitably fall apart, while those with elder plurality thrive.[22] So the aim to establish shepherd leaders is never optional for missionaries and church planters.

One reason is quite clear: church members are sheep who need shepherds to direct them toward spiritual maturity. They should not be as "sheep without a shepherd" (Matt. 9:36). Following the lead of the Lord (Acts 20:28; 1 Pet. 5:2; cf. John 21:16), both Paul and Peter used the verb "to shepherd" (*poimainein*) to describe the work of caring for, protecting, and nurturing the church.[23]

In general the New Testament apostles and elders provide a clear model for developing healthy churches, as in Paul's example, "We proclaim him, admonishing every man and teaching every man with all wisdom, so that we may present every man complete in Christ. For this purpose I labor, striving according to his power, which mightily works within me" (Col. 1:28–29). The "We" in "We proclaim him" is plural, which is to say that evangelism and disciple-making belong to the wider church, not just to the apostle.[24] Future generations of shepherd leaders will bear the same responsibilities. These responsibilities, we see from the passage, include "admonishing every man and teaching every man." Proclaiming Christ, it appears, involves a shepherd leader in intense pastoral care and ongoing instruction.[25] Peter O'Brien observes, "As a true pastor Paul will not be satisfied with anything

19 David Dickson, *The Elder and His Work* (Phillipsburg, NJ: P & R Publishing, 2004 from 19th C. reprint, n.d.), 26; italics added to emphasize that elder plurality is not practiced monolithically.
20 Ibid.
21 Philip Graham Ryken, *City on a Hill: Reclaiming the Biblical Pattern for the Church in the 21st Century* (Chicago: Moody Press, 2003), 97–98.
22 Sinclair, *A Vision of the Possible*, 220.
23 *BDAG*, 842.
24 James D. G. Dunn, *The Epistles to the Colossians and to Philemon*, NIGTC (Grand Rapids: Eerdmans, 1996), 124.
25 Peter T. O'Brien, *Colossians, Philemon*, WBC (Waco, TX: Word Books, 1982), 87. See also Eduard Lohse, *Colossians and Philemon*, Hermeneia (Philadelphia: Fortress Press, 1971), 77.

less than the full Christian maturity of every believer."[26] Every shepherd leader must adopt the same goal.

The propensity of Christians to wander into sinful practices, false teaching, heresy, disunity, and even syncretism calls for vigilance and appropriate corrections by shepherd leaders.[27] Sills tells about the syncretism he observed while serving among indigenous Andean pastors, including pouring out the dregs of their drinks to an earth goddess, as well as a funeral service for a toddler incorporating Catholicism, animism, and evangelical traditions.[28] Churches cannot be left to fend for themselves without godly, trained leaders.

Leadership and Church Maturity

Every church needs regular training in Scripture in order to grow. And this requires a church to have maturing leaders who will consistently teach and train them in the Word.[29] J. I. Packer places the knowledge of Scripture at the heart of growth in godliness, identifying genuine godliness as (1) "a life of *faith in God's promises* . . . (2) [that] involves *obedience to God's laws* . . . (3) [and] is always marked by *delight in God's truth.*"[30] Apart from understanding the Scriptures, a professing believer has no ability to grow in godliness.

This means that evangelism and ongoing teaching are not "mutually exclusive efforts," as though one properly exists without the other.[31] Rather, training new believers to grow in godliness protects the purity of the gospel and yields an attractive evangelistic witness. It is not surprising, therefore, that the great evangelistic text, the Great Commission, anticipates the necessity of shepherd leaders faithfully teaching God's flock to observe all that Jesus commanded (Matt. 28:20; see also 1 Pet. 5:1–5).

Maintaining the purity of the gospel stands alongside growth in godliness. Paul rebuked the Galatians because they were "so quickly deserting him who called you by the grace of Christ, for a different gospel" (Gal. 1:6). While the

---

26 O'Brien, *Colossians, Philemon*, 90.
27 See Matt. 18:15–20 which calls for corrective discipline in the church; note also the many examples of the disciples wandering and thus in need of shepherds to correct, warn, and instruct: 1 Cor. 3:1–8, 16–20; 5:1–13; Gal. 1:6–9; 3:1–5; 5:7–9; Phil. 4:2–3; 1 Thess. 5:14; 2 Thess. 3:6–15; 1 Tim. 1:3–7, 18–20; 4:11–16; 2 Tim. 2:22–26; 4:10; Titus 1:10–16; 2:6; Heb. 5:11–14; 6:9–12; 2 Peter 1:8–15; 1 John 5:16, 21; 2 John 7–11; 3 John 9–11; Rev. 2–3.
28 Sills, *Reaching*, 161.
29 E.g., Matt. 28:19–20; 21:15–17; Acts 20:28; Eph. 4:11–16; 5:19; 1 Tim. 4:11–16; 5:17; 2 Tim. 2:2, 14–15; 3:14–17; 4:1–5; Titus 1:3, 9; Heb. 2:1–4; James 1:18–25; 1 Peter 1:22–2:3; 2 Peter 1:19–21; 3:14–18.
30 J. I. Packer, *God Has Spoken* (Grand Rapids: Baker Books, 1979), 126–132, italics original.
31 Sills, *Reaching*, 36.

congregation should be corporately involved, as "the pillar and support of the truth" (1 Tim. 3:15), the elders should be out front in preserving the gospel. Paul shared this concern with the Ephesian elders, warning them about the "wolf-theology" that would creep in and distort the Christian faith. He also instructed Titus to make establishing elders among the Cretan churches a major priority. Elders would work against those "who must be silenced because they are upsetting whole families, teaching things they should not teach for the sake of sordid gain" (Titus 1:11). John Stott sums up the New Testament's defense strategy well: "When false teachers increase, the most appropriate long-term strategy is to multiply the number of true teachers, who are equipped to rebut and refute error."[32] Young believers in rapidly multiplying churches need the direction and doctrinal training offered by shepherd leaders. Without this they are far more likely to fall into false teaching.[33]

Examples to the Flock

Not only do young churches in hard places need doctrinal protection, they need good models of the Christian life to flesh out how to live in line with the demands of the gospel, as we considered earlier in the book. John Hammett includes this as he identifies four responsibilities of church shepherds: (1) the ministry of the Word; (2) the work of pastoral ministry; (3) exercising oversight or leadership; and (4) serving as examples to the flock.[34] It is possible for leaders to do excellent work in teaching and oversight, yet fail as shepherd leaders by neglecting to model the Christian life.

Paul told Timothy, his delegate with the Ephesian church, "show yourself an example of those who believe…. Pay close attention to yourself and to your teaching" (1 Tim. 4:12, 16). In a later letter he explained what this meant, even as Timothy followed his example: "Now you followed my teaching, conduct, purpose, faith, patience, love, perseverance, persecutions, and sufferings, such as happened to me at Antioch, at Iconium and at Lystra" (2 Tim. 3:10–11). Paul exhorted the Philippians, "Brethren, join in following my example, and observe those who walk according to the pattern you have in us" (Phil. 3:17).[35] Doctrine

---

32 John Stott, *Guard the Truth: The Message of 1 Timothy & Titus* (Downers Grove, IL: InterVarsity Press, 1996), 179.

33 See Witmer, *Shepherd Leaders*, 45–73 as he traces historically the ebb and flow of elder leadership in local churches with corresponding effects on congregations.

34 John S. Hammett, *Biblical Foundations for Baptist Churches: A Contemporary Ecclesiology* (Grand Rapids: Kregel Academic & Professional, 2005), 163–166.

35 The use of *summimetai* or "fellow-imitator," and *tupon*, "type, pattern, model, [moral] example," demonstrate Paul's concern that concrete examples be set for the church. BDAG, 958, 1019–1020.

is not enough. Shepherd leaders must show how the Christian life touches every aspect of relationships, community, family, and work life.

Leadership: Always a Priority

Amidst the rapid expansion of American churches, it is important to remember that the need for spiritual leadership is just as acute in other places around the world. Yet a major difference exists. North American churches possess a larger pool of available spiritual leaders and nearly limitless resources that can assist the new churches until leaders are raised up from within.[36]

The Majority World is another story altogether. Most church leaders have no formal theological education. "In fact, there are approximately two million pastoral leaders in the Majority World," according to research by mission educator John Balmer, Jr., "and 1.8 million (ninety percent) of them have had no formal ministerial training."[37] The lack of theological education often results in syncretism, as animistic practices continue within a twisted, sub-Christian framework.[38] The answer is not necessarily found by forming Western-styled seminaries. Costs, political regulations, and other logistics can make this impractical. Even more, the tendency toward ethnocentrism causes Western viewpoints to neglect contextualizing theological training to appropriately adapt to a given people group.[39] Theologian David Clark explains that biases toward certain forms and hermeneutical approaches can lead missionaries to naturally "exert powerful shaping influence" on how the Majority World thinks theologically, instead of helping them engage the biblical worldview directly.[40] So the answer to training shepherd leaders is not to move Western structures into the Majority World. Instead, missionaries will need to amplify content, while being flexible in form, within the cultural context of new churches.[41]

---

36 Nearly 70,000 students were enrolled in ATS seminaries in Canada and the US in 2009; "Annual Data Tables," accessed September 15, 2010; http://www.ats.edu/Resources/Publications/Documents/AnnualDataTables/2009-10AnnualDataTables.pdf.
37 John Balmer, Jr., "Nonformal Pastoral Ministry Training in the Majority World: Four Case Studies" (D.Min. diss., Columbia Biblical Seminary and School of Missions, Columbia International University, 2008), 1, referencing Ramesh Richard, "The Challenge Before Us," address given at Trainers of Pastors International Consultation (TOPIC) Conference, December 1–3, 1997. Wheaton, IL [lecture given December 1, 1997]; Ralph Winter, "Will We Fail Again?" *Mission Frontiers*, 1993, 15:7–8; Winter, "Editorial," 1994, 16:1–2; Winter, *The Challenge of Reaching the Unreached* (Pasadena, CA: William Carey Library, 1996), n.p.
38 Sills, *Reaching*, 161–162.
39 David K. Clark, *To Know and Love God: Method for Theology* (Wheaton, IL: Crossway, 2003), 100.
40 Ibid., 112–113.
41 Sills, *Reaching*, 168.

Leadership without Seminaries

There is a special need for shepherd leaders where little gospel work has taken place. In such settings, biblical understanding is low, and issues of syncretism and false teaching are acute. Christians in the United State might observe plenty of seminary-trained people in their own nation without church positions, and might suppose that there is a global glut of trained personnel. But that is not the case. Campus Crusade's Steve Clinton has made a staggering observation: though global seminary graduation levels are expanding, they are totally inadequate for global needs. Even if graduation levels held steadily at fifteen thousand graduates per year for the next forty years, there would only be 600,000 new graduates. "However, if the church's growth rate continues, we will need five million new pastors in the next forty years. Thus, eighty-five to ninety percent of the world's new churches will have pastoral leadership that is not seminary trained."[42] Of course, seminary training is not the major objective, but it does illustrate the need.

The early church consolidated their gains. A layered approach ensured that the churches matured in the faith. "The Apostles revisited their converts," explains scholar Michael Green, "they set up presbyters to look after them, they wrote letters to them, they sent messengers to them, and they prayed for them."[43] This is the pattern for modern missionary church planters: continued visits, leadership training, correspondence, delegated messengers, and prayer. Establishing a similar pattern allows the missionary to continue teaching through layered means until he has "trained trainers" who will maintain effective pastoral leadership.[44]

If missionaries and church planters train the trainers in local churches set in hard places, seminary training, while advantageous, is not essential. Leaders can be taught sound doctrine, pastoral skills, and contextualized ecclesiology over time. Missiologist Jim Slack reported that one group of researched CPMs had few seminary-trained leaders. Rather, leaders arose from within the churches or communities. "Pastoral leaders in each assessed CPM were lay leaders who came from the locales where the churches were started. In only one CPM were there even a few theologically trained, full-time pastors . . . the majority of pastoral

---

42 Steven Clinton, "Twenty-first Century Population Factors and Leadership of Spiritual Movements," *EMQ*, April 2005, 41:2, 191.
43 Michael Green, "Methods and Strategy in the Evangelism of the Early Church," J. D. Douglas, ed, *Let the Earth Hear His Voice: International Congress on World Evangelization, Lausanne, Switzerland* (Minneapolis: World Wide Publications, 1975), 167
44 Sills, *Reaching*, 46.

Elders in the Life of the Church

leaders emerged from within the new church being started."[45] This seems to be the same pattern observed in the New Testament (Acts 6:1–7; 14:21–23; Titus 1:5).

Churches must be trained for ministry to the body and to the unbelieving world (Eph. 4:11–16). Green reinforces the biblical approach of equipping a church to conduct the full gamut of Christian ministry: "God's supreme method is man, man regenerated, sanctified, committed, mobilized, trained, and equipped. God's chief instrument is the church, the church as a body of dedicated people. Spiritual leadership and a mobilized, trained membership are God's demand for the advancement of his cause."[46] Seeing the church reproduce itself is a major aim in training. Churches will effectively evangelize only to the degree that they train and mobilize the body of Christ, and that will happen primarily through effective shepherd leaders.[47]

First Things

Whether involved in CPMs or persecution settings, the missionary church planter will need to immediately assess potential leaders for new churches. To do this he should consult the cultural insiders who have observed a potential leader's standing in the community.[48] Certainly, training leaders will slow him from moving on to plant the next new church, but the last demand of Christ in the Great Commission anticipates the need to train leaders who will regularly equip the new church. This was the Apostle Paul's practice, as pioneer missiologist Roland Allen pointed out: preaching for five or six months in one place and then leaving behind an established church with elders. Paul focused on indigenization rather than leaving behind a church dependent on him.[49] His return visits to churches he planted gave evidence of established congregations that could exist without the apostle looking over their shoulders. He trained leaders in the basics of the Christian faith so that they could commit those things to others (2 Tim. 2:2).[50]

What is training? Colin Marshall and Tony Payne wisely explain, "In the New Testament, training is much more about Christian thinking and living than about

45 Jim Slack, "Church Planting Movements: Rationale, Research and Realities of Their Existence," *Journal of Evangelism and Missions*, vol. 6, Spring 2007, 41–42.
46 Green, "Methods and Strategy," 195.
47 Ibid.
48 Correspondence with Bruce R. Ashford, 30 September 2010.
49 Roland Allen, *Missionary Methods: St. Paul's or Ours?* (Grand Rapids: Eerdmans, 1962), 83–84.
50 Contra Allen, 19th century Presbyterian missionary to China, John Nevius, *The Planting and Development of Missionary Churches* (Phillipsburg, NJ: P & R, 1958), 27–28, counsels for a slower, more deliberate approach to training, taking years, if necessary. Nevius also framed a Western model for Chinese churches, 32–44.

particular skills or competences."[51] So the missionary may have no opportunity or even need to mimic his academic training. His concern must be for developing pastoral leaders who know how to think biblically and apply the Scripture to life's demands. "The heart of training is not to impart a skill, but to impart sound doctrine,"[52] which is the opposite of some Western approaches. "Paul uses the language of 'training' to refer to a lifelong process whereby Timothy and his congregation are taught by Scripture to reject false religion, to conform their hearts and lives to sound doctrine. Good biblical training results in a godly life based on sound, health-giving teaching."[53] The missionary cannot simply offer potential leaders a workbook on elders and hope for the best. Training is "deeply and inescapably relational."[54] One need only take a look at the relationship that Paul had with Timothy and Titus to understand this relational necessity. "This close relationship was a vehicle for one of the key elements of Paul's training of Timothy—imitation."[55] Paul was essentially imparting a way of life, and that could only be understood by seeing it modeled by the apostle.[56] Modern missionaries must follow the same pattern.

A church tends to mirror its leaders. If leaders fail to apply sound doctrine to daily life, the church will likely follow the same detrimental step. Though a leader may be a relatively young believer, if he has learned well from the missionary's relational investment in his life, he will be far along in helping others in the new church to see how the gospel applies to life. "The relational nature of training means that the best training will often occur by osmosis rather than formal instruction. It will be caught as much as it is taught. Trainees will end up resembling their trainers, much as children turn out like their parents."[57] Marshall and Payne narrow the nature and goal of training to three foci: "*Conviction*—their knowledge of God and understanding of the Bible; *character*—the godly character and life that accords with sound doctrine; *competency*—the ability to prayerfully speak God's word to others in a variety of ways."[58] A missionary who trains potential leaders may prefer to teach church history, systematic theology, and apologetics to the potential shepherd leaders. While that may seem ideal, he may be prevented from offering such expansive training by time and circumstances. He will need to

---

51 Colin Marshall and Tony Payne, *The Trellis and the Vine: The Ministry Mind-Shift That Changes Everything* (Kingsford, Australia: Matthias Media, 2009), 70. See 1 Tim. 1:11–12, 18–20; 4:7; 6:11–14, 20–21; 2 Tim. 2:2; 3:16, 17.
52 Ibid., 71.
53 Ibid.
54 Ibid., 71–72.
55 Ibid., 72.
56 Ibid.
57 Ibid., 76.
58 Ibid., 78.

prioritize conviction, character, and competency. Or, to adjust to what theology professor and pastor Timothy Witmer calls the "essential elements of an effective shepherding ministry," a missionary to a hard place should emphasize the basics of being biblical, relational, accountable, and prayerful.[59] He will teach potential leaders the Scriptures. He will model Christian relationships. He will demonstrate the need for ongoing accountability. And he will show by precept and practice the vital role of prayer in shepherding ministry.

Discovering Potential Leaders

How should the missionary discover potential shepherd leaders? He must look for those who embrace responsibility, love the flock, show some ability to teach, and demonstrate faithfulness. This necessitates investing time with the new church, asking questions of potential leaders, and cultivating those potential leaders. The demand of hard places causes one to focus on bare minimums rather than the ideal, and on qualities rather than a checklist of qualifications.[60] Instead of comparing potential leaders to the more mature leaders that the missionary knows from established churches, he should look for qualities that show their development in Christian walk and practice.[61]

What if a potential leader is a very young convert to Christ? How long should a missionary invest before putting a new believer into a leadership position? The pressing need for leaders in hard places demands a different approach than commonly practiced in the West, one that will speed along the process of establishing elders. The New Testament dealt with plenty of hard places where churches were planted. Since Paul was with most congregations six months or less, and yet set apart elders to serve in those churches (e.g. Acts 14:21–23), Allen concludes that such a timeframe is adequate for establishing eldership. He admits that if someone proposed to do the same today "he would be deemed rash to the verge of madness. Yet no one denies that St. Paul did it."[62] Allen further explains that, for the most part,

---

59 Witmer, *The Shepherd Leader*, 193–224. He also adds that the effective shepherding ministry should be systematic, comprehensive, and functional, but in light of training leaders in hard places, the four identified above should be priority in leadership training, and if time and circumstances allow, expand to include the other elements.

60 Sinclair, *A Vision of the Possible*, 228; Sills, *Reaching*, 64, identifies bare minimums as teaching "the Scriptures, sound doctrine, and godly living to those who follow."

61 Sinclair, *A Vision for the Possible*, 228–231, adds, "Throughout the centuries God has expanded the boundaries of the church through extraordinarily deficient church planters and imperfect local believers. We are all damaged goods that God is in the process of healing and restoring. That's encouraging to me" (pp. 230–231).

62 Allen, *Missionary Methods*, 85.

the new converts had no special advantages in terms of understanding the gospel or the Christian faith. Though some might have been acquainted with Jewish law or Greek Philosophy, "the vast majority were steeped in the follies and iniquities of idolatry and were slaves of the grossest superstitions. No one knew anything of the life and teaching of the Saviour."[63] If Paul was able to establish effective leadership structures in a brief time with the new churches that he planted, certainly present day missionaries can do the same. So how do modern missionaries balance the urgent need for leaders with the biblical qualifications for shepherd leaders? Observations from the Pastoral Epistles will inform our thinking.

OBSERVATIONS FROM THE PASTORAL EPISTLES

Paul planted the church at Ephesus early in his third missionary journey, spending three years preaching, teaching, and making disciples (Acts 18:22–23; 19:1–10; 20:31). Elder leadership was established, as evidenced by Paul's visit with the Ephesian elders in Miletus (Acts 20:17–38) before his fateful journey to Jerusalem where he was arrested and eventually transferred to Rome to appear before Caesar (Acts 21:27–40; 25:10–12; 28:11–31). The trip to Jerusalem led to his first Roman imprisonment, which lasted from AD 60–62, after which he was free for approximately two and not more than three years for additional ministry labors.[64] During this time he appears to have visited Crete along with Titus, whom he then left behind to put things in order, possibly going onto Spain himself.[65] Paul's visit to the island, though long enough to establish a number of congregations on the island (Titus 1:5, "appoint elders in every town"), lasted less than a year.[66] Mounce makes several observations on Paul's

---

63 Ibid.
64 Thomas D. Lea and Hayne P. Griffin, Jr., *1, 2 Timothy, Titus: An Exegetical and Theological Exposition of Holy Scripture* (NAC, 34; Nashville: Broadman Press, 1992), 41.
65 William D. Mounce posits that the apostle visited Crete prior to the supposed trip to Spain. In *Pastoral Epistles* (WBC, 46; Nashville: Nelson, 2000), lix. The idea that Paul went to Spain comes from Clement, who wrote that Paul preached "both in the east and west, . . . having taught righteousness to the whole world, and come to the extreme limit of the west." 1 Clement 5:7; *ANF* 1:6; A. D. 30–100. Eckhard Schnabel explains that the phrase "to the limits of the West" was a common designation for Spain. Eckhard J. Schnabel, *Paul the Missionary: Realities, Strategies and Methods* (Downers Grove, IL: InterVarsity Press, 2008), 116, citing 1 Clement 5:6–7, along with the *Acts of Peter* and the *Muratorian Canon* as further indication of a Spanish mission, 117. Other scholars, pointing out the lack of internal biblical evidence, are less confident than Schnabel that the Spanish mission actually took place; see James D. G. Dunn, *Romans 9–16* (WBC, 38B; Dallas: Word, 1988), 871–873; Ben Witherington, *Paul's Letter to the Romans: A Socio-Rhetorical Commentary* (Grand Rapids: Eerdmans, 2004), 362–363; Douglas J. Moo, *The Epistle to the Romans* (NICNT; Grand Rapids: Eerdmans, 1996), 899–902.
66 Ibid., lix. Schnabel, *Paul the Missionary*, uses slightly different dates, placing the first Ro-

Cretan mission that are pertinent to the question of 'how recent is too recent to establish elders with young congregations.'[67] He bases his observations on internal evidence that the Cretan churches were relatively new, which means their potential elders were newer believers. What follows is my own explanation of Mounce's points:

1. Paul instructed Timothy to appoint elders but did not mention deacons (Titus 1:5), which suggests that deacons came later after the church began to grow (Acts 6:1–6).
2. Titus is not told to remove offending overseers, as Timothy was in Ephesus (1 Tim. 5:19–21), but merely to appoint them (Titus 1:5). This seems to indicate that overseers did not exist up to that point, so no correction was necessary.
3. Paul does not repeat the injunction that an overseer cannot be a recent convert (cf. 1 Tim. 3:6). This suggests that either there were no recent converts, which is unlikely, or that all were new converts, which seems more likely according to the internal evidence.
4. The majority of the epistle is basic catechesis appropriate for young converts, drawing out the day-to-day implications of the two salvific sayings around which the epistle is formed (Titus 2:11–14; 3:3–8). This seems to indicate that the churches were new, and the believers lacked maturity.
5. The teaching of the opponents, while successful (Titus 1:11), does not play as significant a role here as it does in 1 Timothy, suggesting that the problems were not as advanced.[68]

Further, New Testament scholar Benjamin Merkle highlights the significant distinction between the two character lists for elders in 1 Timothy and Titus: "Titus omits the qualification of not being a new convert."[69] Why was this omitted? "This omission may have been a necessary modification due to the early stage of development of the Cretan churches. Relatively new converts would then be needed in leadership of the younger churches."[70] This modification,

---

man imprisonment from AD 60–62 and consolidation of the new churches in Crete around AD 63.
67 Ashford, "A Theologically-Driven Missiology," 203.
68 Mounce, *Pastoral Epistles*, lix–lx; aided by comments from Benjamin L. Merkle, "Ecclesiology in the Pastoral Epistles," in Andreas Köstenberger and Terry Wilder, eds., *Entrusted with the Gospel: Paul's Theology in the Pastoral Epistles* (Nashville: B & H Academic, 2010), 183–186.
69 Benjamin L. Merkle, "Ecclesiology in the Pastoral Epistles," 185.
70 Ibid.

along with other qualities listed in 1 Timothy, may indicate Paul's flexibility "in certain matters of church organization as the local situation dictated,"[71] as Thomas Lea and Hayne Griffin Jr. observe. Yet within the brief span of Paul's time in Crete, followed by the few months leading up to penning his epistle to Titus, the apostolic delegate had sufficient time to evaluate qualified elder candidates and ready them for appointment to the churches in Crete.[72] Paul intended to rendezvous with Titus in Nicopolis prior to the start of winter, so he anticipated his instructions to be carried out quickly (Titus 3:12). How young were the converts that Titus appointed as elders? One could speculate that (1) they were indeed "elders," that is, older men in the Christian community, (2) that they were schooled in the OT Scriptures since there may have been extensive Jewish communities on the island, or (3) that they were among those converted thirty years earlier at Pentecost, having returned to establish at least a semblance of Christian community on Crete (Acts 2:11). But these are speculations. Internal evidence, especially in Titus 2:1–8, suggests that the churches of Crete were newly formed, and their members were of mixed age.[73]

Timothy and Titus arguably served, not as elders in their respective Christian congregations, but as temporary, apostolic delegates or missionaries.[74] Timothy's ministry had already grown more complicated than Titus's. He was to engage in instructing "certain men not to teach strange doctrines, nor to pay attention to myths and endless genealogies" (1 Tim. 1:3–4). He also had responsibility to pass along the pastoral instructions that Paul had given for the congregation (1 Tim. 4:6, 16). The authority given to him included public rebuke of unrepentant elders who might have fallen into sin, as well as appointing men to the pastoral office (1 Tim. 5:17–22).

Likewise, Paul had entrusted Titus with setting in order what remained from his ministry among the churches and appointing elders in every city, as Paul had previously directed him, presumably while they labored together in Crete (Titus 1:5). Did Titus and Timothy's use of authority cut the congregation completely out of the decision making process? Both Timothy and Titus likely involved the congregation in their decisions regarding elder appointment, for, as Stott observed, "His emphasis on their need to have a blameless reputation indicates that the congregation will have a say in the selection process."[75] This follows the same pattern noted earlier in our reflection on selected passages in Acts.

---

71 Lea and Griffin, *1, 2 Timothy, Titus*, 278, fn. 11.
72 Mounce, *Pastoral Epistles*, lx.
73 Ibid., lix-lx.
74 Merkle, "Ecclesiology in the Pastoral Epistles," 196–198.
75 Stott, *Guard the Truth*, 174.

More broadly speaking, the Pastoral Epistles present some basic patterns regarding the New Testament's teaching on local church leaders.[76] First, elders are chosen from within the church and are well known by reason of their faithfulness, respectability, and involvement. Second, elders are to be chosen carefully. Particular characteristics identified in 1 Timothy 3:1–7 and Titus 1:6–9 narrow the list of elder candidates. Common to both epistles are significant qualities: being above reproach, blamelessness, husband of one wife, managing families well, believing (or faithful) children, self-control, hospitable, not given to drunkenness, not violent, able to teach or exhort in sound doctrine, and not a lover of money.[77] And, as I have already suggested, the fact that Paul does not instruct Titus to exclude Christian novices as elder candidates suggests "flexibility in church organization required for different church situations."[78] Third, shepherd leaders are to be "plural in composition (i.e., not a leadership dominated by one personality)."[79] Obviously, these churches had no concept of a monarchical bishop ruling them, as would emerge in post-biblical generations.[80]

The pattern continues for new churches in rapidly developing and persecution settings. Missionaries should look for potential elders from within the new church, giving careful attention to biblical qualities outlined in the pastorals (particularly in Titus since these characteristics appear more streamlined for a younger church), and always seeking to establish plural leadership unless only one man is qualified.[81]

ESTABLISHING A PLAN FOR LEADERSHIP

A consistent plan for missionaries to follow in CPMs and in persecution settings will help to conserve the fruit of disciple making. Churches must have shepherd leaders. In some settings, because none are available, missionaries will face the difficult decision of recommending someone young in the faith to serve as an elder. How can he do this with confidence that he is following the Lord's leadership? To help establish a workable plan, we will identify ten focal points in the process for establishing local church leadership.

---

76 Lea and Griffin, *1, 2 Timothy, Titus*, 276–277.
77 Gene Getz, *Elders and Leaders: God's Plan for Leading the Church: A Biblical, Historical and Cultural Perspective* (Chicago: Moody, 2003), 157.
78 Lea and Griffin, *1, 2 Timothy, Titus*, 278.
79 Ibid.
80 Merkle, "Ecclesiology in the Pastoral Epistles," 185.
81 See discussion of elder plurality and the rationale for it in W. B. Johnson, "The Gospel Developed through the Government and Order of the Churches of Jesus Christ," in Mark Dever, ed., *Polity: Biblical Arguments on How to Conduct Church Life* (Washington, DC: Center for Church Reform, 2001), 192–195.

First, major on character in potential leaders. Though the behavioral qualities called for in 1 Timothy 3 and Titus 1 are not identified in Paul and Barnabas' appointment of elders in the Galatian region (Acts 14:23), the details given to Timothy and Titus offer assurance that character must never be overlooked. Since the missionary will likely not find many men who have reached a high level of Christian maturity, he must consider how the potential leaders' character has developed in the time he has observed them. Specifically, he should look for faithfulness, availability, personal integrity, and teachability, with special emphasis on the last quality.[82]

Second, due to the focus on newer congregations in Titus, a missionary should especially attend to the character qualities described in Titus 1:6–9 when identifying potential elders. Ideally, a candidate would exemplify all the qualities listed in 1 Timothy 3 and Titus 1. But reality sets in when considering new believers, new churches, and hard places. Dickson also offers this helpful comment:

> The office and work being spiritual, it is necessary that elders should be spiritual men. It is not necessary that they be men of great gifts or worldly position, of wealth or high education, but it is indispensably necessary that they be men of God, at peace with him, new creatures in Christ Jesus; engaged in the embassy of reconciliation, they must be themselves reconciled.[83]

When considering elder candidates, the following four questions may prove useful for summarizing what Paul requires of Titus 1:

1. Is he a faithful family man, devoted to his wife and managing his children well? (1:6)[84]
2. Does he exercise self-control over his affections, desires, and relationships? (1:7)
3. Does he get along well with others, treating them as one living out the gospel? (1:8)[85]
4. Is he able to exhort and correct others through proper use of Scripture? (1:9)

---

82 Lea and Griffin, *1, 2 Timothy, Titus*, 279; Sinclair, *A Vision of the Possible*, 235, uses a helpful acrostic: "Some talk about finding those who are FAT: faithful, available, teachable."
83 Dickson, *The Elder*, 30.
84 See Getz, *Elders and Leaders*, 163–171.
85 Concerning living out the gospel, see J. Mack Stiles, *Marks of the Messenger: Knowing, Living and Speaking the Gospel* (Downers Grove, IL: InterVarsity Press, 2010), 49–60.

Third, look for two or three men whom the church will recognize as worthy of authority by virtue of their character and service. This is authority to lead, shepherd, rebuke, train, teach, and govern. Age is not the issue as much as the congregation's level of respect.[86] As Ray Steadman notes, this respect should be "aroused by their [the elders] own loving and godly example."[87]

Fourth, if only one person is qualified to lead the church, the congregation may set him apart and plan to add another man as soon as they can. Plurality may be more difficult in areas of persecution where a few families or individuals meet in a small house church. Yet, when functioning properly, plurality helps to keep authoritarianism and dictatorships from developing. It leads to greater effectiveness by multiplying ministry gifts and provides a strong support system for the demands of ministry.[88]

Fifth, if only one man is qualified to serve, the lone elder may want to have an accountability partner or team to assist him. Those holding him accountable do not share the same authority, but they can help the elder to guard his walk and doctrine.[89]

Sixth, the missionary should invest intensive time with potential elders, observing how they respond to instruction and noting their humility, personal growth, discipline in the Word and prayer, faithfulness to family, and reputation in the community. Sills points to one missionary tool that has been effective: MAWL (model, assist, watch, and leave). "It calls for the apprentice to learn from a master by watching and doing...When the apprentice is 'soloing' without incident, the master may leave."[90] Sinclair suggests that this process will take from two to six months, particularly focusing on "intense character work."[91] In this fashion, the missionary is able to closely monitor how potential leaders are developing before releasing them to the new churches.

Seventh, the church planter should not attempt to insist a Western-style seminary education on the potential shepherd leaders but to offer a few essentials for training in ministry.[92] Allen probes the issue: "The question before us is, how he [Paul] could so train his converts as to be able to leave them after so short a time with

86 Getz, *Elders and Leaders*, 287–289.
87 Ray Steadman, *Body Life* (Glendale, CA: Regal Books, 1972), 82.
88 Getz, *Elders and Leaders*, 241–242.
89 Ibid., 273, 276.
90 Sills, *Reaching*, 49.
91 Sinclair, *A Vision of the Possible*, 236.
92 See David Bosch, *Transforming Mission*, 5–6, for an insightful look at models of Western imposition.

any security that they would be able to stand and grow."[93] So what are the essentials to be considered? Here are seven possibilities:

1. The basics of the Christian faith with emphasis on biblical theology. Teach them the gospel.[94]
2. Simple rules of hermeneutics.
3. Patterns for the spiritual disciplines.[95]
4. Accountability with one another for personal walk and obedience.
5. Basic responsibilities for spiritual leaders: doctrine, discipline, direction, and modeling the Christian life (e.g. Acts 20; 1 Peter 5; Titus 1:5–9).
6. Church discipline in practice—how and when (Matt. 18:18–20; 1 Cor. 5, etc.).
7. Discipleship of the congregation.

Eighth, the missionary should outline for the new leaders prescribed areas of instruction and ministry to the church. Gene Getz identifies six important priorities: "teaching the Word of God, modeling Christlike behavior, maintaining doctrinal purity, disciplining unruly believers, overseeing the material needs of the church, and praying for the sick."[96] These constitute the major "duties" of the elders in the new churches.

Ninth, if the missionary and the congregation have concerns that the newly appointed shepherd leaders are too new in the faith, then appoint them on a temporary basis until they prove themselves, heeding the warning of 1 Timothy 3:6: "And not a new convert, so that he will not become conceited and fall into the condemnation incurred by the devil." Missionary Brian Hogan recommends establishing "provisional elders" or "elders-in-training," who serve until more mature men are qualified to lead the congregation.[97]

Tenth, after sufficient training and observation, the congregation should set apart the men as the congregation's shepherds or elders, while the missionary commends them to the Lord, following Paul's example in Acts 14:23–24 and 20:31–32.

---

93 Allen, *Missionary Methods*, 87.
94 Ibid.
95 Donald S. Whitney, *Spiritual Disciplines for the Christian Life* (Colorado Springs: NavPress, 1991).
96 Getz, *Elders and Leaders*, 266.
97 Brian Hogan, "Distant Thunder: Mongols Follow the Khan of Khans," in Ralph Winter and Steven Hawthorne, *Perspectives on the World Christian Movement* (3rd ed., Pasadena, CA: William Carey Library, 1999), 694–695, 696.

CONCLUSION

Even in CPMs and persecution settings, training leaders must remain a priority for missionaries. Otherwise, the Great Commission remains unfulfilled despite zealous efforts at evangelism. Remember the Rwandan church's failure to develop faithful shepherd leaders to teach their people. The missionary/church planter must not neglect Christ's command in order to reach the largest numbers, as seems to have happened in Rwanda. Nothing in the New Testament gives credence to pursuing greater numbers while neglecting to teach all the things that Christ commanded his disciples. True disciples seek to obey Jesus Christ as Lord, even in hard places.

Obviously, teaching is an ongoing process. As missiologist Jonathan Chao insists, the missionary "must recognize the rightful rule of Christ over all his churches."[98] After establishing a biblical foundation, he must entrust the governance of the church to local elders who will bear responsibility for teaching, leading, and shepherding. Though he may struggle over idealistic desires to establish fully matured leaders in the new church, he will likely need to demonstrate something of the flexibility Paul demonstrated toward the Cretan churches. Some of the elders he appoints may appear "too recent" in the faith, but here he will need much discretion and direction by the Holy Spirit. As Roland Allen wisely pointed out, if Paul could stay for six months in one city, plant a church, and set apart elders, commending them to the Lord, then modern missionaries may do the same.[99] While no one can offer an arbitrary age or time in the faith as a prerequisite for being an elder, the missionary will need to be judicious in considering the basic qualities necessary in spiritual leaders and then move forward, commending the church to the Lord's care. It is also wise for him to continue relationships with the new leaders and church, not as one exercising external control but as a spiritual father who can offer counsel and encouragement, even as Paul did when he returned to visit churches he had planted.

---

98 Jonathan T'ien-en Chao, "The Nature of the Unity of the Local and Universal Church in Evangelism and Church Growth," in Douglas, *Let the Earth Hear His Voice*, 1111.
99 Cf. Allen, *Missionary Methods*, 81–107.

CONCLUSION

Galatians 6:9 issues both a warning and a promise that is particularly relevant to elders: "Let us not lose heart in doing good, for in due time we will reap if we do not grow weary." We would like to conclude this book by reissuing the same warning and promise.

Do you remember how we said earlier that the office of elder is a burden-bearing office? Burdens weigh down. Burdens are taxing. Burdens borne for extended periods of time can become wearying. You might be younger and weary from an extended "church fight." Or you might be older and simply uncertain how much "fire in the belly" or "gas in the tank" is left. Here's the real problem: Too often we have seen the weary laborer, no matter what age, fall into sin and subsequently become disqualified—no longer exemplary. Fatigue often causes us to fall out of the spirit and feed the flesh.

Many newly expectant mothers have been given the advice, "Rest before you get tired." That is just as easily applied to pastors, elders, and deacons. How do you stay rested with all the needs clamoring for one's attention?

Really, if you just get one thing right, everything else will flow from it. We're called to "abide" (ESV) or "remain" (NIV) in Christ (John 15:4). If fact, our fruitfulness is completely dependent on this act of abiding. "Abide in Me, and I in you. As the branch cannot bear fruit of itself unless it abides in the vine, so neither can you unless you abide in Me."

Other verses get at the same idea, but in different ways. Luke 12:21 commands us to be "...rich toward God." Psalm 37:4 exhorts, "Delight yourself in the LORD..." And Philippians 4:4 says, "Rejoice in the Lord always."

In your laboring, work hard at keeping your First Love your first love. Keep your relationship with God from becoming secondary to anything. Relatively speaking, all other matters are simply unimportant.

You've probably heard the expression, "You cannot impart what you do not possess." We elders first and foremost want to possess Christ and impart Christ. Everything else pales in comparison. Should we do this, there is reward. Go back to the promise of Galatians 6:9, where we're told "we will reap if we do not grow weary."

There's a lot riding on this idea of being a faithful elder: a reward for us; the spiritual health of believers; the church's witness in the community; the name of Christ in the world…

Let us not grow weary.

APPENDIX

Below is a suggested elder questionnaire that may be adapted for your own church context.

ELDER QUESTIONNAIRE

1. Please briefly explain how you came to faith in Christ.
2. Please describe your own practice of spiritual disciplines as a believer.
3. How do you characterize your relationship to your wife and children? Tell a little about your family life, priorities, and what the Lord is teaching you in marriage and parenting.
4. What is the gospel of Jesus Christ? Please give a brief explanation or detailed outline of the gospel as you might present it to someone in need of Christ.
5. Explain your understanding of the Church. What is the church, what is its purpose, how is it ordered by Christ, what is its future, etc.
6. In this regard, what are the offices of a New Testament church and how are these offices to function in local church life?
7. Explain the biblical doctrine of man (briefly).
8. Briefly explain the biblical doctrine of sin.
9. Briefly explain each of the following terms and their importance in the Christian life:
   A. Justification
   B. Redemption/Reconciliation
   C. Adoption
   D. Propitiation
   E. Predestination/Election
   F. Regeneration

SELECT BIBLIOGRAPHY

Anyabwile, Thabiti M. *Finding Faithful Elders and Deacons.* IX Marks Series. Wheaton, IL: Crossway, 2012.

Ascol, Thomas K., ed. *Dear Timothy: Letters on Pastoral Ministry.* Cape Coral, FL: Founders Press, 2004.

Dever, Mark E. *A Display of God's Glory: Basics of Church Structure.* Washington, DC: Center for Church Reform, 2001.

_____. *Nine Marks of a Healthy Church.* Revised edition. 2000. Reprint, Wheaton, IL: Crossway, 2004.

_____, ed. *Polity: Biblical Arguments on How to Conduct Church Life.* Washington, DC: Center for Church Reform, 2001.

Dever, Mark and Paul Alexander, *The Deliberate Church: Building Your Ministry on the Gospel.* Wheaton, IL: Crossway, 2005.

Dickson, David. *The Elder and His Work.* Phillipsburg, NJ: P&R, 2004.

Getz, Gene. *Elders and Leaders: God's Plan for Leading the Church—A Biblical, Historical and Cultural Perspective.* Chicago: Moody, 2003.

Hammett, John S. *Biblical Foundations for Baptist Churches: A Contemporary Ecclesiology.* Grand Rapids: Kregel Academic & Professional, 2005.

MacArthur, John, Jr., ed. *Rediscovering Pastoral Ministry: Shaping Contemporary Ministry with Biblical Mandates.* Dallas: Word, 1995.

_____. *The Master's Plan for the Church.* Chicago: Moody, 1991.

Merkle, Benjamin. *40 Questions about Elders and Deacons.* Grand Rapids: Kregel, 2008.

_____. *The Elder and Overseer: One Office in the Early Church.* Studies in Biblical Literature 57. Hemchand Gossai, gen. ed. New York: Peter Lang, 2003.

Piper, John. *Biblical Eldership: Shepherd the Flock of God Among You.* http://www.DesiringGod.org/library/tbi/bib_eldership.html

_____. *Biblical Eldership.* Minneapolis: Desiring God Ministries, 1999.

Ryken, Philip. *City on a Hill: Reclaiming the Biblical Pattern for the Church in the Twenty-first Century.* Chicago: Moody, 2003.

Strauch, Alexander. *Biblical Eldership: An Urgent Call to Restore Biblical Church Leadership.* Revised and expanded. Littleton, CO: Lewis and Roth Publishers, 1995.

Wills, Gregory. *Democratic Religion: Freedom, Authority, and Church Discipline in the Baptist South, 1785–1900.* New York: Oxford University Press, 1997.

Witmer, Timothy Z. *The Shepherd Leader: Achieving Effective Shepherding in Your Church.* Phillipsburg, NJ: P&R, 2010.

SCRIPTURE INDEX

SUBJECT INDEX